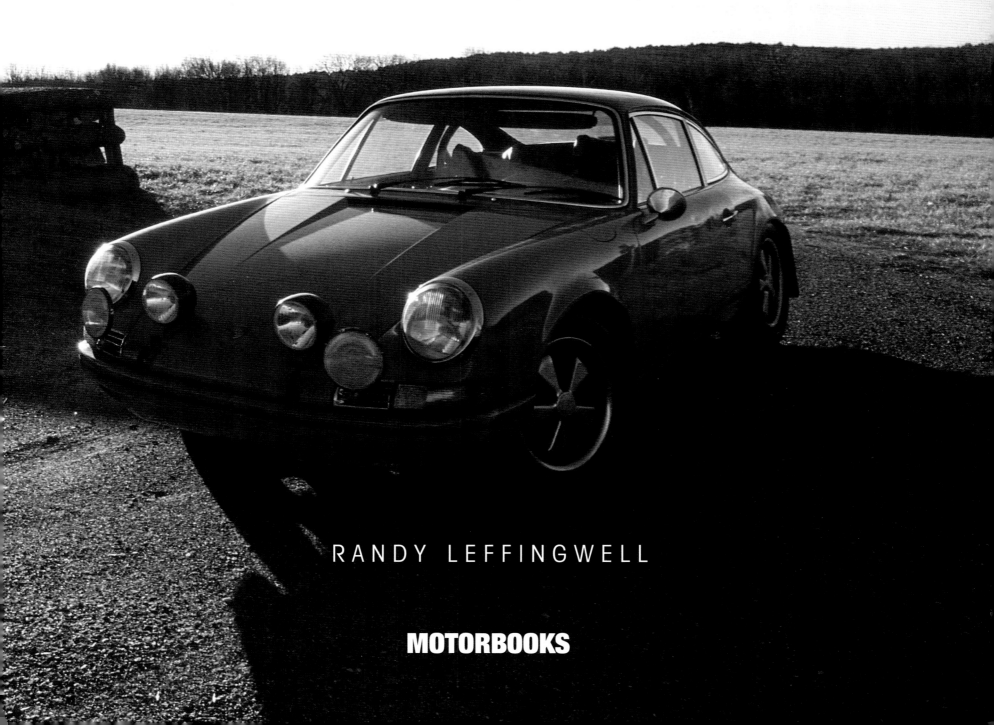

PORSCHE 911

Perfection by Design

R A N D Y   L E F F I N G W E L L

MOTORBOOKS

This book is dedicated to my friends Jerry Reilly and Otis Chandler, who admire the design and engineering of the Porsche 911 as much as I do.

First published in 2005 by Motorbooks, an imprint of MBI Publishing Company, Galtier Plaza, Suite 200, 380 Jackson Street, St. Paul, MN 55101-3885 USA

Motorbooks titles are also available at discounts in bulk quantity for industrial or sales-promotional use. For details write to Special Sales Manager at MBI Publishing Company, Galtier Plaza, Suite 200, 380 Jackson Street, St. Paul, MN 55101-3885 USA.

ISBN-13: 978-0-7603-2092-1
ISBN-10: 0-7603-2092-6

Editor: Darwin Holmstrom
Designer: Mandy Iverson

Printed in China

Endpaper: As good as a 911 looks standing still, the view from behind the steering wheel is the one most owners prefer.

Frontis: There was nothing subtle about the whale-tale rear spoiler on the 911 Turbo, but given the prodigious power output of the boosted engine, the Turbo was not about being subtle.

Front cover: The 993 represented the ultimate evolution of the air-cooled 911.

Back cover: Although every part has changed since the original air-cooled version, today's 997 is still unmistakably a true 911.

CHAPTER ONE   6
THE LEAP FROM 356 TO 901 ■ 1953–1964

CHAPTER TWO   32
THE FIRST GENERATION ■ 1964–1969

CHAPTER THREE   74
RESURRECTION OF THE CARRERA ■ 1969–1973

CHAPTER FOUR   108
THE SECOND GENERATION ■ 1974–1983

CHAPTER FIVE   162
A GENERATION ENDS, ANOTHER BEGINS ■ 1981–1989

CHAPTER SIX   208
PORSCHE'S THIRD GENERATION—THE 964 ■ 1989–1994

CHAPTER SEVEN   248
THE FOURTH GENERATION—THE 993 ■ 1994–1998

CHAPTER EIGHT   284
PORSCHE'S FIFTH GENERATION—THE 996 ■ 1999–2004

CHAPTER NINE   324
THE SIXTH GENERATION—THE 997 ■ 2004–TODAY

ACKNOWLEDGMENTS   348

INDEX   350

CONTENTS

CHAPTER ONE

THE LEAP FROM 356 TO 901
1953 – 1964

"It's about time!"

Motor Sport, December 1963

The chance to create a new sports car represented many things to the small automaker Porsche. The company's first decade manufacturing its own cars had put it on solid financial footing, making a new model possible. The evolutionary development from the first Gmund-built coupes to the 356A models in 1956 and 1957 had advanced and improved the car, but it still lacked some things. Erwin Komenda's body design provided well-heeled buyers with an intimately proportioned automobile that fit well within the reticent nature of postwar Germany. Franz Reimspeiss' engine and Leopold Schmid's chassis had given them power and pleasure in driving.

But customers had begun to communicate to the factory their desire for more luggage capacity, for larger "jump seats" in back, for less noise, and for even more power. When the B series first appeared in late 1959, engineering had addressed each of these issues. By lowering the rear seat cushions, they allowed larger rear passengers or more luggage to fit inside the car. Within the company a superb foundation existed in personnel. Chief designer Karl Rabe led a team that included head of body design Erwin Franz Komenda, engine chief Franz-Xaver Reimspeiss, and chief engineer Wilhelm Hild. Josef Mickl, a former aircraft designer, worked for decades as the company's resident aerodynamicist, and Leopold Schmid served as chief of engine, transmission, and chassis design. All of these men were veterans of dozens of projects with Professor Porsche and his now 49-year-old son Ferry.

A new generation of designers joined this august mix of venerable talent, experience, and personalities in the late 1950s. Ferry Porsche's young son, Ferdinand Alexander, or Butzi, as he was known to family and friends, led the way. Butzi was one of the first graduates of a new design school, the *Hochschule für Gestaltung* (HfG) the upper school for art in Ulm, some 50 miles southeast of Zuffenhausen.

Cofounded in 1953 by Max Bill, a former student at the Bauhaus in Dessau, the new institute originally aimed to teach the public to be politically well informed. His cofounders, Inge Scholle and Otl Aicher, had been persistent Nazi resistance fighters whose goal in the early 1950s was to enlighten politicians and writers. However, Bill pushed his own agenda vigorously, advancing the curriculum of the long-shuttered Bauhaus to concentrate aesthetically progressive designers in an open-minded atmosphere that

1957 356 CARRERA SPEEDSTER

The twin-cam 1,500-cc Carrera engine sits underneath the louvers at the rear of this Speedster. Conceived as a racing engine, its street version answered customer requests for more power.

emphasized design of objects and spaces. Thus the HfG soon focused on the aesthetics of everyday objects, while emphasizing mathematics in the design process. What resulted was a university that set out, as Chantel Blakely, a doctoral candidate in architecture at Columbia University, recently put it, "to change the alphabet of design to fit the world of experience," and to make communication, not just written or spoken words but also the language of design, "more rational." In practice, Bill and his fellow instructors taught Porsche and his fellow students to "reduce ornament to a fundamental and pure geometry of form."

As this school took shape, throughout Germany the country was cleaning up and rebuilding. German design historian Bernd Polster characterized it best. "Cities were in ruins," he explained. "It was more than disaster. All the German traditions were wiped out. And this was reflected in Ulm. They said, 'Here we start completely new.' This project was to clear up the minds and to clear up the surroundings of Germany. The big word was

not 'design,' but *gute form.'* It means the same . . . well . . . just like in other languages, the words can mean the same, and like in other languages, the words are completely different. *'Gute form'* is very moralistic."

Some historians have characterized HfG as a "reform school for good design." Jörg Petruschat, the editor of the German design review *Form + Zweck,* which devoted an entire issue to the school, declared that it was the "last institute to assemble under one roof artists and academics from the world of design who had one important thing in common: They sought to bring about profound changes in modern society . . . . Its independence remained an objective that could only be attained by combating forces from the outside world."

Into this heady environment, young Butzi Porsche took his place and his design aesthetic took shape. He not only learned philosophies and techniques of design but he also absorbed the intellectual world of international politics and culture, science, and art. This taught him to question how older techniques applied

While the idea for these Speedsters originated in the United States, Porsche paid attention to other ideas and concerns from outside the factory. By 1957, buyers wanted more luggage and rear-seat space.

Porsche's evolution from its earliest roadster to the Speedsters reveals significant advancements and improvements. Erwin Komenda's body design provided well-heeled buyers with an intimately proportioned automobile.

to newer products, and it gave him the courage to develop independent thought and ideas and to express his views. In 1957, as he finished up his education in this volatile mix of ideas and ideals, his family's firm approached the brink of change itself.

Back in Stuttgart, Porsche engineers Wilhelm Hild and Leopold Schmid worked to improve the suspension of Porsche's current car. They intended to use their results on a new, larger model. A customer's badly damaged 356 became the test bed onto which Schmid and Hild installed a Mercedes-Benz-derived front suspension. Hild, Schmid, and Karl Rabe sought a suspension that would support the larger car that Porsche's sales department wanted. Sales had watched 356 production quantities ebb and flow, and sales chief Wolfgang Raether had expressed his fear to Ferry Porsche that the worldwide market for an expensive two-seat sports car might be reaching saturation.

1959 356A CARRERA GT
The last of the A-series bodies appeared in 1959 as Porsche introduced the B series with lower rear seats that offer more space for larger riders or extra luggage in the rear of the passenger compartment. This is one of the most desirable versions of the A-coupe.

Years earlier, in 1952, Ferry had asked Erwin Komenda to design a larger, four-seater car as part of project 530. In the late 1950s, the term "design" barely existed. At that time in Germany according to historian Polster, engineers and technicians were like gods. While Max Bill called his new students at Ulm the "design heathens," Polster explained that when they graduated, they had become "design gods." Ulm's "*gute form*" was gaining acceptance. Yet Erwin Komenda's correct job title was most accurately "*blechtechnik*," or thin-metal technician. He had developed Porsche's sheet-metal technology and had done all body design since 1931. His decades-old technical education and his decades-long experience had taught him that strong curves gave thin metal its strength. Floating door cuts, for example, well inside the surface edges caused less stress to the metal.

When Ferry Porsche looked at Komenda's candidate for a 356 replacement, he saw a larger 356. This reflected the body chief's philosophy that any new Porsche must resemble what has come before. Yet, as Ferry looked across town to Sindelfingen, where Mercedes-Benz produced its cars, he saw their lithe

Porsche conceived the Carrera coupes as dual-purpose cars that owners could race around the track and then drive home. The Carrera seats offer superb support.

new 1955 190SL. It was a scaled-down version of the company's powerful 300SL and, while it carried over styling cues from the bigger sports car, it appeared trimmer. Looking to Munich, he saw BMW's striking Type 507. It seemed aggressive yet graceful.

Through Max Hoffman, his U.S. distributor, Porsche contacted Count Albrecht Goertz, who had designed the 507 for BMW. Goertz was a German living and working in New York City. Porsche gave him a set of dimensions and asked him to design a car with more interior space and an unbroken fastback roofline. Goertz spent eight months on the design, known internally as Project 695. His design prominently featured

Erwin Komenda defined the Porsche shape. Ferdinand Porsche wanted to be able to see where the front tires were. Komenda's prominent "stovepipe" made that possible.

1962 TYP 804 FORMULA ONE

Butzi Porsche's first design project was this simple racing car, which was essentially a thin aluminum and fiberglass skin covering a tubular space frame. Porsche produced only four, one of which won the French Grand Prix at Rheims with Dan Gurney driving.

quad headlights in the style of General Motors and Ford Motor Company. The roofline tapered down to rear fender height, but it ended abruptly in several angled surfaces adorned with three taillights per side. In profile, however, the Goertz roof shape and front fender forms hinted at what was to come. It just was too American for Ferry.

In 1957, Butzi joined the family business, reporting to overall design chief Karl Rabe. Rabe sent young Porsche to Franz Reimspeiss, who ordered him to learn the 356 engine.

"I had the assignment to memorize every piece from the engine parts list," Butzi Porsche recalled. "All the screws, the cylinder heads, the cylinders themselves, crankshaft, camshaft. Then I had to draw the engine in profile, the Carrera engine. It took quite a long time but in this way, I 'constructed' the engine by means of the parts list drawings. It was after that, after nine months with Mr. Reimspiess, that I went to the car body division to work with Mr. Komenda." Once Butzi was there, Komenda put the young designer to work in car body construction. "It was my father's wish that I get to know the car body division," Butzi explained, "and simply gather knowledge from scratch with the people there.

"Mr. Komenda was very strict. He naturally had formal views about steering wheels, about everything. He would say to me, 'No, no, it's not done like that. That's not the way to do it.' But despite all this, I was already sure what I was going to do one day. It was definitely to work with the car body in relation to the engine, and in connection with that, the design.

"'Design' means to me that every designing engineer becomes an 'artist' at some stage. When you speak of 'art' in this context, and that these designers are 'artists,' then I must say that every craftsman who can do more than what he was trained to do is an 'artist.' Because he develops a degree of perfection that surpasses the level of the acquired skills."

Butzi's first car, designed for Wilhelm Hild and Hubert Mimler in the racing department, was Porsche's Formula One car, introduced in 1962 as the typ 804. It was a relatively simple cigar shape. While the car body was aluminum, Butzi watched technicians cast seats in fiberglass for their factory team drivers and for customer racers. The success of this system led them to conceive of doing an entire car in fiberglass, the racing Carrera 904 GTS of 1964 and 1965.

This car had to meet specific FIA regulations for wheelbase, width, wheel track, and the interior, including a storage location for a mandatory suitcase of set dimensions. Butzi Porsche, who has characterized himself as a designer who cannot draw well, preferred to sketch quickly and then put his ideas to work in plasticine, a kind of car modeler's clay.

"The most important parameter for us with this car, however, was aerodynamics. But the most exciting feature of the 904 was really that it took only four months from making the plasticine model to completion of the one-to-one car model that was ready to drive.

"That was the beauty of this project. That's the reason the car body remained unchanged, because we were told, 'Nothing can be changed. There is a deadline by which this car must be completed.' For that reason, nobody had the chance to tell us what to do. Hans Tomala (the engineer who would take over technical directorship from Klaus von Rücker while both the 804 Formula One car and 904GTS projects were under way), wanted to lengthen the car body. The aerodynamics would have been slightly better that way. But there simply was no time.

"The most important thing is always to make a beeline for a goal, and not go looking for all the variants. When I make a drawing, I can already feel through the line that I am drawing the correction that needs to

This extraordinarily complicated flat-eight engine displaces just 1.5 liters (90 cubic inches), yet it develops 180 horsepower. It would inspire several future engine concepts for production cars.

Butzi Porsche's wind-tunnel model of the typ 695 reveals many of the shapes and forms that he would call on to develop the 901/911. The horizontal rear vents above the bumpers were moved to the top of the rear deck lid.

be done, because the line isn't doing what I want it to do. It is in my mind. I see it. I start it off. And that's when I start drawing."

Butzi Porsche's success with the racing 904 led him back into Erwin Komenda's car body department model shop. He arrived while Heinrich Klie, the company's chief modeler since 1951, struggled to modify Albrecht Goertz's design into something Ferry Porsche liked. Goertz had come up with a new concept, still within the typ 695 designation. As Klie executed it, he made half of it as Goertz designed it. But Klie did his own variation on the other half of the large form. Each of these got closer to what Ferry Porsche wanted. By this time, all seven designers in Komenda's department were hard at work. Gerhard Schröder, who had designed and created convertible tops for Speedsters and the A and B series 356, presented his own ideas. Konrad Bamberg and Fritz Plaschka joined Butzi in developing new forms. While Komenda had insisted that the new Porsche must resemble the existing cars, Butzi, the graduate of Ulm where the faculty emphasized independent thinking toward new decisions, wasn't so sure. "I was never convinced that we must build a new Porsche just like the old one.

"I could take nothing from the 904," Butzi explained. "This new car was required to have emergency seats, the rear jump seats. With those, it was impossible for me to build an offset tail as the 904 had. Also, there was the rear engine, where the 904 was a mid-engine. And there had to be headlights for the car. Driving at night was much more important for this production car than for the 904. Aerodynamics was given a higher priority in the 904, while headlights had the priority for the new car."

By early October 1959, Butzi had completed his first scale model. Designated the typ 754 T7, he based his concept on the 2,400-mm, 94.5-inch wheelbase specified for Komenda's four-seat typ 530 prototypes. Shortly afterward, Ferry set out to recapture the car's sportier nature, and he shortened the wheelbase by 200 mm to 2,200 mm or 86.625 inches. Ferry accepted Butzi's judgment that a full four seater would require a longer, flatter roof. Still favoring a fastback, the older Porsche agreed that rear seats in the new car would be occasional use only, so the roofline, too, could be more sporting. He based his decision on Germany's car industry, which had divided itself into companies that did economy compact cars, others that did family cars, still others that did its luxury models, and his own that did two-seat sports cars. A year later, in late 1960, another prototype, the 644 T8, took shape as a pure two-seater on a 2,100-mm, 82.69-inch, wheelbase. A vexing front suspension system left little room for a fuel tank, so that ended up in the rear. In October 1961, Porsche even tentatively set production start for the two-seater in July 1963. This target quickly became unrealistic, as Ferry understood that all the other problems could not be solved by then.

Working for Leopold Schmid, chassis engineer Helmuth Bott developed Porsche's new MacPherson strut front suspension, which was more space-efficient than what was originally carried over from the 356. This additional space allowed a safer, larger fuel tank up front and more storage capacity, so by 1962, Ferry Porsche returned the car to its 2,200-mm wheelbase, (111.72 mm, or 4.4 inches, longer than the 356). Now it was a 2+2 seater in what would become its final form. Aerodynamicist Josef Mickl worked with Butzi on the front end with its faired-in bumper and the elegant sweep of the roof angle. Tests in the University of Stuttgart wind tunnel with a 1:7.5 scale model of this latest version were encouraging.

While the nose barely changed, Porsche reconfigured the side and rear windows most noticeably. Angling the center pillar (B-pillar) backwards allows easier rear-seat access.

By July 10, 1963, drivable prototypes were out on public roads, masked with false panels to confuse anyone who might have seen the new two-door. The raised front lip hints at a radiator opening to mislead curious viewers.

Around Stuttgart, the automobile design world whirled. Alfa Romeo showed a Super Sprint coupe designed and constructed by Carrosserie Touring for 1960, and England's Aston Martin had introduced its DB4 coupe in 1958. In France, Citröen had startled the design world with its ID19 sedan in 1955. Flaminio Bertoni's futuristic shapes for the sedan blended sensuous curves with hard edges. Pininfarina's bodies for Ferrari hid headlights behind plastic, much like what Goertz had proposed in one of his prototypes. Butzi had used such a design on his 904. Throughout the industry, stylists thinned roof profiles, enlarged window glass, dipped windowsills lower, and made shapes such as Jaguar's racing-derived XKSS and production XK150 more sinuous. In contrast, across the Atlantic, automotive stylists working for flamboyant directors such as Harley Earl, Virgil Exner, Richard Teague, and Frank Hershey had turned to aircraft motifs that produced zaftig shapes with fins, hard edges, and sharp angles.

"I just think," Butzi Porsche said, "that you start creating edges when the body of the car is bad. This is true, too, for protective stripes or styling stripes. They are lines that support something that ties the designer down." For inspiration, Butzi looked closer to home, to the auto shows at Geneva, Frankfurt, Turin, and Paris.

"I've always found that when you go to automobile shows and come home afterward," he explained, "you subconsciously do things that you had seen there." (Butzi likely would have seen Pininfarina's inventive body for a custom Ferrari destined for actress Ingrid Bergman in newspapers and magazines throughout Europe. One of its most striking features was its upright rear window supported by two elongated buttresses, the "sugarscoop" shape that he improved on for his 904. Years later he recalled that the inspiration for the 901's

1964 PRODUCTION 901

A stunning collection of shapes, forms, and lines. The curves are easiest to recognize under this kind of soft, indirect light.

inset rear window came from Pininfarina's prototype for Lancia's Flavia 2+2 he saw at a show in 1957.) The bulging roundness of Komenda's shapes was slipping from design jargon. So was his dictate that any new Porsche *must* be like the old one. An era was passing. Butzi's car had slender pillars and a thin roofline with large windows all around. He designed in a big-opening rear window just ahead of the engine compartment.

Yet even as Komenda's aesthetic aged, his influence and personality remained strong. Siegfried Notucker, part of Komenda's seven-man design team, took care of the interior, most notably the instrument panel. As Notucker struggled to reckon with the information a driver needed and the desire to eliminate glare from those

Butzi Porsche added the roofline rear inset to create visual interest in the long curve from the windshield to the rear bumper. This also provides adequate bodywork to install slots to exhaust interior air.

gauges, Komenda came up as he did each day to see how his designers were working. Otto Soeding, a young design engineer from Hamburg's *Wagonbauschule* whom Komenda recently had hired to work on interiors, listened as his boss proposed forming the escutcheon into which each instrument fit around a large sphere. "It's a case of sitting a flat circle against a ball," he recalled Komenda telling his colleague. "It always will fit." Soeding watched as Notucker set two large gauges into the curved surface and gave birth to one of the car's iconic design solutions. By 1963, this had grown from a two-gauge cluster to Notucker's three- then five-instrument versions, symmetrically flanking a central tachometer, each clinging to a portion of Komenda's gently curved ball.

Otto Soeding contributed the 911's glove box, from the assignment through to production. Komenda looked over his work every day. "He had me work over every detail, time and again," Soeding recalled. "As I worked on a hinge, Mr. Komenda said it might take me seven iterations before I had it right. But if I returned to my initial concept, then that would tell me it was the right one." Unlike Butzi's intuitive "beeline for a goal without all

From their earliest production, 901 and 911 models featured this new five-instrument panel. Erwin Komenda suggested forming its elliptical shape around a very large ball to angle each gauge toward the driver.

the variants," Komenda advocated a more painstaking and exhaustive approach to the work. Soeding was a skilled and talented draftsman, and Komenda soon promoted him to the task of making engineering drawings for Butzi's 904 and for the new production model.

Earlier in the process, not every encounter with Komenda went smoothly. As Butzi's boss, Komenda advanced the young designer's concepts from paper and plasticine to engineering drawings. En route, he modified Butzi's drawings to coincide more closely with his own ideas.

"These were only the prototypes," Butzi recalled. "But come to think of it, some of it was absolutely crazy, just for the sake of giving a door a greater resemblance to a proper door, that the door had to go down relatively low and be round at the bottom. Mr. Komenda insisted on that.

"I think that the advantage of my time," he continued, "was the fact that I was the son, which can entail advantages and disadvantages. People would pay more attention to what I said due to the fact that I was the son, and had a direct line to the boss. I would be able to work out a proposition, put it in front of him and say, 'See! That's it!'"

Watching Butzi's designs change in the hands of an old and trusted friend was a hard message for Ferry Porsche to accept. As he explained to former Porsche Presse staff member Tobias Aichele, "I had to realize that a body designer was not necessarily a styling man, and vice versa." In response, Ferry took his son's propositions not back to Erwin Komenda but to Porsche's neighbor, Reutter Carrosserie, with whom Ferry and his father, Ferdinand, had worked more than a decade building Porsche's car bodies. Walter Beierbach, Reutter's managing director, assigned his own design department to complete Butzi's engineering drawings. Within a few months, by mid-1960, Komenda, who had been stunned by Ferry Porsche's action, came to accept

Hans Mezger did most of the design and development of this 2-liter, 130–brake horsepower, opposed-six-cylinder engine. Porsche selected Solex carburetors initially, but their soft metal housings soon proved to be a challenge to keep adjusted.

1964 904 CARRERA GTS

Decades after Butzi Porsche sculpted this beautiful racer, enthusiasts still praise its appearance. His successors have commented that one reason for Porsche's styling success is that the company allowed its designers "to work the surfaces to perfection."

Butzi did this design about the same time he created the 901/911. For this racer, engine access was crucial, while the 901/911 had to meet international headlight regulations and provide interior comfort.

it and he contributed to the new direction with his characteristic grace. Still, Komenda and Beierbach worked together to dissuade Ferry from adopting Butzi's opening hatchback rear window. Events next door with Reutter conspired to eliminate this feature and to delay other variations on the new car. (As a result, Butzi redesigned the coupe's B-pillar door-opening from one that angled forward to a door frame that canted rearward to allow easier rear passenger and luggage access.)

Reutter was vital to Porsche's plans for its new model. Beginning in 1949, Reutter Carosserie had produced Porsche's body shells and completed the trim. As Ferry Porsche calculated the costs of introducing this new car, he allocated a sizable portion to Reutter. For the coachbuilder, this would entail a large investment in new tooling, if not new buildings. This time Reutter said no. While founder Wilhelm Reutter had died in 1939, his son Albert perished in wartime bombing of Stuttgart. The family's outside manager had run the company successfully but, facing a sizable financial commitment, they chose instead to put the company up for sale. For Porsche there was little choice. Ferry invested nearly 6 million deutsche marks (about $1.5 million at the time) to acquire the coachbuilding firm; Porsche now employed its staff of nearly 1,000 and owned the business arrangement that it previously had enjoyed by contract. (The Reutter family retained its seat and seat assembly business, giving it a new name that abbreviated the original. Reutter Carosserie became Recaro.)

On top of this expense, Porsche then added another 6 million deutsche marks during 1963, to pay for tooling and a new building. As Ferry Porsche did his sums after this purchase, he saw the cost of his new model reaching 15 million deutsche marks (nearly $4 million at the time,) before it would reach the market. For a small company, this was a huge expense, and it led Ferry to concede that Porsche might have to withdraw from the 1963 Formula One Grand Prix season. It also affected some of Butzi's other ideas for the new car.

On the early cars, these engine and rear-brake cooling vents were discrete interruptions to the side of the car. By the time Porsche installed its flat-six racing engines in the last run of these cars, the intakes had nearly tripled in size.

Between late June and Christmas 1963, the younger Porsche designed a full line of models. This range included a sunroof coupe, the removable roof Targa, and a full cabriolet. Packaging problems put the cabrio on hold even as Butzi finished it. His side views did not allow enough space for the new 2-liter six-cylinder engine that engineering had developed for the car. But with 15 million deutsche marks committed, that much additional work was a luxury the company simply could not envision.

At the beginning of 1961, Ferry Porsche had named Butzi head of the model department, promoting him over Heinrich Klie. (Within a year Butzi changed its name to the styling department.) From then through 1963, he and fellow designers completed the myriad design and engineering drawing details on the new car. Butzi and his father sat in on meetings to sort out the new suspension. Leopold Schmid, suspension and engine design chief, and Erich Stotz, rear suspension system designer, worried that they had insufficient time to fully develop it. Yet Ferry and Hans Tomala, who replaced Klaus von Rücker in early 1962 as technical director, viewed the new, up-to-date MacPherson strut configuration as equal in importance to a new engine and Butzi's lean car body. The new car was becoming very expensive; delays throughout the company, from completion of floor-pan and suspension drawings to the suspension design itself, were making it more so, and Ferry Porsche wanted to do a new suspension now rather than later. Chassis engineer Helmuth Bott took the first drivable 901 prototype out for a run at 9 p.m. on Friday, November 9, 1962. Ferry Porsche had recently promoted Bott to head of the road test department, and he chose the late evening hour so fewer motorists would see the new car. Bott was pleased with what he drove.

It had been a battle worth fighting. As father and son looked around them, they saw startling new cars from Mercedes, especially Paul Bracq's handsome 230SL with its airy "pagoda" roof, Malcolm Sayer's stunning new Jaguar XK-E, Nuccio Bertone's handsome BMW 3200CS coupe, and even Chevrolet's striking Stingray, the collaborative multiyear effort of Peter Brock, Chuck Pohlman, and Larry Shinoda. Citroën showed elegant DS19 convertibles that Henri Chapron styled from the sedans. Everywhere, car designers had yanked forms out of the 1950s, simplified them, tidied them up, and made them more representative of the modern engineering technologies that worked beneath the sheet metal.

The whirlwind of auto industry activity in these three years brought a new parts distribution and sales agreement between Porsche and Volkswagen. This led to the 901 model designation for the new car. While Ferdinand Porsche labeled his very first outside project as number 7, so his first client would not know he was first, the company had fairly reliably followed the sequence upward from there. There were skips and gaps. However, the jump to 901 resulted from a computer's searching VW's parts number inventory and finding the only sequence still available was the nine hundreds.

Helmut Rombold, Porsche's chief of testing and Helmuth Bott's new boss, had introduced a rack-and-pinion steering system for testing in early 1962 after its success on the Grand Prix Model 804. This fulfilled a Porsche desire to provide right-hand steering for customers in the United Kingdom as well as affording a collapsible steering column for front crash safety. Work progressed designing and producing car body dies. Wilhelm Karmann Carosserie in Osnabruck joined the body production team along with Reutter, as Ferry Porsche anticipated increasing the manufacturing run. Soon after, Karosserie Weinsberg came on board for another portion of the manufacturing process. Now Porsche had to create not just two sets of some of its body stampings and parts casting dies, but a third set as well. The race was on to meet an absolute deadline of September 12, 1963. Porsche had contracted

Hans Tomala conceived the Carrera GTS as a race-tuned version of the new 901/911 six-cylinder engine. It wasn't until near the end of the assembly run that Porsche fitted those engines and began to describe the car as the prototype for the 906.

1965 356SC CABRIOLET

The 356 for the public road never got any better than the SC coupe and cabriolet versions. These cars used the 95-horsepower, 1,582-cc, 96.5-cubic-inch SC engine derived from the previous generation Super 90. Reutter manufactured the cabriolet car bodies.

The 356C series, including these SC or Super C models, introduced disc brakes to production Porsches. As *Illustrated Porsche Buyer's Guide* author, the late Dean Batchelor, said repeatedly, this was the 356 model that gave drivers the most of Porsche's good qualities.

a 211-square-meter floor space, stand 27, in Hall 1A at the 41st Annual IAA Frankfurt Auto Show, which opened that day, and the company intended to show off the new 901.

The car would not run in time for the show. It could not. Ferry Porsche's original target for Rabe, Komenda, von Rücker, and the rest of his staff was that the new car should perform like the 2-liter typ 587/1 overhead cam Carrera 2 model. He also wanted its 130 brake horsepower, but without its complex engine or its noise. Butzi's first running prototype 754 T7 utilized a 2-liter opposed four-cylinder engine mounted below the floor. This engine dictated the horizontal air-intakes on the car's sides behind the rear wheels. This engine, with overhead valves, needed two cooling fans to keep oil temperatures down. But it was even noisier than the Carrera engine it meant to replace.

Franz Reimspeiss experimented with Kugelfischer fuel injection on the old reliable typ 616 four-cylinder pushrod engine in 1961. But this package didn't meet Ferry Porsche's horsepower goal. Technical director von Rücker led efforts to devise an all-new opposed six-cylinder engine. Discussions in Ferry's office overruled any eight-cylinder engine, whether opposed or in V-configuration for the new car. It was too expensive to develop and it had too many pieces for economical manufacture for series production. For racing it was fine, and von Rücker and Reimspeiss began work on the typ 753 and typ 771 opposed-8s for racing.

Reimspeiss' next engine, designated the 745, displaced 1,991 cc through six cylinders of 80-mm bore and 66-mm stroke. With overhead valves and its side-draft carburetors outside the heads mounted nearly horizontally, it proved to be a bulky engine, and it was nearly as complex as the overhead cam racing typ 753 flat eight. On its bench tests, it developed 120 brake horsepower at 6,500 rpm, below Ferry's goal. Reimspeiss and

his staff enlarged the bore to 84 mm, which increased displacement to 2,195 cc. This delivered 130 brake horsepower, also at 6,500. However Reimspeiss and von Rücker concluded that its 60 mm stroke limited its potential. Such long pushrods would not survive higher engine speeds, so any future development toward more horsepower would require displacement increases. This, however, was the engine in the first drivable prototypes in early 1962, as von Rücker left to join BMW, and Hans Tomala, an engineer with farm tractor design in his background, took over as technical director for Porsche's factory, its experimental department, and its design office. Tomala reexamined every ongoing engineering project, including those relating to the new production car. One of Reimspeiss' earlier hires, Hans Mezger, got the next engine assignment.

Mezger joined Porsche in 1956 after graduating from the Stuttgart Technical Institute at age 30. He cut his teeth developing the valve gear on the typ 753 flat eight. This Grand Prix powerplant was an incomprehensibly complicated dual-overhead camshaft engine of just 1.5 liters displacement. It was durable and powerful, and for a time Ferry Porsche had contemplated using it in a high-end limited-production road car variation. Unfortunately, the engine required 220 hours to assemble, rendering it impossibly costly. Mezger had

The 356 was a very successful and long-lived model. When Porsche ended production in September 1965, the company had manufactured 86,303 of its 356C series. Little did anyone imagine that the next series would last many more decades.

1964 PILOT PRODUCTION 901 PROTOTYPE

As late in the process as this preproduction model was, Porsche still was developing details such as engine exhaust. This prototype showed a dual exhaust system that later would appear only on racing models while street models got a single left-side pipe.

established Porsche's computer program to design camshafts. So once he completed work on the intricate 753, it was a much easier task to conceive the intake system and valve gear for a 2-liter production car engine.

This interim engine followed the 616 and 745 models. Designated the 821, it had Mezger's dual-overhead camshafts, but it used a wet sump lubrication system. With Porsche's air-cooled engines being partially oil-cooled engines, the sump requirement was too large. This made the engine too tall for the body that Butzi had designed. The next improvement, the typ 901 engine, carried over many of the ideas of the 821, but it used dry sump lubrication. Engineers could build and install the engine lower in the car and closer to the ground, improving the car's balance and road holding. This made the car's long sweeping roofline a sure thing. Butzi's cousin, Ferdinand Piëch, the son of Ferry's sister Louise Piëch, supervised the 901 engine development and got it production-ready in time for late 1963 testing and the 1964 manufacturing start-up. Mezger and Piëch specified a three-barrel Solex overflow carburetor over each bank of cylinders, equipped with one float chamber for the three 30-mm venturis. This controlled the rate of fuel as it flowed from the fuel tank, metering it as it flowed through the jets into the cylinders. It offered enthusiastic Porsche drivers the benefit of no float to hang up from centrifugal force in hard cornering situations. This condition normally would interrupt fuel supply and cause the engine to stumble or stall. In this configuration, after Mezger's work and Piëch's testing and development, the 901 engine developed

130 DIN horsepower at 6,100 rpm. In the United States, the Society of Automotive Engineers measured gross horsepower and, using this SAE standard, the engine put out 148 horsepower.

This power led to another of the last-minute decisions just before the September auto show. Egon Forstner, from Porsche's calculating department, had determined the size of the cooling air intake that this engine required. Butzi Porsche immediately set his fellow designers to work. They came up with six different grille configurations covering this 0.75-square-foot opening. Final dimensions had to await actual driving tests, which Helmut Rombold's testing staff completed just days before the Frankfurt show opened.

In sheer numbers, most everything about the new car represented an improvement. Butzi's larger greenhouse provided 58 percent more glass area than the 356. With the front trunk and rear storage, the 901 offered nearly twice the luggage capacity. While its frontal area increased to 17.9 square feet from 17.4 for the 356, Josef Mickl's aerodynamic work brought the car's coefficient of drag down to 0.380 from 0.398 for the earlier car. The new car carried over Alfred Teve's Ate disc brakes tested on the 695 project and introduced on the 356C models. At the last minute, as Porsche and his engineers worried over final details, Ferry authorized the latest rear suspension for production. This retained the trailing steel arms and the transverse torsion bars, but engineer Helmuth Bott's new system used open half shafts connected to two universal joints per side from the transaxle instead of the axle tube as the primary means to constrain rear wheel movement. While it cost more, it was necessary. The 901 engine, fully equipped with starter, clutch, generator, and other accessories, weighed 405 pounds. (The intricate 185-horsepower typ 753 flat-eight racing engine weighed 341 pounds.) This was the heaviest engine Porsche ever had produced. No one was sure how customers of average driving skill would do with so much weight so far back.

Delays compounded costs. Running prototypes hit the roads in March and April 1963, just months in advance of the Frankfurt show. The company completed just seven by the day the show opened. (The show model displayed number 5; it was assembled at Karmann in Osnabruck, and painted yellow.) Ferry Porsche looked at totals of 15 million deutsche marks beyond the purchase of Reutter as September approached. Three things were clear to the man whose father had founded the company and whose name emblazoned every car that left its plant: Porsche could not return to Formula One racing. The convertible could not possibly happen for years. And this new car could not fail. ▤

It's an instrument panel used in no other known 911. Only the very earliest 356s provided just two large instruments, but that configuration disappeared nearly a decade before design and engineering fabricators completed this unique automobile.

THE FIRST GENERATION
1964 – 1969

"No contest.

This is the Porsche to end all Porsches

or, rather, to start a whole new generation

of Porsches."

Car and Driver, April 1965

By the time the guards locked the doors on the final day of the 1963 Frankfurt show, more than 800,000 people had filed through the halls. Certainly not all of them came to see Porsche's new 901, but the impact the car had on automotive enthusiasts and journalists was out of proportion to the company's size. It was, however, in perfect balance with Porsche's reputation and status in its industry.

Five years earlier, Porsches virtually had ruled the autobahns. Few German drivers experienced a Ferrari, Maserati, Aston Martin, or Jaguar passing them. A Mercedes-Benz 300SL was a rarity. Yet most natives recognized the 356 shape and knew they should whole families riding in comfortable Mercedes-Benz 220SE sedans found themselves drawing up on the 356s, and it was Porsche drivers who watched their mirrors. The new car with its sleek body, its powerful engine and five-speed transmission, and its innovative suspension, restored the hierarchy of the roads. However, for a company that had completed only seven prototypes of its new model, the workload it faced would call for all its resources.

There was development to finish and more money to be invested in this new 901 before the first customer could take delivery. What had Ferry Porsche been thinking, showing this car so long before anyone actually could take delivery?

If Ferry's crucial decisions to push for the better suspension—for Butzi's startling body shape, and for Mezger's clever engine, each had been a wise choice—his reasoning for the 1963 show premier revealed his smartest strategy. With one single yellow coupe, Porsche put the sports car world on notice: In a few months (although it actually would be nearly a year), they could purchase one of these. Do they really want that French Alpine Renault A110 with its meager 87 horsepower? The new British Aston Martin DB5 is nice, but even with more than twice the 901's horsepower, it's staggeringly expensive. (It would prove to be twice the price of the 901.) And where do they get it serviced? The new BMW 2000CS, well, what's to say? BMW continues to put that 100-horsepower engine in the wrong place in its cars? A Ferrari? Great cars for dukes and princesses and movie stars. The Mercedes 230SL? Well, yes, 10 more horsepower, but one fewer gear, and so costly!

Porsche counted its orders and prepared its show car for the next display at the Paris Salon in October. There it captivated a French motoring population even as it elevated eyebrows at *Automobiles Peugeot*, who found themselves at unexpected odds with the German carmaker despite the vastly different autos each produced. In 1929 Peugeot had introduced its low-priced Model 201. The company registered with the French government's office of copyrights and patents the right to use three-digit model designations incorporating a zero in the middle. The 201 represented chassis series 2, with the 1.1-liter engine. By 1963, Peugeot had advanced through its 301, 401, and 601 series to its latest models, the 403 and 404. After the Paris show closed, Peugeot let Porsche know it could not use the 901 designation in France.

France represented a large enough market for Porsche's cars that it chose not to antagonize the nation or the other carmaker. It did not remind anyone that its Carrera 904GTS already had raced in France, and its 804 Formula One car had won there at Rheims circuit without any comment from Peugeot. Porsche renumbered the new production car as the 911. Parts numbers and internal designations at Zuffenhausen and VW's headquarters at Wolfsburg remained 901 but those were out of the public eye. Then, following a brief wait, Porsche's venerable racing and public relations director, Baron Huschke von Hanstein, appealed to the Fédération Internationale des Automobiles (FIA), the world auto racing governing body with its headquarters in Paris. Von Hanstein pointed out that Porsche's racing models, not regularly sold to customers, should be able to retain the 804 and 904 middle zero configuration. The FIA, flummoxed by this dilemma, agreed. Von Hanstein quickly announced development of a new model, the 904 successor known as the 906 Carrera 6. Peugeot remained mum.

1965 911

Porsche started series production on the 901 in September 1964. French automaker Peugeot protested the "0" in the designation, so since November 10, 1964, the new coupe has been known as the 911.

Right: ZUFFENHAUSEN PRODUCTION, CIRCA 1966

Porsche's 911 assembly line was not entirely automated or mechanized. Cars awaiting their engines line up on the left, while those with front and rear suspensions and full running gear are moved around by manpower on seemingly precarious three-wheel carts. *Porsche Archives*

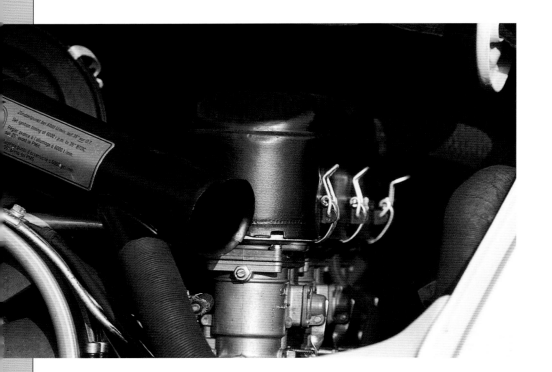

All through 1965 production, and up until March 1966, Porsche fitted Solex triple-choke carburetors to the 911s. But when Solex had trouble with its castings, Porsche switched to Webers, which it used until fuel injection replaced carburetors.

Not only did potential Porsche 911 buyers have to wait nearly a year for their dream car, but the company tested the automotive media's patience as well. There simply were no cars that were enough like final production models to let journalists have their way with them. In fact, one of the delays came from Porsche's need to complete the customer 904 race cars as well as to ensure production of the final edition 356, the C and SC versions that had shared Frankfurt floor space with the new 911.

Both England's *The Motor* magazine and America's *Car and Driver* ran Frankfurt show preview stories that appeared as the show opened. With typical reserve, the writer for *The Motor* announced that, "For the enthusiast, perhaps the most notable car at the Frankfurt Show is the new typ 901 Porsche, with a six-cylinder 2-liter engine." It concluded a few short paragraphs later by stating that, "Production of this typ 901, which is planned to give a 120-mile-per-hour-plus performance with much greater refinement, cannot begin 'for some time.'" *Car and Driver*'s writer, limited to slightly more than half a page beneath a large photo, was awe-struck:

"Wipe that drool off your chin; it's not going to be ready for almost a year and it won't be cheap when it gets here. We're talking about the Porsche 901, to be introduced after a long, rumor-filled gestation period . . . . "

Road & Track, the most British of U.S. magazines, got correspondent Hansjörg Bendel into one of Porsche's earliest production models for a test it published in March 1965. Bendel commented that, "The new Porsche 911, née 901, is the first entirely new Porsche in 16 years. All previous models were developments of the typ 356 that first saw daylight in 1948 . . . .

"Inside the car," Bendel continued, "the theme, 'completely new yet unmistakably Porsche' is played in many variations. The overall impression is that this car was built by men who know something about fast motoring and that it is destined for owners who feel the same."

A month later, in April, *Car and Driver* let its entertaining sense of dramatic overstatement loose on its readers. "No contest," it began. "This is the Porsche to end all Porsches—or, rather, to start a whole new generation of Porsches. Porsche's new 911 model is unquestionably the finest Porsche ever built. More than that, it's one of the best *Gran Turismo* cars in the world, certainly among the top three or four. . . .

"Only yesterday," the unidentified writer gushed, "the 356 seemed ahead of its time. Today you realize its time has passed; the 356 leaves you utterly unimpressed and you can't keep your eyes off the 911. The 911 is a superior car in every respect . . . the stuff legends are made of." Readers almost needed to pause and catch their breath after such prose. Elegant photos from Porsche's own Julius Weitmann illustrated the Frankfurt

1966 BERTONE 911 ROADSTER

California racer and Porsche dealer Johnny von Neumann felt strongly that Porsche needed to build an open-model 911. When he got no response from the factory, he commissioned Italian designer Nuccio Bertone to create a prototype. This is his concept.

show car arcing through body-swaying turns or parked on endless cobblestones. Each magazine pushed and punished its test cars, recording 0–60-mile-per-hour elapsed times, standing-start quarter-mile times, and observed top speeds. *Car and Driver*'s times always beat *Road & Track*'s (*R&T*) results, but it was not that one magazine got a faster or slower car. *Car and Driver* performed its acceleration tests with a driver and minimal test instrumentation only, and its testers ran the engine well up in revolutions before abruptly releasing the clutch. *R&T*'s tests carried not only the driver but also the test instrument operator and gear, and their clutch treatment was less brutal. *Car and Driver* got the 911 to 60 miles per hour in 7.0 seconds while *R&T* got there in 9.0. Quarter-mile times ranged from 16.5 for *R&T* down to 15.6 seconds for *Car and Driver*, while *R&T* saw 132

miles per hour top speed against *Car and Driver*'s 130. Reviews from other magazines around the United States and Europe were equally as positive, if slightly less categorical than *Car and Driver*. In all, these were the kind of responses that racing and press boss Huschke von Hanstein and sales chief Harald Wagner prayed for.

Reutter, Karmann, and Weinsberg body works wasted no time getting production up to Porsche's pace. To meet the unexpectedly high demand, Karmann assumed a greater role in assembling and trimming out complete 911 car bodies. With manufacture of both 356C and SC coupes and cabriolets continuing in the shadow of such enthusiastic praise and support for his new car, Ferry Porsche looked to discontinue the older models by the end of the 1965 model year.

While striking in appearance, Bertone's open-model 911 is much more Italian in character than German. The roadster's lack of "Porsche-ness" is one of several factors that killed it.

Butzi Porsche had completed a full car line when he added drawings in late 1963 for the sunroof coupe, the removable-roof Targa, and the cabriolet. His father and sales director Wolfgang Raether had conceived the 911 as a full-range line, just as the 356s had been. They planned a deluxe version. This would be the car shown at Frankfurt but fitted with a leather interior. A Sport or "S" model with 150 horsepower would top out the line. An entry-level or standard version utilizing the four-cylinder engine from the 356 would be their third variant. Porsche had designated the four-cylinder model as the 902. This became the 912 after Peugeot voiced its objections.

About the time *Car and Driver* published its road test on the 911, Porsche began manufacturing the 912, in April 1965. American magazines announced this new model almost immediately and got their chances to drive it during the next winter. *Road & Track* liked their version and found its road manners gentle and forgiving. "Now, oversteer is a thing of the past, and one no longer need be an expert of any kind to keep from losing it?even in the wet. Fact is, it's well nigh impossible to trip up the 912 on a winding mountain road. Both ends grip tenaciously, and about the only way to break the back loose is the same technique applied to front-heavy cars: brake in the middle of a tight turn." With 1,600-cc displacement (this was the 1600 SC engine in the 356SC models) and only 102 brake horsepower, even with its optional five-speed transmission, it just wasn't powerful enough to kick out the back end of the car. That would await the arrival of the upper end of the 911 range, the S model.

By the end of 1965, Porsche had manufactured 3,390 of the 911 models and 6,401 of the four-cylinder 912s. Wolfgang Raether and Harald Wagner cut frills on the 912 in order to bring its price close to the 356C coupe. Many customers enthralled by the 1963 Frankfurt show car realized they could have 911 looks and handling for about $1,000 less if they could do without the 911's engine. (The optional five-speed transmission added 300 deutsche marks, about $75.) But nearly all these 912 purchasers were in Europe. To best serve its loyal customers at home, Porsche decided to not export the 912 to North America until the company ended production of the 356C models. This came in September 1965 at the start of the 1966 model year.

Ferry Porsche's wish for an open version of the 911 brought about the next new model announcement. The company's first automobile had been a roadster, and following its Gmund coupes, it had offered open cars continuously. Making room for a collapsible top infringed too greatly on the engine compartment of the new car. In addition, while Helmuth Bott had tamed some of the 911's handling peculiarities, removing the steel roof would bring some back and make others worse. The 911 simply was not stiff enough to support a fully open version at this early stage. Yet in late 1961, Ferry asked Reutter's Walter Beierbach to consider how to develop a cabriolet from Butzi's typ 745 T7 styling proposal. That request got lost in the hustle of developing the

To create the sleek, low body, Bertone dropped the cowl height by relocating the instruments to a vertical console. Bertone used leather lavishly.

coupe. A year later, scale drawings and a model went to Karmann at Osnabruck to determine the feasibility of manufacturing an open car. Butzi's first variation with convertible stylist Gerhard Schröder's input on folding systems and retractable bows showed a car with a collapsible padded top that stored beneath a boot that provided a low silhouette. Another idea used a removable top that the owner stretched over bows stowed in a small boot. The final option showed a removable two-piece roof with one panel over the driver and passenger and a second as the rear window. These pieces attached either to a fixed-in-place roof bow, or to something collapsible offering a clean profile.

While von Neumann and Bertone worked on this car, Porsche was applying finishing touches to its own variation with a built-in roll bar. Porsche engineers realized that an open 911 needed chassis stiffening, a fact von Neumann had not considered.

ZUFFENHAUSEN PRODUCTION,
CIRCA 1967

A technician assembles the front steering rack and suspension. Behind his back, dozens of other Zuffenhausen mechanics and technicians complete the variety of tasks necessary to produce 1967–model year 911s. *Porsche Archives*

Butzi favored the true cabriolet. "Open cars at Porsche," he explained, "always have been roadsters or speedsters. These have followed a distinct shape for the roof that is not the same fastback form as our coupes. I wanted a clear break in the roofline to the rear of the car so as to reemphasize that roadster character." His cabrio roof silhouette required new body panels for the rear end of the car. It was too expensive.

Making the roof bow collapsible, whether as a single stout one or several typically slender ones, required body modifications that Butzi had not foreseen. Nor had Erwin Komenda recommended them when he ordered engineering drawings of the 911 car body. Gerhard Schröder's experience with Komenda's other convertibles showed him clearly where the problems lay. "With the engine in place," Schröder explained to Tobias Aichele, "the folded top would have stood above the body, like a VW Beetle cabriolet, and that would not have been acceptable for a sports car of Porsche's stature." That left only one alternative. The broad center bow would remain fixed rigidly. It could support two individual removable panels while offering additional stiffness to the open car body.

There was another consideration that influenced the configuration. The U.S. government threatened to define vehicle safety. Consumer activist Ralph Nader had crippled sales of General Motors' Corvair. Chevrolet built this car with a rear-mounted air-cooled engine, just like Porsche, and with independent swing axles, like the 356 Porsche. However, the Corvair never got the rear anti-sway bar that its engineers vigorously recommended. The car suffered several bad crashes and disastrous publicity followed. GM's smear campaign against Nader set auto buyers on edge, embarrassed the U.S. auto industry, and stimulated Congress to contemplate design and engineering mandates. As Helmuth Bott explained in an interview in 1992, "There were several reasons we did not introduce a true cabriolet at the beginning. We were worried that the American Congress might legislate against convertibles. That had been a big portion of our market for the open cars. Also, we could not afford the costs to retool body panels to hide the roof and its bows. And, from my point of view, most importantly, the integral rollover bar made the open 911 much stiffer and therefore much safer. And while others did not have this, we would again lead the industry."

By mid-June 1964, Porsche had a styling prototype complete. Six months later, in late January 1965, Bott drove a prototype with additional reinforcement at the base of the A-pillars. "It was," he recalled, "as stiff as I expected, about as stiff as the current 356 cabriolet, but not as much as I would have wished. In time, of course, it became much better."

The roof treatment was similar to an option that English sports and compact car maker Triumph introduced in 1962 on its new TR4 two-seater. This car, styled by Italy's Giovanni Michelotti, introduced a hardtop in which owners could remove its solid center section and drive with it open, or replace the rigid panel with a canvas top. Porsche's patent expert Emil Soukup learned about this innovation, but he determined it differed enough from their own to allow Porsche to patent its version. Sales chief Harald Wagner had christened it the "Targa" during a conversation with other sales executives. They had discussed how automakers used racetrack names for some of their models. Porsche already had used "Carrera," after the Mexican road race. In the 1930s, Alfa Romeo had a Monza and more recently Opel in Germany used the Monza name. Its parent company GM had named a performance version of its Chevrolet Corvair after the Italian track as

1965 PROTOTYPE TARGA

While Butzi Porsche's concept for the 901/911 included several open variations, engineering considerations delayed model introduction. In mid-1965, both design and engineering had a prototype ready for wind tunnel testing prior to its Frankfurt Auto Show introduction in the fall. *Porsche Archives*

1967 911S TARGA

The 911S or Sport package was another exciting introduction for 1967. This model offered competitive drivers a 160-horsepower version of the 2-liter engine, as well as Fuchs alloy wheels.

Porsche answered ongoing customer demand for an open car with this model they named the Targa. Its integral roll bar serves to stiffen the chassis and provide solid top closure.

well. "Targa" was a word easily spoken in any language. When Wagner and others learned the word meant "shield" in Italian, it resonated well with Butzi Porsche who had insisted that the central bar remain highly visible. He highlighted its function using a brushed stainless-steel finish. Press director Huschke von Hanstein capitalized on the feature in his press release in September 1965: "It is Porsche's privilege to be the first auto manufacturer in the world to offer a roll bar on a production car." Targa manufacture began a year later as a 1967 model. Porsche started cautiously, assembling just seven Targas each day out of every 55 cars that came off the assembly line.

The Targa wasn't convertible enough for some of Porsche's dealers. Californian Johnny von Neumann had contributed his ideas and opinions to Max Hoffman as early as 1953. Von Neumann sold Porsches in southern California that he got through Hoffman, Porsche's U.S. importer. Summers in southern California were hot, and von Neumann believed his customers wanted "a Speedster, a boulevard race car." They wanted a car that on any Saturday evening in the summer they could drive "down Sunset Boulevard with their elbow over the door and the

girls can see them in the car . . . and they can see the girls on the walks!" Von Neumann visited Hoffman, who talked to Germany. In September 1954, Porsche introduced a 1,500-cc, 1,675-pound, $2,995 Speedster. Initial production came directly to Hoffman, who shuttled most of them across the country to von Neumann. Europeans couldn't even get one for the first nine months. They were popular with West Coast racers, boulevard cruisers, and movie stars. The Speedster established a Porsche icon and it gave von Neumann credibility.

Johnny von Neumann looked at Butzi Porsche's new 911 and by October 1965, he had gotten another idea. With Max Hoffman dead, and Porsche's Targa now public information, von Neumann bypassed New York and Stuttgart on his way to Turin, Italy. He approached Nuccio Bertone with his idea of doing a series of at least 100 Porsche roadsters. Von Neumann would supply as much of the 911 as Bertone wanted and he and his staff would design, assemble, and finish the open car. Bertone made sketches and began working on a prototype. Von Neumann went to Porsche and spoke to Ferry and to sales boss Harald Wagner.

Porsche selected the name Targa to commemorate its frequent victories in Italy's challenging Targa Florio open road race. This roof system consists of a removable top over the driver and passenger and a zippered plastic back window to create a truly open car.

1967 911R PROTOTYPE

These "R," or *rennsport*, models are Porsche's first attempt at disguising a race car in production clothing. The R was the brainchild of brilliant engineer Ferdinand Piëch. He conceived these competition cars for events that allowed production-based vehicles with unique modifications.

"They kept saying, you know, you would have to sell this car for about $7,000," von Neumann recalled in an interview in 1991. "That's what came out of their price calculations. My idea was to have them deliver the platforms to Bertone with, let's say, wiring and that stuff in it." Bertone would fit the body and interior and then ship the car back to Porsche for the engine and drivetrain. Porsche had done that before with 356 cabriolets built in Switzerland, and 356 racers produced by Carlo Abarth in Italy.

Ferry Porsche was wary. "Well, you know," he told von Neumann, "it has our name on it, so we are concerned to be sure it is going to be right." At that point, von Neumann recalled, he felt that his project was doomed. But it was a while before he understood the cause of death.

Bertone introduced the car on their stand in March 1966 at the Geneva International Auto Show. It was a striking Italian-looking Porsche. They had finished it just hours before the doors opened, similar to Porsche's own experience with its 901 at Frankfurt. On another stand, Porsche had its Targa with its body-reinforcing roll bar.

"The thing that killed it," von Neumann recognized 35 years after its debut, "was something they already knew . . . when you make a convertible out of a coupe, there's some chassis movement, flexing."

At Geneva, von Neumann and Bertone received some interest but not a single order ever materialized. Perhaps like Count Albrecht Goertz's typ 695 prototypes that were "too American," this one was too Italian a

solution to the question of how to make a 911 cabriolet. Or perhaps the Swiss and other European visitors to the show looked at the Targa and saw Porsche's own perfect answer.

As Helmuth Bott worked to reinforce the Targa's chassis, he split his time with another project that the true Porsche performance enthusiasts anticipated. The "S," or sport model, bore most of its improvements in its engine. Small but significant changes elevated output to 160 DIN brake horsepower at 6,600 rpm, or 180 horsepower using SAE's gross rating. To achieve this 30-horsepower increase, engineer Paul Hensler enlarged valve diameters and extended valve timing to bring more fuel mixture in and move the exhaust out more thoroughly.

Weber carburetors marked another major change, although this was an improvement bestowed on the standard 911 as well. The "base" model began using three-barrel model 40IDA3C carburetors starting March 2, 1966. The throttle bodies of the overflow Solexes had proven too soft, and Porsche mechanics experienced difficulty keeping them in tune. For the new S model, Porsche selected Weber's 40IDS3Cs, with 32-mm venturi, compared to the base models' 30-mm intakes. All of this combined to increase torque output to 132 ft-lb at 5,200 rpm. This higher level, nearly 1,000 rpm above the peak on the base engine, made it clear this car was the new autobahn runner. The five-speed transmission (with a higher top gear and a lower first, along with torque and horsepower arriving well up in the engine range) ensured good acceleration at high speed. With its top speed at 141 miles per hour, only Ferraris, Maseratis, Aston Martins, and Lamborghinis, at twice the price, were faster.

New forged-aluminum wheels from Fuchs let more cooling air reach the brake rotors while saving almost 5 pounds at each corner. To better keep the wheels and tires on the road, Bott and his colleagues fitted larger front and new rear anti-sway bars along with adjustable Koni shock absorbers from Holland. Interiors had vinyl seats that had inserts in either corduroy or houndstooth cloth, or optional full-leather seats. Leather wrapped the steering wheel, and the dash lost its wood trim, replaced in the S with embossed padded vinyl.

Huschke von Hanstein got a test car into reviewers' hands in early August 1966, almost two full months before its public introduction date as a 1967 model. The magazines had mixed feelings about the new car.

Above: The heart of this wolf in sheep's clothing is the twin-spark-plug typ 901/22 flat six, a variation of the racing Carrera 6 engine. With its two Weber 40IDA3C carburetors, the engine develops 210 brake horsepower.

Above, left: Porsche's racing department stripped everything from these cars to cut their weight. In their leanest trim, the cars weigh just 823 kilograms (1,810 pounds).

Porsche's racing manager, Huschke von Hanstein, advocated a large production run for the 911R models, perhaps 500 or more. But the noisy stripped-down cars frightened marketing and sales managers, who believed that regular customers may admire race cars but would never buy one.

It certainly was quicker. *Car and Driver* got theirs from 0 to 60 miles per hour in 6.5 seconds, a half-second less than the base 911, through the quarter-mile in 15.2, compared to 15.6 seconds, and up to an overall top speed at 140 miles per hour compared to 130. However, *Car and Driver*, *Road & Track*, and even some of the European magazines found the car more challenging to drive in urban settings, where its high torque and horsepower curves didn't favor stop-and-go realities.

Porsche offered the base 911, now with a four-speed gearbox, for $5,990 in New York City, and the four-cylinder 912 came in at $4,790. The S, priced at $6,990, topped the model line in performance and features. Porsche established the Targa as a $400 option for any of its models, and both the 912 and base model 911 could get Fuchs wheels for $375 and the five-speed transmissions for $80.

Model year 1966 was Porsche's first full year with 911 and 912 production only. If Ferry Porsche still had any concerns, 1966 went a long way toward eliminating them. The company experienced record production at

12,820 cars. Nearly three-fourths, 9,090, were the affordable entry-level 912s. More than half of all its cars came to the United States, a sales and manufacturing feat aided greatly by Porsche's completion of its emissions test facility at Zuffenhausen. This was the first in Europe that the U.S. Environmental Protection Agency (EPA) had approved for vehicle certification over its official driving cycles.

In 1967, with three complete model lines, Porsche manufactured a total of 11,011 cars. Of these, 6,472, or more than half, were 912s. Of this same total, the United States swallowed 5,400, slightly less than half the company's entire output.

Porsche's emissions lab proved necessary for model year 1968. With its large Weber carburetors, its bigger intake and exhaust valves, and its slightly rich fuel mix, Porsche could not get the 911S to meet new exhaust emissions standards that went into effect in the United States. As a result, the company chose to not export the high performance model. Instead, it created a 130–DIN horsepower 911L variation, "L" meaning luxury,

Ferdinand Piëch's mechanics assembled four R prototypes, of which this was the third. Each advanced his ideas on weight reduction and power increase. Once he was satisfied, Piëch approved assembly of another 20 "production" models.

1967 911R

While this is perhaps the most significant of the R models, it's also one of Porsche's most important racers, even in its rough, unrestored state. Over four days, this car ran flat out and collected five world and eleven international speed records. The car has subsequently been restored.

or *luxus*. This utilized the interior and trim features of the S but packaged them into the base model. As the top U.S. offering, Porsche fitted the L with ventilated disc brakes but also with the EPA's mandatory emission-reducing air-injection pump. The base 911, with the same 130-horsepower engine, had solid brake rotors. In Europe, the new 911L fit between the 911S and another new issue, the 911T. Porsche's sales department targeted the 911T as a six-cylinder model to sell in Germany for less than 20,000 deutsche marks (about $5,000 U.S. at the time.) Introduced with a four-speed transmission, solid disc brakes, and no anti-sway bars, these differences along with its detuned engine kept the price down. Its flat six developed 110 DIN brake horsepower at 5,800 rpm, and 116 ft-lb of torque at 4,200 rpm. Its SAE power rating was 125. Devoid of trim and luxuries that were standard even on the base model, this reduction in features provided Porsche's competition department with a benefit: The 911T was about 35 kilograms—some 77 pounds—lighter than the base 911. Amazingly, this lightweight combination offered performance near the base model. Germany's *auto motor*

und sport magazine achieved 0-to-60-mile-per-hour acceleration times of 8.1 seconds and a top speed of 129 miles per hour.

Some of Porsche's most interesting models in 1967 and 1968 were those it not only did not sell in the United States, but that it kept for itself or released only to well-known customers. These were special variations created in Ferdinand "Beurly" Piëch's experimental department, in Peter Falk's competition department, and in Hans Mezger's racing engine shop. They had letter designations that few outsiders recognized until years later, the 911R in 1967 and the 911ST and 911GT in 1968 and later years. These were cars made *for* Europe's long distance rallies, endurance races, and speed record trials, and then made famous *by* their victories on them.

The "R," or race, models began as Ferdinand Piëch's challenge to see how lean a 911 could be. Four prototypes endured a severe weight loss program, with each successive example using thinner fiberglass panels and Plexiglas windows, and metalwork that was drilled and perforated like Swiss cheese. Rolf Wütherich, a

Unearthed in a Paris suburb, this 911R had campaigned in countless races after its 96-hour endurance run at Monza, Italy. Widened rear wheels and bodywork were not part of Ferdinand Piëch's original configuration, but these modifications helped keep the car competitive for decades.

Like a pipe organ, these 46-mm Weber triple-choke carburetors make beautiful music. The exhaust freely flows through resonators and creates a tone that's easily recognized by racing enthusiasts throughout the world.

talented mechanic in Peter Falk's race shops, had developed a system and a device for precisely placing and drilling holes in almost any body panel, seat rail, or foot pedal. With painstaking patience, he shaved away ounces all over the cars.

Porsche had campaigned its 911s and helped customers race the cars on road courses, and in hill climbs and rallies starting in 1966. The 911S model opened a new horizon, and Porsche published a special catalog that included new venturis and jets for the Weber carburetors as part of Sport Kit I. Larger diameter anti-sway bars, different compound brake pads, and a virtually open racing exhaust were part of Sport Kit II. Belly pans and stone deflectors, Recaro seats, and 911L cylinder heads with 911S cams comprised the meat of Rally Kit I. Rally Kit II gave the buyer the full 160 horsepower 911S engine, making the car a 911ST. But these were options for limited-production-based racing applications (a minimum of 500 built), those in the FIA's Group 4, Special GTs. Production S models modified for racing qualified for Grand Touring Group 3 (for production

GTs). In this under-2-liter category, the 911 raced against Alfa Romeo 1600 Giulia GTs, BMW 1800 TISA sedans, Ford's Lotus Cortina, Lancia Flavias, and MGBs. It seldom was a fair match for Porsche's competition. This was a large category that required a minimum of 1,000 identical cars from a manufacturer in order for homologation, that is, to qualify the car for competition. Porsche's goal was to race its 911 in Group 2, (the touring car category), a much larger group that still called for 5,000 identical cars but for which homologation was based on measurements that, as a two-door coupe, Porsche couldn't meet.

It made no sense for Porsche to manufacture 500 of its R models unless they would be homologated and yet, in its best catch-22 circular reasoning, the FIA would not homologate the model without evidence that Porsche had produced 500 of them. While Huschke von Hanstein and his new press and racing deputy Rico Steinemann appealed for admission, Ferdinand Piëch began his experiments. Lightening the 911 wherever possible, he and his engineers replaced standard steel panels with thinner gauge steel or fiberglass whenever they could. Glass windows went out and wafer-thin Plexiglas replaced side and rear windows. Peter Falk in the competitions department and his colleagues sealed the front quarter windows in place but drilled large holes which they fitted with circular aircraft-type vents. They glued louvers into the rear quarter windows in an effort to get some air circulation into the stark cockpits. All the sound and weather insulation got discarded and Scheel's lightest-weight competition bucket seats replaced the stock models. Karl Baur in Stuttgart assembled the bodies of these lightweights for Porsche. Piëch's engineers lowered ride height 50 mm, slightly less than 2 inches, and fitted 6-inch-wide front wheels and 7-inch rear ones. This increased front and rear track, the better to cope with the greater pendulum-effect handling challenges that a lighter body coupled to a much more powerful engine would guarantee. This 1,991-cc engine was more similar to the racing typ 906

The sound inside the car rivals the sound outside because all of the sound insulation has been stripped away. Paper-thin Plexiglas side and rear windows, as well as thinner laminate windshields, contribute to weight loss.

Carrera 6 than the 911S. Mezger fitted giant 46-mm Weber carburetors, and domed pistons provided 10.3:1 compression. The engine developed 210 DIN brake horsepower at 8,000 rpm with 156 ft-lb torque at 6,000. In a car that Piëch and his colleagues had whittled down to just 823 kilograms—1,811 pounds—in its fighting trim, this represented, for its day, awe-inspiring performance potential.

Most memorably, the 911R provided Porsche a record performance that targeted every other automobile in production at the time. Ford had held these titles for some time, running 180 kilometers per hour (112.5 miles per hour) for four days at Daytona, reaching 20,000 kilometers at the end. More recently, Toyota had averaged 206 kilometers per hour (126.75 miles per hour) for three days around Fujiyama, knocking down the 10,000- and 15,000-kilometer records. Rico Steinemann and Dieter Spoerry, Swiss racers and co-owners of a 906 longtail, enlisted factory team driver Jo Siffert and their friend and twice-Swiss national champion Charles Vogele. Steinemann and Spoerry calculated that they could beat all these. FIA-sanctioned runs required that the contestant vehicle carry all its replacement parts and necessary tools on board. Only spare tires, jacks, spark plugs, gas, and oil could remain in the pits. After just 1,000 kilometers, 625 miles, Siffert pulled in with a broken shock absorber mount. The banking had beaten the overloaded 906's suspension and jeopardized the run until Ferdinand Piëch came up with a solution: He could provide a 911R if they wanted it, two in fact. He would fill one with spares and factory advisers.

Siffert already had driven an R and knew the car to be fast and robust, the two things this Monza run needed. A day later, Heinz Baüerli, the company's chief mechanic, and Albert Jünginger from Piëch's experimental department arrived in the sacrificial parts car. The next day, just hours before their FIA permit expired, Peter Falk and engines chief Paul Hensler arrived in the car the quartet would run. They had delayed long enough to install a rebuilt twin-plug typ 901/22 engine, the same as in Steinemann's 906 longtail. To be sure the gearbox would survive, drivetrains chief engineer Richard Hetman fitted two 5th gears, the one in fourth position just slightly shorter than the other.

At just before 8 p.m. on October 31, 1967, the R pulled out onto the track. Through rain, fog, night, and day the drivers piled up distance, lap after lap, at 1 minute 11 seconds each, averaging 210 kilometers per hour (131.25 miles per hour.) At 7,000 kilometers (4,375 miles), a front suspension MacPherson strut assembly failed. In the pits, mechanics replaced it quickly but Falk and Steinemann understood that the next would go at around 14,000 (8,750 miles) and they hoped to accomplish 20,000 (12,500.) Baüerli and Jünginger had completely dismantled the other spare in the car, preparing for individual pieces failing rather than the whole unit. When it went out, scrutineers allowed Falk to substitute it with a complete unit removed intact from the parts car, ruling that carrying the assembly in pieces made it legal.

After 73 hours, the R had covered 15,115 kilometers, or 9,446.9 miles. The drivers had another 24 hours and 5,000 kilometers, 3,125 miles, to go. On the last day, fifth gear failed, and so they shifted into the other fifth gear in fourth. Just after 8 p.m. on November 4, the car slowed to a stop and the pit crew and drivers popped champagne. In 96 hours, Piëch's 911R, the "wolf in sheep's clothing," as Jo Siffert called it, had met the task. The drivers and car set five world records, including 10,000 miles at 210.32 kilometers per hour,

This epitomizes the loneliness of a long-distance run performed by a single car on a large oval. Each of four Swiss drivers ran two-hour sessions to total 96 hours through rain and fog, day and night. Their performance opened the way for decades of endurance events with 911s.

1968 911L

This version of the L, or Luxus, was a U.S.-only model because European engine specifications did not meet American pollution-control standards. As a result, this was essentially a 911S body and interior with the Weber-carbureted 911 base engine.

131.43 miles per hour; 20,000 kilometers at 130.77 miles per hour; and 96 hours for 20,086 kilometers, 12,505.38 miles. Before he and Peter Falk had left Zuffenhausen to drive to Monza, Paul Hensler learned something that made him anxious through the entire run: The engine in their car had run on a test bench for 100 hours. Mechanics took it apart, measured it, and reassembled it. No one knew how carefully, and there hadn't been time to build a fresh new one. The world record motor already had run another world record in the race shops before arriving at Monza.

After this success, Huschke von Hanstein pushed for a larger run than Piëch's 20 copies. The baron believe there would be a market for perhaps 500, but Lars Schmidt, Harald Wagner, and Wolfgang Raether in sales remained unconvinced as they monitored routine production models during that year's sales slump. Before and after the Monza records, Porsche's 911Rs won races. Vic Elford drove them repeatedly, and a month before Steinemann & Co. drove theirs for 96 hours, Elford, along with Hans Hermann and Jochen Neerpasch, won an equally grueling 84-hour event at the Nürburgring, the Marathon de la Route. In that car, another Porsche innovation proved itself as well: Porsche's new Sportomatic transmission. Porsche still campaigned its Rs into 1969, when Gerard Larrousse and Maurice Gelin won both the Tour de France and the Tour de Corse in an R fitted with a fuel-injected engine. Perhaps Ferdinand Piëch created these R models as his own fleet to test his ideas, and he never cared whether any sold or not. Their secrecy proved Wagner and Raether right. As late as 1970, some of the original 20 cars still were available at the factory.

Another of Ferdinand Piëch's 1967 ideas was much grander, and it went through to fruition. Porsche already had a test track and skid pad at nearby Weissach. In late 1960, Porsche's secretary, Ghislane Kaes, and his finance chief, Hans Kern, had secured a 93-acre patch of undulating farm land. Helmuth Bott designed and soon constructed a 1.8-mile test track hugging its boundaries and taking advantage of its contours. Now Piëch's grand vision incorporated a $20 million building program there, with the intention of "putting everyone needed for the design and engineering of a car within 100 meters of each other." (Over time, that boundary has stretched to 300 meters, and the racetrack has curled and twisted in accommodation.) Porsche's research and design engineers and stylists had enough outside work, primarily from Volkswagen as a carryover from Professor Porsche's relationship with his old friend, VW Chairman Heinz Nordhoff, that VW used Porsche as its own R&D facility. Its annual contracts virtually would support the new facilities at Weissach. In an atmosphere isolated from sales, marketing, and even series production cars, engineers and stylists could create without interference. Paul Hensler planned the buildings and their layout, and he supervised the entire project.

Porsche's idea with its Sportomatic transmission certainly was sales. These targeted the U.S. market, where Porsche and others had observed the arrival at driving age of an entire generation who could not operate a clutch and manually change a gear. But Porsche was aware of the un-sports-car-like connotations of a full automatic transmission. It did not miss journalists' disparaging remarks about the first Corvette 14 years before. But this was a new decade, and Porsche had a different idea. Its Sportomatic was a semiautomatic transmission. Drivetrain chief Richard Hetman's staff made this work by mating Porsche's four-speed gearbox to a hydraulic torque converter. The clutch disengaged

Porsche charged $6,790 for the 911L coupes and added another $400 for the Targa body style. The interior was standard 911S equipment. This particular model was also air conditioned.

This is the 130–brake horsepower engine that U.S. buyers got in either the 911L or in the base 911 models. U.S. emissions regulations required the addition of an air pump, and Porsche had not yet developed that version for its S model.

automatically whenever the driver touched the gear lever. There was nothing automatic about the Sportomatic. The driver had to change gears or risk over-revving the engine. In place of a manual clutch, however, Porsche substituted a micro-switch-activated automatic clutch and the torque converter.

Ironically, European journalists took much more favorably to the new transmission than the Americans for whom Porsche intended it. Perhaps what helped Porsche's home markets were racing enthusiasts who knew that Texan Jim Hall had won the 1,000-kilometer race at Nürburgring in 1966 in his own semiautomatic transmission Chaparral. *Car and Driver* rushed to get their hands on Porsche's Sportomatic, publishing their first story in March 1968.

"Follow the reasoning of Porsche's product planners," the writer urged early in the story. "The traffic situation in metropolitan areas gets worse by the day, and there's no relief in sight. People are here to stay, and people drive cars, and more and more of them, and those cars clog the highways . . . .

"Porsche's answer was the Sportomatic. Trouble is, Porsche should have held out. Porsche is *the* enthusiasts' car. It's not cheap, but it's not up there with Lamborghini either. It's comfortable, it handles, and it goes . . . . So we're unhappy." Perhaps after *Car and Driver*'s experience, other Americans took their time getting to the transmission. It wasn't until the April 1971 issue that *Road & Track* published a full road test with the transmission in a 911T.

"There's no such thing as a nonsporting Porsche," the unsigned story began. "But now that the 911 comes with a choice of three engines and three transmissions, some 911s are more sporting than others, and the factory would admit that a 911T with Sportomatic is the least sporting model in the line." The three models referred to the 911S, back in the lineup after its one-year absence in 1968, the 911T, and a midrange 911E, the "E" representing *einspritzung* (fuel injection).

"We are inclined to consider the Sportomatic an excellent answer to a question that hasn't been asked," the *R&T* writer continued. "In its favor, it detracts only slightly from the pleasures of driving. Maybe not at all; it is fun to develop any skill. There is a small loss in performance and efficiency, but not much."

Inside Porsche and outside, the automotive design and engineering world had not stagnated. A new trend from a concept born in auto racing was apparent. At the Geneva Auto Show in March 1966, Ferruccio Lamborghini had captured auto journalists' attention with his handsome mid-engined Miura, styled by Marcello Gandini at Bertone studios. A year later in 1967, Ferrari introduced its new Dino 206GT designed by Pininfarina, with its 2-liter V-6 installed behind the seats and ahead of the rear axle. Across the hall, Alejandro de Tomaso showed his mid-engined Ford V-8-powered Mangusta. Lotus had its new Europa. Had

Porsche shown a street-version of its 904, it could have bragged about being years ahead of the others. What it realized instead was that this interest in mid-engine sports cars offered them an option for their next partnership with Volkswagen and Porsche's possible replacement for its 912. VW had relied on Porsche for research and design work since 1948 under a loose agreement between Professor Ferdinand Porsche and VW chairman Heinz Nordhoff. Porsche's 904 inspired Volkswagen's 914, a project the two companies launched soon after the Geneva show. Volkswagen would use its 411 engine, nearing the end of its development cycle, and Porsche would design the car so it was large enough to house its own flat-six as a 914/6 model. A design assignment for BMW that came from Hans Gugelot, a former faculty member at Ulm's *Hochschule für Gestaltung* (HfG), Butzi's alma mater, served as Porsche's design studio inspiration.

This was a very successful model despite offering less performance than the previous year's 911S. More then 10,000 copies sold in the United States, in both coupe and Targa models. Cars for the U.S. market also used rectangular marker lights on the front and rear.

Through 1968, Porsche offered the 911, 911L, and 912 coupes and Targas in the United States. The factory manufactured a record 14,300 of these A-series cars. The six-cylinder cars had taken over the production lead from the four-cylinder 912s the year before by a slim margin. Just as the company introduced its 1969 models, Butzi Porsche attended an award ceremony at the October 1968 Paris Auto Salon. France's *La Comité Internationale de Promotion et de Prestige* made its first-ever automotive award for the "overall aesthetic conception in the creation of a Porsche body."

For 1969, the B-series cars introduced major changes to the 911 and 912 lineup. Most dramatic was engineering's decision to move the rear wheels back 2.25 inches, 57 mm. Lengthening the wheelbase (to 2,268 mm, 89.3 inches) without changing the body moved some weight off the rear wheels and onto the front to improve weight distribution and handling. This called for longer rear suspension trailing arms and new half-shaft universal joints to handle the slightly greater angle from the engine to the wheels. Up front, Porsche introduced a self-adjusting hydropneumatic suspension strut on the 911E. Manufactured by Boge, this system automatically accommodated front-end load changes as minor as additional fuel in the gas tank or as significant as luggage for a week-long road trip. One by-product of this system brought Alfred Teve's ATE aluminum front brake calipers to 911s. Helmuth Bott's engineers designed the Boge strut system with these race-proven calipers that accommodated pads 50 percent larger than the original steel calipers. Porsche's decision to switch from one 12-volt battery up front to two 12-volt units, one beneath each headlight housing, further improved weight distribution and car balance.

Porsche resumed offering 911S models to American markets because it no longer needed to use an air pump on U.S. models. Bosch mechanical fuel injection made this possible. Porsche provided this system on both S (now at 170 DIN horsepower, 190 SAE, at 6,800 rpm) and the 911E version with 140 DIN horsepower (158 SAE) at 6,100 rpm. Beginning this year, Porsche cast all its crankcases in aluminum rather than magnesium as it had previously. Eliminating the air pump permitted Porsche to carry on with carburetors in the lower-performance 911T and 912 models, though this would be the last year for the 912 in this guise. Paul Hensler, the engineer whose 911R motors were strong enough to win world records even after a 100-hour bench test, examined both Bosch's new electronic fuel injection system (that Volkswagen used) and its mechanical system. The diesel-type mechanical system worked better with Porsche's high-speed engines to provide equal distribution to each cylinder. This closed system also eliminated the fuel evaporation problem that vaporizing carburetors permitted and against which states such as California had begun to mandate.

In February 1969, *Road & Track* published its owners' survey of 911 and 912 models. Of the 158 owners who responded, 106 or two-thirds drove 912s and the rest 911s. Half of all these owners reported that they ran their cars hard and 39 percent explained that they put 15,000 to 25,000 miles a year on them. Most of them claimed they bought the car for its handling (48 percent), and 77 percent of them claimed it was the car's best feature. Butzi Porsche's styling was the reason another 34 percent of them bought the car. Perhaps most interesting was that 94 percent of those who replied used their 911 or 912 every day, with 75 percent of the total taking their cars on long trips. In a field of automobiles where the 911 competed

with Corvette Stingrays, Jaguar XK-Es, and Mercedes-Benz 280SLs, the magazine reported that 95 percent of these individuals would buy another Porsche.

In 1969 Tony Lapine joined Porsche from GM's Opel design in Russelsheim, having completed the striking Opel GT before leaving. In Zuffenhausen, Lapine found prototypes in development for a mid-engine sports car for Volkswagen, the 914. This project had become something of an orphan. Long-time VW Chairman Heinz Nordhoff, who authorized and encouraged the project in 1967, died in April 1968. His successor, Kurt Lotz, was a sharp businessman but one with no auto industry experience. He was not a sports car enthusiast. But worse, he didn't understand the full nature of Porsche's relationship with VW.

1968 911S GT

The Monza endurance-record runs proved that 911s could take on challenges. Within a year of Monza, this hybrid S GT model won the Marathon de la Route, the aptly named 84-hour race around the Nürburgring.

For pleasure or in competition, this may be a Porsche driver's favorite view: nothing but the fascination of an open road ahead. With no signs, your only limitations are imagination and experience.

1968 911T/R

Vic Elford initiated the idea of Porsche going after international rally titles. Racing director Huschke von Hanstein offered him a single car, this 911T, stripped and prepared as the 911R had been. When Elford asked about spare parts, von Hanstein informed him that "Porsches don't break." Elford made history, winning the Monte Carlo Rally as well as many other races.

"VW had a standing order with Porsche," Tony Lapine explained, "to reserve a capacity of development time in Zuffenhausen in those days—later on in Weissach. It was understood that this was VW's time and we could not make other commitments for that time, as though they said, 'Do what you want, but 40 percent— for example—of your development capacity belongs to us over the next so many years. This was the agreement with Mr. Nordhoff."

Lotz focused on basic transportation, and he was willing to let Porsche continue to do VW's R&D. As Lapine looked at more drawing boards, he saw sketches for the next generation Porsche, the 911 replacement. It took its inspiration, and its engine and location, from a project Porsche was doing for Lotz.

"VW, Mr. Lotz, wanted to replace its tried-and-true Beetle," Lapine continued. "Their assignment was that this car had to be within the same dimensions as the Beetle but it had to be much bigger inside, much more powerful, yet even more fuel efficient. Quite a few challenges?"

Ferdinand Piëch recalled a prototype idea that had surfaced and then sunk while his uncle and cousin were devising the 901. Butzi's first prototype, the 695, had a flat-four-cylinder engine mounted under the floor of the rear seat between the rear wheels. It offered the benefit of a surprising amount of interior space within a modest exterior package. Piëch resurrected the idea for the VW project, now named EA266. Lapine's stylists created a simple, smart two-door sedan with large windows and engineering's new, water-cooled, inline four cylinder engine, mounted horizontally under the rear seat between the rear tires.

1969 911S TARGA

To improve handling and stability on its 1969 models, Porsche lengthened the wheelbase of the 911 by 2.4 inches (61 mm) without stretching the body. Slight fender flares accommodate 6-inch (150-mm) wheels on the S models.

The 225-kilometer-per-hour (140-mile-per-hour) top speed of the S made it a favorite among Europeans driving on roads without speed limits. In the United States, where most drivers measure performance from one stop light to the next, the lower torque of the S and its higher gearing made it less appealing to anyone but purists.

This was the last year that Porsche offered the zippered rear window, and it was only available as an option. Cold weather shrunk the plastic, which made reinstallation very difficult. Porsche introduced an optional solid glass rear window in 1968, and made it standard equipment in 1969.

"But Mr. Piëch took this idea much farther," Lapine went on. "He looked at the heritage of this company, and he recalled a prototype that Professor (Ferdinand) Porsche and Mr. Rabe and Mr. Komenda had done for Auto Union. They proposed taking the mid-engine Auto Union Grand Prix car, the V-12, and making a production road car out of it. A coupe, with three seats. The driver in the middle." Lapine paused to let the words sink in. He was talking about 1936.

"The programs worked this way. Porsche did the work, the research and development. The contract we made with anybody we ever worked for was that they would get the product they asked for, and of course, they owned the research we did along the way. But we reserved the right to use it if they chose not to. And of course, we wouldn't sell it to anyone else to use. But as you can imagine, this gave us some opportunities to do some testing or to develop some ideas that we might not have done otherwise if we'd had to pay for them all the way from scratch. This was the arrangement that we had with Mr. Nordhoff, but since it wasn't spelled out in our contract with them, Mr. Lotz objected, and that's what stopped the 914. With this one, we spelled everything out.

"One of Mr. Piëch's ideas was to take VW's underseat flat four and use it as the foundation of a new line of Porsche sports cars, the next 911. His engineers designed the four-cylinder engine as a modular package, rather like he had done with the 917 racing engine. And he reasoned that if you could make a four, you could make two fours by putting them together at the crankshaft, making an opposed eight. And if eight, why not add cylinders at each end to make twelve?

"He knew most of Porsche's customers hardly ever took extra passengers. He liked the idea of Professor Porsche's three-seater coupe. And so we made sketches. We designed a mid-engine coupe and roadster, three seaters with the driver in the middle. Good sto-age up front, more storage over the engine." Lapine smiled. "It was beautiful," he said, "like nothing you've ever seen. Mr. Piëch wanted three lines, just like the T, the E, and the S, but as a four-cylinder, an eight-cylinder, and for special customers, or for racing, a twelve. He even built a prototype flat-eight-cylinder engine. This was to be the next 911. Mid-engine. The current one would expire in 1972 or 1973, and this would appear. We worked on it. Internally we called it the typ 1966. We definitely knew it as the 911 replacement. The 911 was gone." ▪

For 1969, both the S and the E models got Bosch mechanical fuel injection to replace the Weber carburetors (though these remained in use on the T models). The new induction system boosted output to 180 DIN brake horsepower.

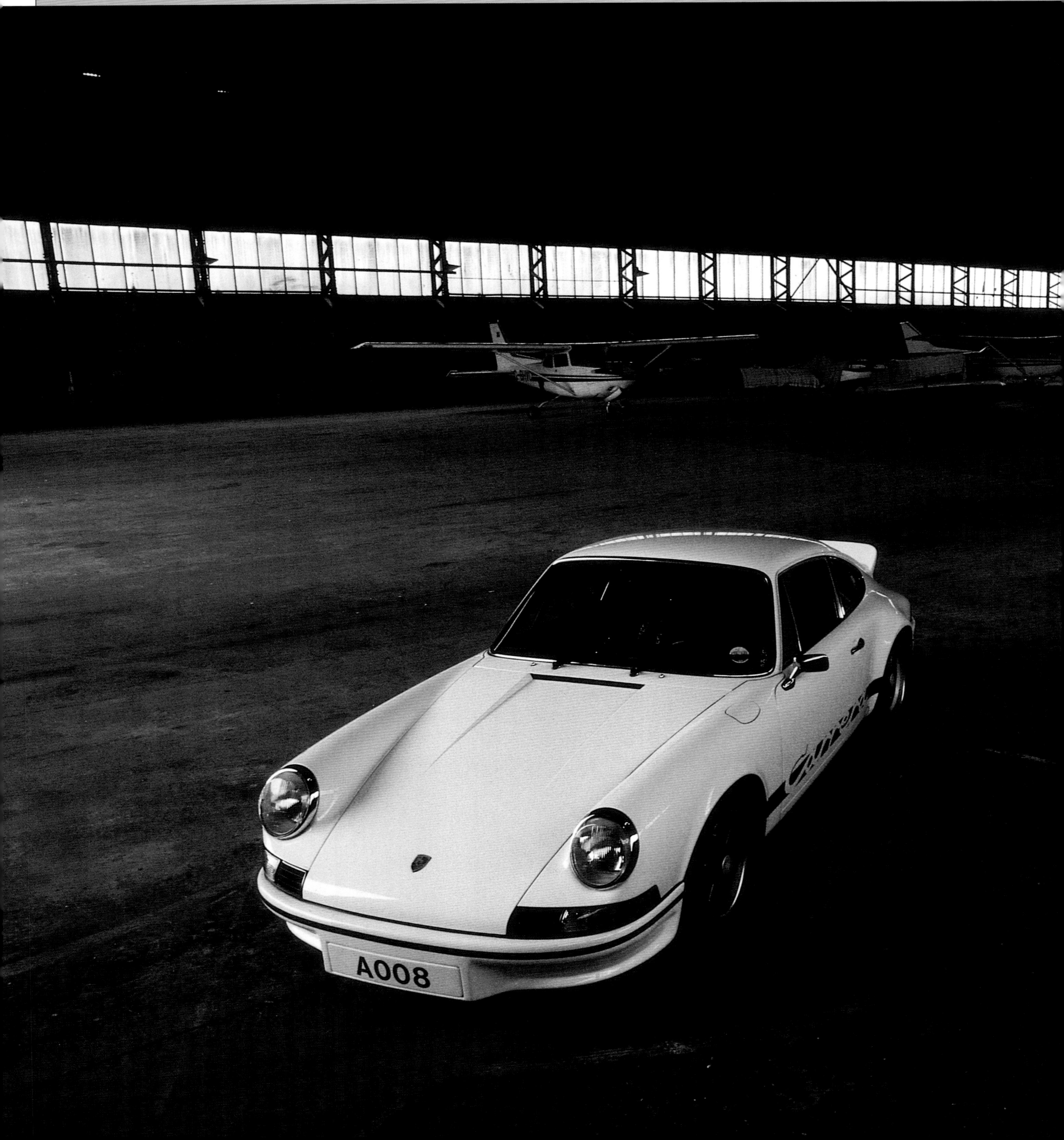
A008

"For the driver who really wants to get with it, the 911S is bound to be even more fun than the 911."

Road & Track, April 1967

The engineers and designers were excited by new offices and the prospect of a "new" 911. VW's ongoing research and development projects offered Weissach and Porsche some security. World politics made the job slightly harder as the American Congress passed the Clean Air Act in 1970: All automakers planning to sell cars in the United States had to control the evaporation of hydrocarbons. Porsche's engineers moved forward with the 1970 models, the C series, and part of Paul Hensler's solution to coming U.S. regulations was a new 2.2-liter engine, designated the typ 911. Hensler's staff enlarged cylinder bore to 84 mm from 80, increasing total displacement to 2,195 cc from 1,991 in the old

Previous pages: Porsche conceived the RS Carrera as a production homologation special to qualify a lightened 911 for international competition. They needed to sell 500. Marketing wasn't sure about the car, but Porsche very quickly manufactured and sold 1,590 of the RS lightweight and touring models.

typ 901 engines. Power for the 911T (still with its black fan shroud) now reached 125 DIN horsepower, 142 SAE, at 5,800 rpm at 8.6:1 compression, and 130 ft-lb (DIN), 148 SAE ft-lb of torque at 4,200 rpm. For the 911E (using a green shroud) Porsche achieved 155 DIN, 175 SAE horsepower at 6,200 rpm with 9.1:1 compression and 141 DIN, 160 SAE ft-lb of torque at 4,500 rpm. The red-shrouded 911S hit 180 DIN, 200 SAE horsepower at 6,500 rpm. Torque figures reached 147 DIN ft-lb and 164 SAE at 5,200 rpm, with 9.8:1 compression.

Porsche completed the 18-month-long construction of its new 160,000-square-foot assembly plant in Zuffenhausen shortly before starting to manufacture its 1970 models. This new facility incorporated a paint shop and an interior trim facility. The paint shop made custom color possible and Porsche now offered nine standard exterior choices. Dealers in Newport Beach, Hermosa Beach, and Beverly Hills, California, quickly concocted special orders in custom shades and hues for cars they ordered on speculation. But the colors attracted entertainment industry people and wannabees, and the cars sold rapidly and profitably. Porsche, pleased with the way these colors looked as they left Zuffenhausen, added many of them to optional catalogs and it began to invite its better dealers to submit custom orders for more personalized cars.

The world economy in 1971 affected Porsche more than emissions regulations or requests for odd colors. As the value of the deutsche mark climbed against the dollar, Porsche saw its prices rising in the United States. The 911S now sold for $8,975 in New York, $9,075 in Beverly Hills. The E went for $7,995 and the T for $6,495, on the East Coast, plus another $100 out West. The Targa option climbed to $675. The exchange rate affected other German exported cars as well and led to a sales slump at Porsche that slowed production to 60 cars a day from 70 and put year-end manufacturing at 11,715 cars, lower than any year in the past five.

1969 PININFARINA
4-SEATER PROTOTYPE

Commissioned to design a four-passenger model, Pininfarina delivered this four-seat prototype in the fall of 1969. The Italian designer's roofline on this 911S chassis is very similar to what Butzi Porsche and his father had discarded in 1962.

As Ferry Porsche prepared to move his stylists and engineers, in three waves, into the new facilities in Weissach in the coming summer, he understood clearly how forces beyond his control could affect sales to his biggest single market. He had done a stringent job of controlling the costs of his production cars. The price increases American buyers suffered largely were currency exchange matters. But where Ferry had been frugal, his nephew, development chief Ferdinand Piëch, had treated Porsche's racing department as if it had endless financial reserves. His philosophy had earned Porsche successive world championships for the racing 908s and the phenomenal 917s. As Butzi Porsche had experienced benefits in "being the son," with the ability to deliver an idea and have it approved, so Ferdinand Piëch, as the nephew, held out for highest quality pieces, materials,

and workmanship. The difference between second tier and best might register a minimal improvement in quality, a percent or two, but the cost often was 5 or 10 times as high. Piëch built new race cars from one event to the next where other manufacturers rebuilt last week's winner. He hired engineers such as Norbert Singer, Tilman Brodbeck, and others for their expertise in fields as arcane as aerodynamics.

These extraordinary costs, plus the intermittent arrival at the administration doorstep of Butzi's and of Piëch's siblings expecting their own role in company management, put Ferry Porsche and his sister Louise Piëch, Ferdinand's mother, under strain. Porsche's management board in 1970 consisted of Ferdinand "Ferry" Porsche II (who was 60 years old), his son, Ferdinand Alexander "Butzi" Porsche III, who was 35, Ferdinand "Beurly" Piëch, 33, and his younger brother Michael, 28, as well as the firm's chief financial officer, outsider Heinz Branitzki, then 41. Butzi's younger brother, Peter, 29, had joined the firm in 1963 and by 1970 was head of production; he was not part of this management board but he played a significant role in company direction and profit.

1970 911E

Porsche introduced its 2.2-liter flat-six engines in 1970 for all models and T, E, and S variations. This E made excellent use of 155 DIN brake horsepower.

This profile was on its way to becoming a design icon by 1970. Few outside the company had any notion that some insiders were already planning its replacement.

A Piëch dispute over camshafts was typical of the Porsche-vs.-Piëch philosophies. Ferdinand Piëch argued that Porsche's series production cars should adopt the dual-overhead camshaft cylinder heads that he had proven in racing, and for which he already had prepared production tooling. Peter Porsche supported Ferry's argument that existing single-cam heads worked fine, and the company could achieve additional power more affordably by increasing displacement than raising engine speeds. It was a matter, both sides agreed, of who

To achieve the 2,195-cc engine displacement, Porsche increased the cylinder bore from 80 to 84 mm. They did not alter the 66-mm stroke.

was the car's target buyer. But that buyer was what they could not agree upon: racer or enthusiast. Every engineer always wanted the next Porsche to be more powerful than the preceding one. But how much would the company spend to reach that target?

Following a weekend-long retreat at the family home in Austria in the fall of 1970, the families accepted the greatest cost. In a decision that surprised business observers, the Porsches and Piëchs agreed to vacate

1970 911ST

Porsche continued its strategy of developing and assembling limited-production racing and rally-prepared 911s. This lightened 911T (down to 960 kilograms [2,112 pounds] with S running gear) won the 1970 Monte Carlo Rally.

Many stages of the Monte Carlo Rally are run over public roads, albeit during the night. Brilliant supplemental lighting is crucial.

their jobs in the company so that experienced, qualified professionals could serve instead. The transition was gradual and it ultimately benefited family members financially, but it transformed the company, literally and figuratively. It changed from a family-held company to a limited-liability corporation. It began looking for successors for the family members who stepped aside or away as their replacements arrived. Butzi Porsche left his job as chief stylist soon after the weekend decision, to open his own independent design firm in Zell am See, Austria.

In a decision that had profound effects on Porsche's 911, the board hired back Ernst Fuhrmann to fill several roles. Fuhrmann had been with Porsche in the 1950s and as a young engineer, he designed and supervised development of the company's legendary typ 547 Carrera four-cam engine. He had drawn the cylinder heads himself. His Carrera engine brought many of Porsche's early outright racing victories to the company. In 1956, when Ferry Porsche named Klaus von Rücker as technical director, a promotion Fuhrmann believed he deserved, he left Porsche to join Goetze, a piston ring manufacturer in Stuttgart. In a dispute over management responsibilities there, he left Goetze in the early summer of 1971.

"One day the telephone rang. It was Mr. Bott, asking if he and Mr. Piëch could pay me a visit here," Fuhrmann recalled in an October 1991 interview. "They came here [to his home in Teufenbach, Austria] and asked me if I'd like to come back to Porsche. They showed me the designs for the new cars. So," he laughed, "I had nothing else to do. I should say, the position was very simple, and easy to handle. It was no complicated thing."

When he returned in September 1971, Fuhrmann was in charge of all things technical at Porsche, from its new design, engineering, and technical center in nearby Weissach to racing and production operations in Zuffenhausen. He and the board quickly promoted Helmuth Bott to head all development including design and testing. (Branitzki stayed in place to manage commercial and financial matters, and Ferry Porsche remained as chairman of the supervisory board.)

"Then," Fuhrmann said, picking up his story, "four weeks later, the general manager of Volkswagenwerke, Mr. Lotz, had to leave the firm, and the decision was made that VW would not use the Porsche-designed prototype successor to their Beetle." Lotz had cooled down VW's 914 project when he misunderstood Porsche's simultaneous development of its own companion 914/6. But then he had fired up the EA266 Beetle-replacement, and even empowered Porsche to conceive its next sports car, the mid-engined 1966. VW named Rudolf Leiding to replace Lotz, and Leiding promptly reviewed all the company's projects. He immediately halted the EA266.

Standard 911S engines develop 180 DIN brake horsepower, but competition versions built for cars such as this produce 240 at 7,800 rpm. Björn Waldegaard and Lars Helmer won the Monte Carlo Rally in 1969 and again in 1970.

1970 911/C20 PROTOTYPE

Following Pininfarina's four-seater attempt in 1969, Butzi Porsche and the design staff created their own version using an extended 911S chassis. The outside oil-filler cap shown on this prototype would appear again on production models only in 1972.

"But that complicated things," Fuhrmann explained. "The successor to the 911 was by that time already along. The sales people wanted a new car. And the plans from that time were that the 911 should end in 1973. And the new car should come then.

"But then in the VW-werke, the decision was made to not build the Porsche car [EA266] and now Porsche had no successor for its 911. There were other changes in the VW-werke at that time. Porsche had an agreement that the whole costs of the development center were taken over from VW-werke. Weissach *was* their development center. The VW-werke gave enough orders to help support Weissach. This was cancelled within a year.

"So I had no work after the end of one year for Weissach, and I had no successor for the 911. And then the whole family left."

"Overnight, everything disappeared," Tony Lapine remembered. "EA266, the typ 1966 sports car. The next day, it was as if these projects never had existed. All the drawings, all the notes, the papers. Mr. Piëch's prototype engine. I heard it was cut up. And then we had a hell of a job to do, to keep this place going. Mr. Fuhrmann put us to work right away."

Faced with the threat of U.S. government intervention in the design of automobiles, Ernst Fuhrman made a decision: The next Porsche should not be like the last one. Concerns that the 911's air-cooled engine could never meet coming exhaust emission and noise standards had led to the water-cooled eight. Those questions still existed. The typ 928 would have to be a different car from the 911.

Helmut Flegl, who served as project manager of the 928 for two years after his successful 917 developments, remembered the times.

"The thing was regulations in America," Flegl explained, "the discussions about handling. They wanted to control the handling, what the handling had to be like going down the road. You have the steering input, and the rules, as they were in peoples' mind; they were for sure for the American car. But the 911 is absolutely not an American car.

1971 911S TOUR DE FRANCE WINNER
In the final years of the Tour de France de l'Automobile, Porsche owned the event, winning in 1969, 1970, 1971, and finally in 1972, the last year the Tour was run. Staff engineer, racer, and customer sports manager Jürgen Barth won the event in this car in 1971.

While bicycling's Tour de France started in 1899, the race for automobiles was much newer, beginning in 1951. It covered 5,000 kilometers (3,100 miles), with contestants driving on public roads between a number of French racetracks and hillclimb circuits. At those venues, organizers conducted timed events as part of the overall timed and scored Tour.

"So there was quite a bit of nervousness here: 'If that comes to life, we cannot sell ANY car in the United States. Because it is impossible to meet those regulations.'

"Whatever rule they write," he continued, "we cannot say what the handling has to be. It will be defined, but they surely cannot forbid American cars. They can make the rules as they want, we don't know, but somehow American cars will meet their rules. So what is specific with American cars?"

No one at Porsche knew the answer to this question better than Tony Lapine. He had spent 17 years at General Motors, many of them in a basement studio in Warren, Michigan. Underneath the Design Building in the corner of the GM Tech Center campus lay Studio X, the secret shop where he and Larry Shinoda spent their days and nights creating prototype Corvettes for GM's design boss, Bill Mitchell. Now that experience paid off for Porsche. If American legislators never would forbid an American car, Porsche would create its own Corvette, the 928.

Around all this family and corporate drama, 1972 production continued. It was not easy, and morale slipped. The 1970 Clean Air Act in the United States required cars that would be sold here in 1976 to emit 90 percent fewer hydrocarbons than 1971 levels. Manufacturers concluded it would be impossible to reach these targets without catalytic converters that superheated the already-hot engine exhaust in order to bake out the remaining unburned vapors and particles before they reached the atmosphere. Tetraethyl lead, the additive in gasoline that increased its octane rating to give it higher performance, killed the heating pellets within the converter. By the early 1970s, automakers throughout the world had begun redesigning engines to run on lead-free gasoline. Engineers at Porsche understood that its high-rpm, short stroke, big bore engines produced great horsepower but dirty exhaust. Smaller bores coupled to longer strokes offered a double benefit in a changing world. Their longer burn cycle combusted fuels more fully, meeting emissions standards more easily.

What's more, this configuration provided greater torque at lower engine speeds, just the thing urban Porsche drivers needed to survive stop-and-go traffic.

Porsche chose to keep the flat-six's cylinder bore at 84 mm but increase its stroke 4.4 mm to 70.4 mm from 66. This enlarged total displacement to 2,341 cc which Porsche rounded up for marketing and labeling purposes to 2.4 liters. To simplify an otherwise complex process, Paul Hensler's engineers designed one aluminum cylinder head—with a single camshaft—for use on the T, E, and S engines. To meet the ever-increasing U.S. emission standards Hensler fuel injected the T engine for U.S. markets, as well as the E and S. (Other countries still got the Solex-Zeniths introduced on the T.) With a view toward cost-effectiveness, Porsche chose to carry the same engines over into 1973. The 911T now rated 140 DIN horsepower (157 SAE) at 5,600 rpm, and 145 DIN ft-lb (166 SAE) of torque at 4,000. Hensler coaxed 165 DIN horsepower (185 SEA) out of the E at 6,200 rpm along with 152 DIN and 174 SAE ft-lb of torque at 4,500. The S still remained the racer's favorite, with 190 DIN horsepower (210 SAE) at 6,500 with 159 DIN and 181 SAE ft-lb of torque at 5,200 rpm. These torque figures represented an average 10 percent increase over what was available to 2.2-liter owners, making a noticeable difference to city traffic drivers.

(To further confuse ratings, at this time the Society of Automotive Engineers introduced its new formula for calculating horsepower and torque figures. Known initially as SAE net, and now it simply is SAE. They did this in an effort to more closely align their ratings with those of the rest of the world, and in response to red flags American auto insurers were waving about the dangers of excessive horsepower in cars. For the 1973 Porsches, this took SAE gross horsepower figures for the T down to 134 from 157; the E became 157, down from 185; and the S dropped to 181 from 210. Regrettably, these still differed from DIN figures, so both ratings remained necessary.)

This 2.4-liter engine represented one of Ferdinand Piëch's three final production car influences before he left Porsche. The second was a new transaxle targeted at better acceleration. Piëch's new gear ratios sacrificed top speed and increased fuel consumption but made the cars easier to drive in cities and therefore more enjoyable for most of its buyers.

This kind of development was additional evidence of Ferdinand Piëch's character and his near obsession with extraordinarily high standards. Karl Ludvigsen, who has thoroughly chronicled the history of nearly every one of Porsche's cars, put it best: This new transaxle, he wrote, "reflected an almost reckless drive for perfection in Porsche cars, for only two years earlier the change had been made to a magnesium die-casting

The racing 911S versions carry over the concept of the 1967 911R, but engineers Helmuth Bott and Norbert Singer advanced the technology. By 1971, 2.5-liter engines in these cars developed 270 DIN horsepower at 8,000 rpm.

for the housing of the earlier transaxle." Not only that, but the new one added 20 pounds to the car. It epitomized a classic Porsche conundrum: save weight or introduce new technology. But Piëch had not finished in his pursuit of perfection. Always concerned by weight at the car's extremes, for the 1972 model he moved the dry sump oil reservoir to a new position behind the right rear door, ahead of the rear wheel. Body engineers cut a filler cap and lid into the rear fender just behind the B-pillar. It took nearly a year of work for an engineer and a stylist. But achieving this target caused not one but two problems. It had the unfortunate effect of confusing some innocent gas station attendants who, not knowing Porsche's fuel filler was in the trunk, pumped gasoline into the side oil reservoir. For the following year, recognizing that problem and seeing that U.S. regulations for side-impact safety might affect its placement, Porsche moved the tank back in the rear fender behind the engine.

The prototype chin spoiler hints strongly at production versions that would appear in 1973. Slots in the bumper and spoiler vent air to the front brakes and front oil cooler.

For 1972, the Boge hydropneumatic struts shifted from the standard equipment list on the 911E model to optional. The struts were prone to leaking, and owners found them more costly to replace than even the expensive Konis. Deleting the Boges allowed Porsche to hold the 911E's price at 1971 levels, at $7,995. The T settled at $7,367, and the S reached $9,495. The Targa now added $735 to the price of any of the models.

Despite its lower top speed, the 911S still was a potent automobile. Capable of reaching 100 miles from a standstill in just 15 seconds according to *Car and Driver* magazine, the car easily would run on another 40 miles per hour from there. At those speeds, with its wider tires and fenders having increased frontal area to 18.4 square feet from the original 17.4, and the coefficient of drag to 0.41 from 0.38, the 911 had a noticeable tendency toward front end lift. A young engineer in the racing department, Tilman Brodbeck, who had joined Porsche in October 1970 with a technical education in mechanical engineering and aerodynamics, got the assignment early in 1971 to work on the 911S in Stuttgart University's wind tunnel. Design chief Tony Lapine assigned one of his modelers to join Brodbeck in case the engineer came up with something.

A wind tunnel technician moved the oil vaporizer wand up and down over the nose of the car. Brodbeck noticed the tendency for this stream to disappear directly under the front valance below the bumper. He wondered if there wasn't some way to stop the air, to redirect it. He held a finger in the path of the oil stream at the base of the valance, and watched the stream detour around it. He and the modeler looked around the tunnel and the control room for other things that might work—a pencil, a business card. By the end of the first

day, Brodbeck had taped a piece of rope across the bottom lip. The oil stream caught on the rope and shifted it right or left. Technicians in the control room read the results. At the end of the third day, Brodbeck and the modeler had roughed out with fiberglass a piece that provided the same result as the rope but with smoother edges and greater effect. It reduced lift by nearly half, to 102 pounds from 183, and it dropped the coefficient of drag from 0.41 to 0.40.

Piëch put Brodbeck and one of Lapine's stylists on a crash program to produce this front spoiler in fiberglass as a production part and as an accessory piece that owners could buy for their earlier cars. "There were some who wanted this piece made in steel," Tillman Brodbeck recalled recently. "That would have taken a year. They worried that in a crash, pieces of the fiberglass might hurt someone else. Mr. Piëch said it was too important to wait. It improved safety and handling so much."

The Tour de France ran for a week at a pace that allowed drivers and crews to rest overnight at hotels along the way. The event ran with several interruptions from 1951 through 1972. Note the Minilite wheels on the rear of the race car above.

1972 911S TARGA

The S Targa is almost the prototypical summer vacation car. It has enough power—180 DIN brake horsepower— to expedite any escape. Its removable roof lets drivers take best advantage of beautiful weather.

These E-series bodies were ready to yield to 1973 F-series cars that would wrap up Porsche's first generation of its 911. The company had taken in slightly more than 300 million deutsche marks in 1972 under the cost conscious Ferry Porsche. However, its motor sports programs had spent more than 30 million under the quality conscious Ferdinand Piëch. In 1972, as Porsche prepared this next series for production, status quo seemed a thing of the past. The joint project with Volkswagen, the 914, had brought in revenues for R&D, but Porsche's own version, the production 914/6, had been a disappointment. The economic downturn in the United States in 1971 and 1972 had affected sales, limiting resources for future products and projects. The Porsche and Piëch families were departing and new personnel arrived almost weekly. For most of these new engineers, stylists, and managers, there was a lot of work to do.

In the midst of this, Ernst Fuhrmann, now Porsche's technical director and chairman of the executive committee,

Putting an outside oil filler on a mid-mounted dry-sump oil reservoir was a flawed idea. Uninformed gas-station attendants thought it was the fuel tank, and the risk of side-impact oil spills necessitated that it be moved back to the rear fender after this one year.

who did not normally search for new problems, found another one. Recognizing that Porsche no longer could fund expensive prototype racing programs such as the 917 coupes in Europe and the 917/30s in the American Can-Am series, he wanted to see how Porsche 911 racing cars were doing. He knew that the FIA was weighing a new regulation for 1975 based on production cars as a Group 5 category. Racing always was a passion in his life. He had developed the 547 Carrera engine as a racing engine he could have in his own road car. For years, on whatever weekends a Porsche campaigned, he and his wife Elfreida kept a candle lit in his living room window. Uncannily, the candle often expired just as Porsche's cars did on the track. Fuhrmann took a day in the spring of 1972 to get away to a touring car race at the Hockenheimring.

"I was just standing in the pits," Fuhrmann recalled. "I watched many 911s, and the Fords and the BMWs were passing them. Even our fastest 911, I think it was lapped by a Ford and then a BMW!" While Porsches raced in Group 4, the Ford and BMW cars competed in Group 3. Though they were not racing directly against one another, the appearance that a compact Ford had passed a Porsche flustered Fuhrmann. In its own group, Porsches found themselves fighting to stay ahead of Ferrari 365 GTB-4 Daytonas and Ford V-8-engined de Tomaso Panteras. "I went looking for one of our engineers, Mr. Singer, or Mr. Falk, perhaps, to ask him why this happened. I found another one, younger, one of Mr. Singer's protégés."

Wolfgang Berger, the protégé, explained that Ford's racing director in Cologne, Michael Kranefuss, had produced a small group of *rennsport* models, racing prototypes that bent the FIA rules. Kranefuss pulled

everything not needed for racing from the car, cutting its weight greatly. Wings and spoilers, more flamboyant than Porsche's, improved its aerodynamics and enhanced its handling, a feature further aided by dramatically larger tires. Burkard Bovensiepen had accomplished similar feats with his Alpina operation, modifying and preparing BMW 2800CS models for competition Fuhrmann recalled that Berger went further, explaining what Porsche might need to win.

"'Your analysis is interesting,' I told him," Fuhrmann said. "'Think about it,' I told him, 'and then tell me what you will do.'"

Within days, Helmuth Bott called Tillman Brodbeck into his office. "Porsche 911 race drivers," he said, "have a lot of trouble when they go for the curves on the racetrack. Even the Ford Capri and the BMW coupe are quicker through the curves. You must do something. Anything! Without changing the whole car, it must be possible that these racers can buy something to make the car better. Think about it!"

911RSR 3.0
Racing engineer Norbert Singer created a special rear wing, the "Mary Stuart Collar," to better control airflow for this car and its twin. Both racers use a 3-liter 330–DIN brake horsepower flat-six, and this one finished fourth at Le Mans in 1973.

"I'll never forget it," Brodbeck recalled recently. Now as head of Porsche *Exclusiv*, he is surrounded by options and accessories that racers and boulevard drivers alike can buy to make their cars better. "I had no idea what to do. It was in a time when people really didn't know a lot about spoilers. On normal cars, nearly nothing. On racing cars, not much, but on series production cars, just nearly nothing."

During his last year in school, in 1968, he owned a small Fiat coupe, the 850 fastback. He liked its shape particularly. He bought a second one, the GT, because it had five horsepower more. It also had a small lip on the rear, the first one Brodbeck really had noticed. He asked his professor in aerodynamics why Fiat had done it. "Perhaps it has to do with aerodynamics, but I think it is more something from design," Brodbeck remembered his professor telling him.

As early as 1962 Pininfarina had put a slight lip on the rear of Ferrari's Lusso, and a larger one on the 1964 275 GTB Berlinetta, inspired by the racing 250 LMs and GTOs. By 1968, Ford's stylists had mounted massive vertical walls off the back of Carroll Shelby's GT350 and GT500 Mustangs, reminiscent of Peter Brock's Cobra Daytona Coupe and Ford's GT40 Mk IV models. But no one had taken these production car rear lips into a wind tunnel to see what they did beyond turning heads and inspiring sales.

"We went back into the Stuttgart wind tunnel," Brodbeck continued, "the same one where we had done the front lip for the Carrera. Now, we started with welding wire, to make a form. The front had needed such a little bit. We put that onto the rear and we thought about how to change the shape of the rear. Over the next three days, we formed this new shape. We moved it forward and back, up and down the rear end. It was trial and error. It changed things so much with the lift. But you know, in those days, it was still just theory. We had to have a real driver take the car out and test it."

Brodbeck's final version was flat sheet metal wrapped over welding wire. His fellow engineers laughed when they saw it, but it was nervous, stress-releasing laughter: Brodbeck had spent three days in the wind tunnel for something made with sheet metal and welding wire? Günther Steckkönig, a Porsche test driver since 1953 and a factory racer by the mid-1960s, took it out onto Weissach's test track. "Listen," Brodbeck remembered his fellow engineers saying to him as the car disappeared, "This better be good because Mr. Bott is waiting . . . "

"Everyone there thought it looked strange," he recalled, "because of this thing the car had on its back. But Steckkönig came in and said, 'Wait, the car feels *much* better.' From there, Brodbeck went back to Lapine's styling studio. 'You have to do something that is smoother,' I said. We told them the important points for the aero-dynamics, where they have to be. Then they made this little thing, this ducktail, the bürzel." With the ducktail molded in fiberglass, Brodbeck, another engineer, and a stylist went to the wind tunnel again, this time to VW's because Mercedes-Benz had just purchased the Stuttgart University facility. A former classmate, now working at VW in aerodynamics, saw Brodbeck, heard he was there to "manage the lift" on the car and said Brodbeck was wasting his time. "The only thing we are working on is the drag coefficient. That is the most important thing."

Soon afterward, Porsche took the mocked-up prototype to Volkswagen's test track in Ehra-Lessin. In the mid-1950s, working with Zora Arkus-Duntov after one of the Le Mans races Duntov had run in a Porsche,

Helmuth Bott and Duntov had developed a series of handling tests meant to unsettle a car. One of these involved a violent lane-change maneuver. Bott's standard of acceptable chassis and suspension development allowed no more than three fishtail swerves before the car either stabilized or went back for more work. Bott invited Brodbeck to go along for the first ride of the day.

"The first time, he was driving about 180 kilometers (roughly 112 miles per hour) on a straight," Brodbeck recalled. "And then suddenly with the steering wheel he yanked it hard to the right. And you can imagine what that does. I got pale. Without the spoilers it was awful what this car did.

"And with the spoilers, it was amazing. Everybody said, 'Well, something else must be changed, the tires, the suspension. It cannot just be these two small spoilers.' But Mr. Bott had used the same car. He only had the technicians change the front panel and rear deck lid. The difference was so great. With the spoilers, it did three swings and then it went straight ahead."

1973 911 CARRERA RS 2.7

Wind tunnel tests on production versions of the RS 2.7, with its innovative *bürzel* or duck tail, showed most of the taped fabric tufts following air flow over the roof and off the rear wing. *Porsche Archives*

1973 911 CARRERA RS
2.7 LIGHTWEIGHT

The ingredients are few and relatively simple: Front chin spoiler, side graphic, rear *bürzel* or ducktail spoiler, a spartan interior, and a pedigreed engine. That's what it took to put Porsche's race car characteristics into dealer showrooms. Buyers snapped them up.

Meanwhile, Berger had reported back to Fuhrmann. The protégé had direct access; Fuhrmann eliminated Berger's normal chain-of-command reporting hierarchy. Porsche's racing engineers had learned from Ferdinand Piëch's 911R models and the same thinking applied now. Berger gutted a 911T. The Biral cylinders on current production 911s nearly had reached maximum bore, at 88 mm, before making cylinder walls too thin to be reliable. Helmut Flegl and Hans Mezger had used a nickel-silicone carbide, Nikasil, liner on the 917 engine cylinders, and this allowed a couple extra millimeters of bore. Mezger increased bore to 90 mm from 88. This enlarged total displacement to 2,687 cc, moving the 911 up into the next racing class, under 3-liters. The FIA had established this prototype-class limit for 1972 in order to eliminate Porsche's unbeatable 917s. However, even production classifications allowed wider wheels, which led Berger to widen the rear fenders. Wider wheels accommodated 917 brakes with a prototype ABS system from Teldix. Their own variation of the front spoiler Falk, Singer, and Mark Donahue had devised for the Can-Am 917-30s incorporated a low-mounted oil cooler and channeled air off the nose. A larger version of Brodbeck's sheetmetal bürzel reached the height of the rear window. According to historians Dr. Thomas Gruber and Dr. Georg Konradsheim, Porsche asked its old friend Paul Ernst Strähle from nearby Schöndorf to enter the car as his own Group 5 prototype in the 1,000-kilometer race at Österreichring in Austria on June 25. Fuhrmann hoped this tactic would avoid revealing a factory prototype. Tilman Brodbeck's test driver/racer Günther Steckkönig, along with 1969 and 1970 Monte Carlo Rally winner Björn Waldegaard, drove the prototype to 10th place overall, finishing behind open sports racers. The 911 was back.

For Fuhrmann, it was a crucial test. He had no money and no 911 replacement. He had to return the 911 to the company's front burner, to make it viable and rekindle customer interest. Racing could do that. But this racing was best since it cost so little. A production option that picked up the character of this new racer would excite buyers the way Fuhrmann's old Carrera coupes had done. Porsche was corporate proof of two of motor sports' oldest sayings: Racing improves the breed; and race wins on Sunday bring sales on Monday. Fuhrmann had able collaborators in place. Norbert Singer would take on the competition development and racing programs for the new 911. For the production side, the full force of Wolfgang Berger's small production engineering staff and Tony Lapine's styling studio would work on this new Porsche 911S 2.7, as it would be called. Their target was to produce a Group 4-legal production model, devoid of anything that would not help the racing effort yet somehow still appeal to 500 paying customers.

Fuhrmann conceived it as an addition to the lineup, its performance placing it on top of the 2.4-liter 911S already planned and in production. Timing was urgent. He had heard that BMW had a new lightweight coupe with a larger engine, the 3.0CSL, for introduction in September or October 1972. Mercedes-Benz 350SL, already out a year, offered 200 DIN horsepower (230 SAE) and 0-to-100 kilometer-per-hour times of 8.8 seconds. At 32,915 deutsche marks ($11,755) for 1973, the Mercedes was nearly 1,700 deutsche marks ($607) more than the 2.4S. But BMW's 30,450 deutsche marks ($10,875) CSL, with 180 DIN horsepower and a rumored 0-to-100 kilometer time of 7.8 seconds, was a threat to the 31,180 deutsche marks ($11,135) 911, with 190 horsepower and 7.0-second acceleration. Moreover, the 3.0CSL would constitute a serious threat to Porsche's 911 racing

comeback. Fuhrmann needed the 2.7 with its wider tires and rear fenders and its simplified interior and minimal insulation, despite what sales and marketing said. And they had their say.

The naysayers and their successors who had dismissed the viability of the 911R saw a new R here and threw up obstacles as they backed away. There were more of them and they had additional allies now; Porsche and VW had joined sales forces as the VW-Porsche Marketing Company, with new offices nearby in Ludwigsberg. However, Fuhrmann was motivated. What if Zuffenhausen assembled 500 cars, each stripped as Norbert Singer needed them for homologation? What if buyers could order them with an option code that gave them the same interior as a 911S with soundproofing and with steel bumpers? This was harder to reject, so marketing grumbled that "S 2.7" was not a name with any charisma to reach their target customers. Yet within days, they had resolved their own dilemma. Reaching back into their history—and to Fuhrmann's—they christened

Porsche bored out the 2.4-liter flat-six from 84 to 90 mm, but engineers didn't change the 70.4-mm stroke. This provided 2,681 cc (161.1 cubic inches) that yielded 210 DIN brake horsepower.

it the Carrera. They already had participated in discussions that set aside the name for an entire future generation of products. So marketing took this car's competition orientation as a suffix. It added the letters "RS," for *rennsport*, racing sport. Tony Lapine's stylists created a stylish script logo that stretched across each door in a contrasting color that matched its Fuchs five-spoked wheels.

In another olive branch tendered to sales and marketing, Fuhrmann's engineers developed a second trim and interior option level to broaden the appeal. In addition to the severe lightest-weight homologation version with narrow wheels and no sway bars (known internally as RSH, for homologation), option M471, a sports version, fitted wider tires and thick anti-sway bars. For those seeking the style of the new Carrera RS without sacrificing comfort, Porsche offered marketing's favorite, the M472 option. This touring version provided appointments near to the 911S production run. The M491 option came from Norbert Singer for his own factory racing purposes and customer sales. This used a 2.8-liter racing engine, included an installed roll bar, and 11-inch-wide rear tires and flared fenders, as the RSR version, the *rennsport rennen* or race sport racer.

Wolfgang Berger completed his first production prototype in April 1972. Using a 1972 E-series body, the prototype even had the external oil filler cap on its passenger side. The car lacked only preproduction versions of Tilman Brodbeck's front and rear spoilers and Lapine's script logos on the side. Eight more prototypes appeared before production—of 500 units—started in October. Fuhrmann pressured the sales organization, which shifted into high gear. With a single prototype but stacks of photos, they called on dealers and distributors for orders. Prospective 911S customers got personal visits to induce an RS purchase.

Fuhrmann and Berger set the Paris Auto Show, on October 5, 1972, as the public debut. According to Karl Ludvigsen, the effective sales staff already had recorded 51 sales by the opening day, unheard of and very encouraging, for the M471 sport version that sold for 33,000 deutsche marks ($11,785). For an additional 2,500 deutsche marks, about $893, a buyer got the touring package with full 911S luxury. Orders streamed in, and within a week of the closing of the Paris show, Porsche had sold the 500 it needed. But orders continued and Fuhrmann shrewdly agreed to increase the run until buyers were satisfied. That finally happened in July 1973 when number 1,580 rolled off the Zuffenhausen line. After the first 500 sold, the company raised the price by 1,000 deutsche marks, about $330, and no one complained. While that price held to the end, the extra sales allowed Porsche and the FIA to reclassify the car as Group 3 Grand Touring, where it essentially would own the field.

(Quoting prices in U.S. dollars for the Carrera RS is an exercise only in historical context. Porsche made no effort to meet U.S. emission standards with the 2.7-liter RS engine, so the cars remained something longed for in the States. They were unobtainable for years, until EPA standards relaxed enough on older cars to enable enthusiasts and collectors to bring them in.)

While demand for the car surprised the Ludwigsberg sales staff, they did not miss the lessons. Porsche owners were loyal. They recognized and valued something unique. They were willing to pay an additional premium to be part of a small group who could own a Carrera RS or whatever other limited-edition models the company might create.

1973 911 CARRERA RSR 2.8

The purpose for manufacturing and selling the Carrera RS 2.7 road car was to make this 2.8-liter model legal for racing. It was the result of a challenge issued to young engineer Helmut Berger by chairman Ernst Fuhrmann.

The *bürzel*, or tail, grew out of hurried efforts to control the handling of the 911 coupes through high-speed corners while racing. The prototype that Tilman Brodbeck and a stylist developed in the wind tunnel was ugly sheet metal. So Tony Lapine's staff designers refined the shape, making it into a handsome fiberglass innovation.

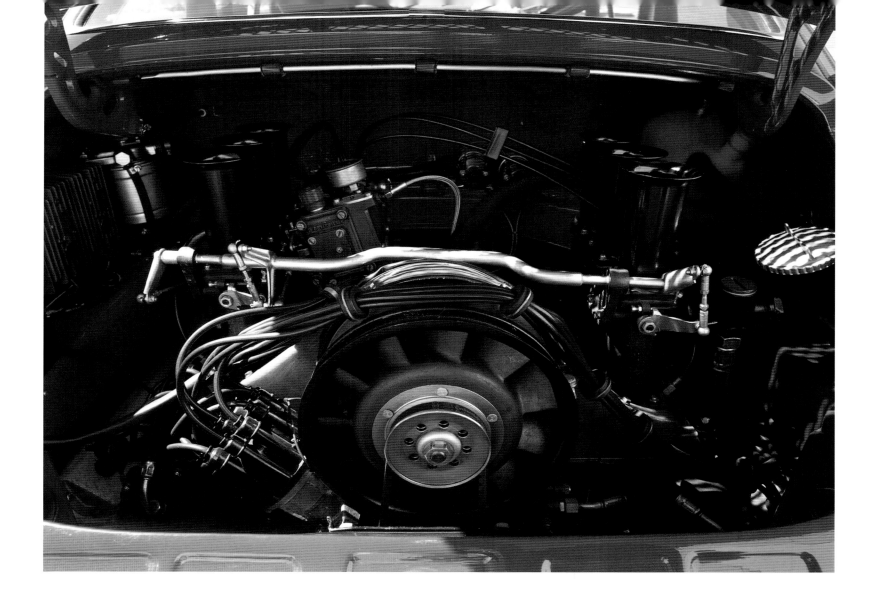

For Norbert Singer, the car's acceptance on the roads, and its shift to Group 3, made his job easier, and this acceptance mirrored his experience on racing circuits around the world. According to Dr. Thomas Gruber and Dr. Georg Konradsheim, Porsche's racing department completed 55 of its RSR 2.8-liter models. The option of the second R, the *rennen* in its designation, cost the customer racer another 25,000 deutsche marks ($8,930) over the purchase price of the RS (for a total of 59,000 deutsche marks, or $22,500 delivered in the United States). Singer's colleagues pulled the inglorious RSH homologation cars off the Zuffenhausen assembly line without engines and transmissions, and rolled them from the new assembly plant to the former racing shops at Werke I, an area set aside for customer service after racing moved to Weissach. There they received Hans Mezger's version of the engine, bored an additional 2 mm to 92 mm, yielding total displacement of 2,806 cc. Modified cylinder heads increased compression, provided larger valves, and twin spark plug ignition. These modifications brought horsepower up to 300 DIN at 8,000 rpm, with 217 DIN ft-lb of torque at 6,300 rpm in a car weighing just 852 kilograms, or 1,875 pounds. After an embarrassing debut at the Tour de Corse in November 1972, Singer and his staff worked through the winter fixing the problems. They dedicated themselves to winning the 1973 World Championship of Makes with their new RSR.

Porsche enlarged the cylinder bore to 92 mm in order to reach a 2,808-cc displacement (171.3 cubic inches). With Bosch mechanical fuel injection, the engine develops 308 horsepower at 8,000 rpm.

Georg Loos and Porsche's Jürgen Barth teamed up to drive this RS 2.8 to a 10th-place finish in the 24 Hours of Le Mans in June 1973. They ran 4,249 kilometers (2,656 miles) at an average speed of 177 kilometers per hour (111 miles per hour).

Martini & Rossi signed on for a three-year contract as team sponsor and Porsche was off to the races, at Daytona, Florida, in early February 1973; Vallelunga, Italy, in late March; Dijon, France, in mid-April; Monza, Italy, 10 days later; Spa-Francorchamps in Belgium in early May; the Targa Florio a week later in mid-May; Nürburgring, the last weekend of May in Germany; Le Mans in early June; Austria two weeks later; and culminating at Watkins Glen, New York, in late July.

A protest, lodged by a Porsche customer-racer named Bonomelli after the Vallelunga event and just before the start of the Monza race, gave Singer and the RSRs an unprecedented chance to move up to prototype class from GT because of a technicality over a rear suspension mount. For the creative racing engineer, this was a gift with enormous potential.

"So as a prototype, there was a lot you could do," Singer said with a laugh. "First was these spoiler things, which were free (of regulations), which helped the car quite a lot. And then we put on wider tires, which was a big discussion at Le Mans.

"There was a practice session at Le Mans in April. We raced with the narrow tires, I think it was 11 inches, or 12. And for the race in June, in between times we had widened the rear tires to 15 inches. Just a little bit! The top speed dropped 15 kilometers or so, which was natural. This got Mr. Fuhrmann upset; he was an engine man basically.

"He wanted to know how he could make us more power and still the car was slower on the straight? How can you do that?" Singer looked over the top of his glasses, smiling. "But the lap times were equal; what we lost on the straight we compensated in the corners. And you got average lap times that were constant. With the narrow tires, you started off fast but then the tires go off. Very fast, after two or three laps, you lost a lot. Therefore, overall, it *was* faster. But, of course, *if* you are looking for a faster lap time *and* a faster top speed, then you have nothing.

"I remember Mr. Fuhrmann was really disappointed about the top speed. On Saturday morning before the race, he came up and said, 'Okay, tell the driver we race flat out from the first lap. Twenty-four hours.'

"And I went to Herbert Müller and said, 'Well, you know, you can make your dinner reservation. Mr. Fuhrmann wants "flat out." It'll be a short race.'"

But Müller's car, shared with Gijs van Lennep, ran a long race, a near-sprint right around the clock. It experienced no problems and finished fourth overall, behind two pure sports-racing Matra-Simca MS670B racers and a prototype Ferrari 312PB. Other Porsche 2.8 RSRs took 8th and 10th as well. When the dust settled at the end of the season, and the FIA counted points, Porsche's road-car-derived 911 Carrera RSR 2.8 had beaten Ferrari's prototype sports racers 27 to 24, with sport prototype entries from Matra, Chevron, Lola, and Mirage, and BMW's feisty 3.0CSL "batmobiles" all trailing behind. With total series production at 14,714 cars, close to a record and most of those as 911s, Norbert Singer, Wolfgang Berger, and Ernst Fuhrmann had resuscitated an automobile that others had sentenced to death at the end of 1973. ▤

Around-the-clock races require more than bright headlights to drive at such high speeds. The cars also need more modest illumination on their numbers so timers and scorers can keep track of each car's position and progress.

CHAPTER FOUR

THE SECOND GENERATION
1974 – 1983

"In spite of a heavy infusion of racing blood,

the Turbo Carrera road car

is easily the fastest and most civilized

Porsche 911 ever built ."

Road & Track, December 1975

"Development of the turbocharged engine was done in a very short time, about half a year or so." Ernst Fuhrmann spoke of adapting the turbo to 911s for racing and production applications. In the racing department, Hans Mezger and Valentine Schäffer already had turbocharged the mighty 917 flat-twelves for both the European Interserie and the North American Can-Am, two series that placed no restrictions on engine size or power output. Porsche routinely reaped more than 1,100 horsepower from the 5,374-cc (327.8-cubic-inch) engine weighing just 617 pounds. While such performance almost defies belief, Mezger and Schäffer worked with Norbert Singer on those projects, for which

1974 911 CARRERA

United States emission standards kept the Carrera RS 2.7 models out of America in 1973. For 1974, Porsche offered a Carrera model using the 175–DIN brake horsepower 911S engine driven by the K-Jetronic electronic induction system.

Opposite: This is the work of talented engineers and designers. Aerodynamics engineer Tilman Brodbeck devised the ducktail wing. Styling boss Tony Lapine turned it over to his staff stylist, Wolfgang Möbius, who shaped it and also devised the accordion-like covering for the impact bumpers.

they could design the racing car body around the engine. For the 911, they had to fit these pieces into an existing shape that had fostered fervent loyalty. "I would say it was a marriage of the development engineers who did this . . . and I did push a little bit on this project." Then Fuhrmann laughed.

"Racing must have a connection to the normal automobile," Fuhrman continued. When he returned to Porsche, the company's turbocharged race cars already performed flawlessly and won relentlessly. Each version improved on the previous car. What's more, compared with nonturbocharged Can-Am cars, Porsches sounded practically muffled. "We were far ahead," Fuhrmann recalled. "So I said to my people, why don't we put this success into our series production cars?"

"They said, 'Oh, this was tried already.'" In 1969, Schäffer had mounted turbochargers onto a couple of typ 901 1,991-cc engines. One went into a 911, the other in a 914/6. On the 911, the turbo hung outside the car body. In the 914/6 there were serious problems with heat dissipation. Both installations suffered tremendous turbo lag, as the long plumbing delayed the arrival of the pressurized fuel to the cylinders.

Michael May, an independent engineer in Stuttgart, had turbocharged Ford Capris reliably enough that local dealers were able to sell them. May consulted with BMW in Munich to help them get their turbo 2002 racing program going. In their own efforts to tame the system for series production models, they experienced

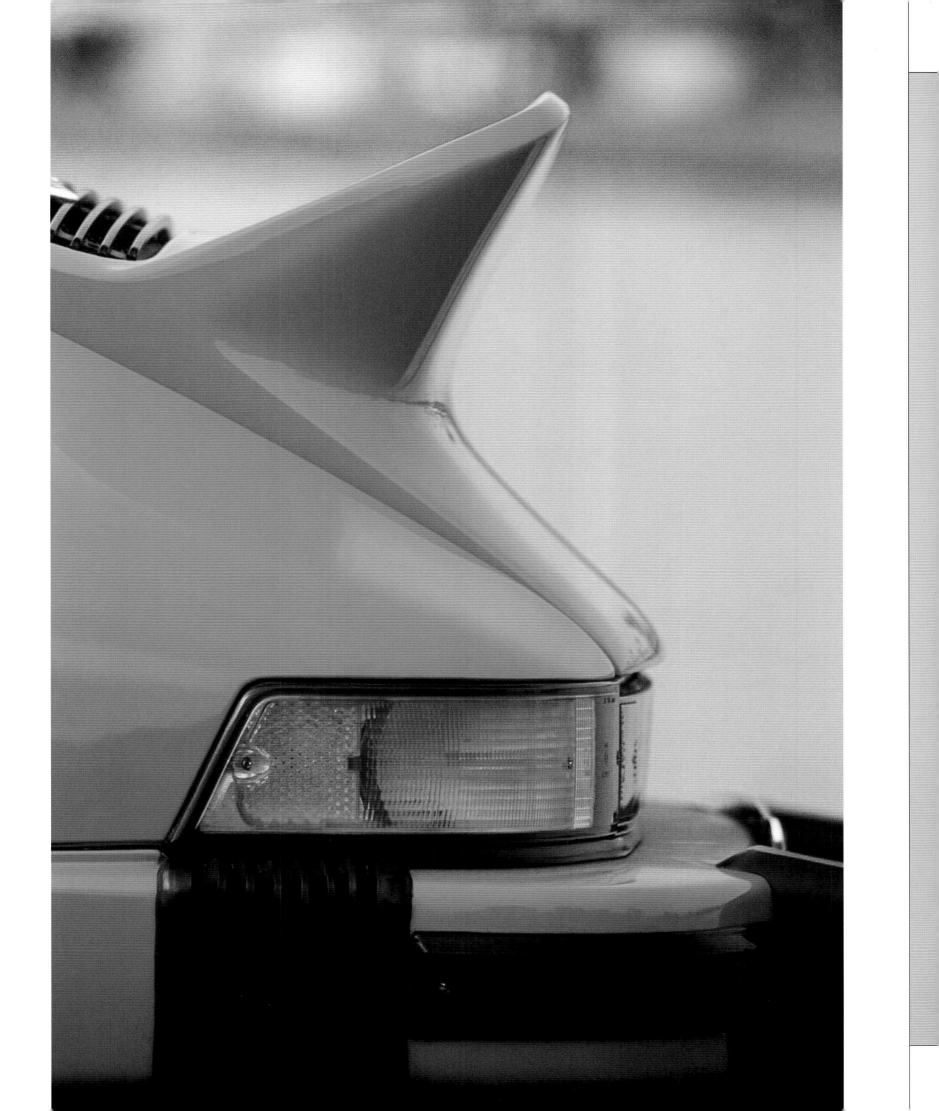

American regulations affected not only engine performance for 1974, but also the car's appearance. New bumpers had to absorb the energy of a 5-mile-per-hour impact, so engineers mounted aluminum bumpers on dampers hidden behind rubber flaps and side bellows.

similar problems to Porsche's, however. Rumors persisted that they had succeeded and with each passing auto show, Porsche expected to see a car displayed. The latest hints suggested that BMW would introduce a turbocharged 2002 for the street as a 1974 model.

"But in our car that was not done right," Fuhrmann countered his engineers. "And it was refused by management at that time. It was impossible. Not enough room." What's more, back then, Ferry Porsche and Ferdinand Piëch had an all-new water-cooled mid-engine car coming with eight cylinders.

"I looked in the engine compartment and said, 'There must be room.' This was my contribution," Fuhrmann explained. The only admonition missing was, "Think about it!"

Schäffer got one running in April 1973, albeit poorly. Fuhrmann drove the experimental car, which suffered long turbo lag, and the 911 chassis wasn't up to the potential of 250 brake horsepower. Fuhrmann pushed ahead, giving his engineers one more target to meet. Whatever system they got to work had to function with the new electronic fuel injection system Porsche just had introduced in late 1972 with the 911T, Bosch's K-Jetronic.

Mid-year introductions previewed full-run production improvements. This was true with Paul Hensler's next induction upgrade for the 911T with Bosch's fuel injection. While it appeared in the 1973 1/2 Ts for U.S. delivery, it spread across the full 911 lineup starting with 1974 models. Schäffer made it work by inducting outside air through the K-Jetronic upward past its metering valve and into the compressor side of the exhaust powered turbocharger. From there, the turbine forced the condensed air/fuel mix to the throttle valve on top of the engine's new cast-aluminum intake manifold. Schäffer and Mezger turned the system over to Herbert Ampferer and Robert Pindar to make it production-ready. Their work was not much easier.

Turbo lag presents different challenges to different drivers in different conditions. To racers who can learn the engine, the car's handling, and the track, it was a matter of remembering at what point in each turn they mashed the gas pedal back down. In some instances, they were hard on the gas even as they still were hard on the brakes. By the time the turbo spun back up to its 80,000 or 100,000 rpm, the racer was at the apex and looking for power. If timing was off, the car spun wildly off track or lurched and jerked slowly out of the turn. The other dynamic that made turbos suitable for racers but a challenge for series production drivers was that racers seldom coast. They never cruise the boulevard at 30 kilometers or 30 miles an hour or run a steady 100 kilometers on an autobahn or interstate highway. That "partial throttle" condition in which production cars run most of the time puts the turbocharger to sleep. When power is needed, a floored accelerator brings unexpected results, sometimes

1974 911 TURBO RSR

Displacing just 2.1 liters, this 480–DIN brake horsepower RSR introduced the racing world to the serious potential of the turbocharged 911. Shown here at Watkins Glen, it had already finished second overall at Le Mans. Its enormous wheel flares and wide wing are just hints of what was coming from Porsche racing.

Engine displacement follows a mandatory multiplier rule, which gives turbocharged engines the equivalent of 1.4 times the non-turbocharged displacement. To qualify, Porsche ran its 2,143-cc (130.7-cubic-inch) flat-six with 83-mm bore and 66-mm stroke.

Porsche chairman Ernst Fuhrmann was embarrassed by the huge rear wing that Norbert Singer used to hold this exaggerated 911 shape on the ground at high speed. Fuhrmann ordered Singer to paint it black so it would be less obvious.

doubling the horsepower within a second, but after several seconds delay. The rule for production car owners was never mash the gas pedal down until you definitely are headed the direction you wish to travel. Ampferer learned the consequences early in his work on turbocharging when he rented one of Michael May's turbo Ford Capris and, as he told Karl Ludvigsen, "nearly ended up in the cemetery." The challenges Ampferer and Pindar faced equaled in difficulty those Mezger and Schäffer had met as they tried to get the things to work on racing engines.

Porsche introduced its production car at the Frankfurt show in September 1973. It showed a striking silver coupe, swollen with RSR flared front and rear fenders shrouding extremely wide tires, and finished with a large flat rear wing. "Turbo" graphics stretched like elastic from the taillights to the top of the rear wheel arches. For motorshow guests who had witnessed the Interserie 917s or the Can-Am cars, this new

1974 911 RSR-IROC

The International Race of Champions (IROC) series was the brainchild of retired racer Roger Penske. He created a four-race program to determine the best driver from several series, including NASCAR, Indy, and sports cars. Twelve competitors raced identical coupes, including Bobby Allison in this car.

show car was irresistible. No matter that, once again, Porsche had shown a car years before the buyer could have one. The 901 introduction in 1963 had served to warn people to save their money. The October 1972 introduction of the Carrera RS told them to order now. Sales had learned its lessons well and no one, neither buyer nor seller, seemed concerned if this car sent a confused message. It was a Turbo with, according to printed materials, 280 brake horsepower from 2.7 liters. This was race car stuff, and civilians could own it.

For the FIA and for Norbert Singer, this *was* race car stuff. Regulations looked certain to restrict the next generation of the Manufacturer's Championship racing to what is known as a "silhouette formula." That meant, generally, that vast modifications to the engine, transmission, brakes, the interior, and even the chassis were allowed, so long as the car retained its series production "silhouette." Much the same way the American NASCAR series lets many things happen under the hood and inside the body, the cars must look familiar to fans in the stands and to track officials.

Throughout the world, Norbert Singer's 3.0-liter RSRs, still bearing an easy resemblance to the previous year's Carrera RS 2.7 models, won races, captured championships, and inspired entire series. In the United States, Roger Penske, already one of Singer's best customers with his operation of the Sunoco 917/30 Can-Am program, stepped up again. He purchased 15 identical RSRs for a race series he and Riverside racetrack owner Les Richter contrived called the International Race of Champions, IROC. Four races, beginning at Riverside, California, in October 1973, and culminating at Daytona, Florida, in February 1974, would determine the world's best driver by pitting Richard Petty, A. J. Foyt, and David Pearson against Emerson Fittipaldi, Denny Hulme, Mark Donahue, and George Follmer. Peter Revson, Bobby Allison,

Porsche tuned and assembled 15 3-liter IROC RSRs to 315 DIN brake horsepower, including three spares. Roger Penske had considered other car makes, but his team driver, Mark Donahue, advocated the RSRs. He went on to win three of the four events, taking the IROC title.

Roger McCluskey, Gordon Johncock, and Bobby Unser rounded out the field. Donahue won the series. Singer and Fuhrmann created the IROC RSRs blending bits of the RS 3.0 body and RSR 3.0 engineering, cloaked in a vivid array of paint colors. The bodies, with Porsche's new large flat rear wing, looked closer to series production cars than pure racers, the better to entice spectators into showrooms on Monday mornings. Porsche assembled, broke in, and tuned each of the cars (to about 316 brake horsepower) as similarly as possible so it remained a driver's match race.

Series production cars continued for 1974 with the G series. Porsche dropped the T and E models, replacing them with a single base model, the 911. This offered 150 DIN brake horsepower—143 SAE net—at 5,700 rpm, with 174 DIN ft-lb of torque, 168 SAE, at 3,800 rpm, with compression at 8.0:1. Both the 911S and U.S. Carrera shared engines and performance statistics: 175 DIN (167 SAE net) brake horsepower at 5,800 rpm. Torque ratings matched the base 911, but at 4,000 rpm

1975 911S

By 1975, U.S. emission regulations were severe enough that Porsche produced its models for the rest of the world with 175 brake horsepower, the 49 U.S. states with 165 horsepower, and a California version with 160 horsepower. California represented 25 percent of its total market, so the company felt that it needed to comply with the state's more stringent regulations.

instead, with compression at 8.5:1. All U.S. market 911 models operated at lower compression than their European counterparts to accommodate lead-free fuels. (Europeans got a Carrera that carried over the 1973 engine and specifications.) Originally the 1974 piston cylinders were lined with Nikasil, but in the middle of the model year Porsche introduced a General Motors/Reynolds Aluminum alloy, 390 aluminum-silicon, or Alusil lining, with Ferrocoated pistons. Alusil offered the benefit of providing an aluminum cylinder block without inserting iron liners.

European Carreras got a five-speed gearbox as standard equipment, while the 911S and base 911 (and the Carrera for U.S. consumption) ran four-speed transmissions. Five-speeds and Sportomatics (with a desensitized shift lever to make it harder to disengage inadvertently) were optional at $250 and $425 respectively. The base car sold for 27,000 deutsche marks in Germany, $9,950 in the United States. The S went for 31,000 deutsche marks ($11,875), while the Carrera tipped the scales at 38,000 deutsche marks, $13,575. *Car and Driver* and *Road & Track* each tested base 911s and the Carrera (slightly less mighty than the unavailable 1973 version). For the Carrera, *Car and Driver* achieved 0 to 60 miles per hour in 5.8 seconds, while *R&T* got there in 7.5. For the base model, *R&T* saw 60 in 7.9 seconds, while *Car and Driver*, with its lighter test load, got there in 6.1. The base car was good for 125 miles per hour in *Car and Driver*'s test, 130 with *R&T*, while the Carrera hit 143 for *Car and Driver*, and 144 for *R&T*.

These automobiles met seemingly impossible standards—including the ability to bounce off a fixed barrier at 5 miles per hour and show no damage. Working with engineers from a variety of disciplines throughout Weissach, Tony Lapine's brilliant designer Wolfgang Möbius produced bumpers that met the challenge without destroying the lines of the 911. As Karl Ludvigsen expressed it, "After the G-series cars had been on the market for about a year, they looked so right and were so familiar to the eye that they tended to make earlier Porsches look excessively light and fragile by comparison." Möbius, fellow styling genius Dick Soderberg, and studio chief modeler Peter Reisinger were among the talent that Lapine brought with him from Opel when he left the GM subsidiary for Porsche in 1969. Möbius' creation, which made no effort to hide its accordion-like

High-backed seats with integrated headrests appeared in 1974, a welcome addition for comfort and safety against rear-end-collision whiplash. For U.S. customers in 1975, Porsche offered only the 911S and the Carrera model. The base 911 remained available throughout the rest of the world.

California cars were fitted with air pumps, thermal reactors, and exhaust gas recirculators (EGRs) to manage exhaust emissions. The other 49 states required only air pumps. Cars shipped throughout the rest of world ran without these additional controls.

1970 930 TURBO

From the front, the only indications that this is not an ordinary 911 are the headlight washers that came standard on the Turbo. The car sold new for $25,850 in the United States.

compression covers, was as faithful to Butzi Porsche's legacy as his own urgings to make the Targa bar apparent rather than hiding it in body color or black, a direction that Lapine's staff chose later. One of Lapine's on-going influences was the slow, steady blackening of highlights, as he took design tastes of the 1960s and moved them into the 1980s. Just as his staff had done with the racing RSR 2.8 and 3.0 models, they now matte-blacked window frames, outside mirrors (that had grown large and rectangular, due to still other U.S. regulations), and door handles. Chrome remained optional. In the interior, new seats incorporated headrests in another effort to accommodate U.S. whiplash concerns. Throughout the interior, Lapine's subtle taste toned down chrome and emboldened knobs, handles, sliders, and grips, including a new 15-inch-diameter, three-spoke steering wheel with a thick leather wrap.

Another performance target these G-series cars achieved was emission, through the K-Jetronic system. Designed to keep fuel mixture lean and reliable, Porsche's engines more easily met U.S. and world exhaust standards while returning better fuel economy. Overnight, in October 1973, that became crucial.

A group formed in September 1960, the Organization of Petroleum Exporting Countries, OPEC, consisting of Iran, Iraq, Kuwait, and Saudi Arabia, began dealing as a consortium with oil refining companies around the

Its appearance was almost scandalous. Porsche had to finish the wide upturned "whale-tail" rear wing in pliable rubber so pedestrians who walked into it wouldn't be hurt.

This view, or a similar angle, was the image that most drivers got to know of Porsche's staggering production 930 Turbo. Introduced in Europe in 1975, it reached the United States as a 1976 model with 260 brake horsepower out of 3 liters in an era when other car makers were selling fuel economy and strangled performance.

Black tubes on the left disappear toward the single KKK turbocharger, and matching tubes return from it. The 3-liter engines carry over the 11-blade cooling fans, while normally aspirated engines introduce new 5-blade versions.

world, negotiating per-barrel prices and delivery schedules. For the next decade, OPEC moved and reacted to world politics without influencing them while generally accepting the prices oil refiners offered. That changed in 1971, when Iran threatened to cut off all supplies to the West and began negotiating the prices it wanted. Qatar and Abu Dhabi joined OPEC, and oil prices surged. On October 21, 1973, OPEC arrested all oil shipments to the United States in protest of American political support of Israel. A month later in the United States, President Richard M. Nixon enacted the Emergency Petroleum Allocation Act, as oil companies announced large price increases for gasoline and heating oil. By December, more than 90 percent of the gas stations in the United States closed intermittently and voluntarily to save gasoline. Lines of cars stretched around the block, and stations began limiting purchases to $2 or $3, 4 or 6 gallons in those days. OPEC lifted its embargo in March, though the now 12-member organization refused to reduce its prices. Estimates put OPEC's earnings at $100 billion for the year. Nixon imposed a national speed limit of 55 miles per hour. In Germany, the autobahns

and all other roads went silent on Sundays, becoming walkways and bicycle paths as the nation banned all but emergency vehicles. It was short-lived, but it sobered up auto company executives around the world, especially at Porsche, where the durability of a sports car market always merited a watchful eye.

The gasoline shortages and increased fuel prices brought Porsche's products into sharper focus. The latest—and last—of its Volkswagen collaborations, the front-engine, water-cooled, four-cylinder 924, designed by Dick Soderberg and newcomer Harm Lagaay, took on a somewhat greater appeal, because it offered the best fuel economy of any Porsche product. The new 928 (also styled by Wolfgang Möbius) suddenly looked inappropriate. Conceived by Ernst Fuhrmann as his 911 replacement, he modified Ferdinand Piëch's mid-engine car concept and gave his 928 a powerful, water-cooled, front-mounted V-8.

1976 934 TURBO

Once the production output of 930 Turbos had qualified the car for competition, Porsche introduced the Group 4 version of the 930, known as the 934. Here George Follmer works his car hard at the Monterey Grand Prix at Laguna Seca in California. *Bob Tronolone*

1976 934 GROUP 4 CHAMPION

While this car raced consistently from 1976 through 1982, its most significant result came to its owner and team in June 1982. English drivers Richard Cleare, Tony Dron, and Richard Jones finished first in Group 4, 13th overall, in the 24 Hours of Le Mans in Cleare's meticulously maintained seven-season-old racer.

Fuhrmann, as company manager and spokesman, joined other German automakers at the podium decrying slower speed limits as not necessarily safer or more economical. "One hundred miles per hour on an empty autobahn with a driver and car in good condition is often better than 55 miles per hour on a rainy night with an exhausted driver on the same road."

Still, the U.S. auto industry embraced the limit. It cost them nothing, and it improved their image. Gasoline mileage went up, and the number of accidents and injuries decreased. The industry spent no more than the costs for speedometers with 85-mile-per-hour maximum readings.

October 1974 brought the 1975 H-series models to shows in Frankfurt and throughout Europe. While an elegant 25th Anniversary 911 (commemorating 25 years of Porsche cars, not the 911) got some attention, it was the production version of the Turbo that turned heads and built lines behind Porsche's order takers at the

shows. Developed off the new 3.0-liter, 2,993-cc racing engine with 95-mm bore and 70.4-mm stroke, Europe got the 260 DIN brake horsepower Turbo with 253 ft-lb torque at 4,000, in 1975.

U.S. buyers did not have the option of buying the Turbo in 1975. To compound matters, they suffered a further indignity: Air pumps were back, and, with 157 SAE net brake horsepower at 5,800 rpm, the cars developed 10 horsepower less than the 1974 U.S.-market S and Carrera. California cars, with additional thermal reactors, heat exchangers, and an exhaust gas recirculation system, lost another 5 horsepower, for a 152 SAE net with the same 166 ft-lb torque at 4,000 rpm.

U.S. and European cars (except the Euro Carrera) got electric blowers for the heater, addressing a concern of 911 owners in colder climates. Additional noise insulation quieted the cockpit, a sensory benefit that

1976 934

Original owner/racer Egon Evertz campaigned this car fairly successfully throughout Europe during the 1976 World Championship of Makes. It changed hands, ultimately ending up with Englishman Richard Cleare for the 1980 season, and he continued racing it through 1982.

Porsche enhanced with taller final drive gears, letting the engine run slower at comparable road speeds than it had in 1974. Tony Lapine took the next big step in toning down the bright work and for 1975, buyers could get the Targa roof bars in flat black as well as brushed stainless steel. Best of all for U.S. customers, a favorable exchange rate made possible a slight price reduction. The 911S and Carrera dropped to $11,700 from $12,000, and to $13,600 from $14,000 respectively. As every year, the two principal U.S. magazines tested the Carreras. *Car and Driver* reached 60 miles per hour in 6.2 seconds and topped the car out at 132 miles per hour. *R&T's* gentler clutch treatment and passenger slowed their California-specification model's acceleration to 8.2 seconds but they reached 134 miles per hour. A record 55 percent of Porsche's sales went to the United States, making it clear to Ernst Fuhrmann and other observers that 55-mile-per-hour speed limits and 60-cent-per-gallon gasoline (it had been 35 cents just two year earlier) offered little deterrence to loyalists who wanted a new car, and to Hollywood's successful television writers who could afford their first 911.

The biggest news for U.S. customers for 1976 was the availability of the typ 930 Turbo Carrera. These I-series cars, with the Carrera 3.0 (called the 911S in the United States so as not to confuse buyers with two Carreras) in the middle, and the 911 as the base model, quickened the pulse of many buyers. Emissions equipment sapped another 10 horsepower away from the 911S engine, so Porsche dropped the S model and put its revised engine in the base model, now with 165 DIN at 5,800 rpm. Yet slightly different gear ratios gave it better performance than the 1975 S had presented. The new 3.0 Carrera used the Turbo's 2,993-cc engine without the turbocharger. A non-U.S.-market car, it developed 200 DIN brake horsepower at 6,000 rpm, and 188 ft-lb torque at 4,200 rpm. (The U.S.-export 911S developed 165 brake horsepower throughout 49 states and 160 for California.) The turbocharged version rated 234 SAE brake horsepower at 5,500 rpm, as well as 246 ft-lb of torque at 4,500 rpm. Porsche created a new four-speed transmission especially for the Turbo to handle the torque.

Rules for Group 4 allowed Porsche to extend rear fenders by 100 mm (4 inches), and the front by 50 mm (2 inches). Despite this aerodynamic encumbrance, Tony Dron routinely saw 325 kilometers (200 miles) per hour along Mulsanne. Dron turned the fastest lap ever for a Group 4 car at 4:04.08.

Both low engine speeds and low compression—6.5:1—were part of the formula to keep production engines from becoming expensive failures. Porsche recommended list price was $25,880 on the East Coast, $26,000 in the West. *Road & Track* saw 0-to-60 times of 6.7 seconds and at 6,150 rpm in fourth gear, and they topped out at 156 miles her hour. This was the same as competitor *Car and Driver*, which may have had more entertainment during its tests as it ripped the Turbo to 60 miles per hour in 4.9 seconds! This kind of publicity helped launch Turbo sales to 500 in the United States out of the 1,300 delivered worldwide.

In a market-protection move, Porsche reinstated the four-cylinder 912, with Bosch's D-Jetronic system now, strictly for the U.S. market for 1976 only. The company discontinued the 914 and wished to hold its place in the

economy sports-car sector until its 924 model debuted for 1977. This 912E used the 914's Volkswagen-designed, Porsche-developed 1,971-cc flat four, developing 86 SAE net horsepower at 4,900 rpm and 93 ft-lb of torque at 4,000 rpm. DIN figures never were released, because it was a U.S.-only model.

Porsche followed its 25th anniversary model from 1975 with a Ferry Porsche "signature" model for 1976. His autograph emblazoned the steering wheel. Marketing and Sales clearly had learned its lessons from the Carrera RS exclusivity. It had also noticed another trend. Throughout Europe and the United States (despite its less valuable dollar) auto buyers who could afford Porsche's cars had developed enough confidence in the economy to reward themselves with cars at this price level. But while they not only expected certain performance and they welcomed the cachet of exclusivity, they came to expect luxury. Chevrolet Corvette

Preparing for the 1982 season, Cleare sent his engine back to Porsche. They suggested he change from the CIS electronic to mechanical fuel injection, which gave him about 620 horsepower, up considerably from the original specification of 485 at 7,000 rpm. Still, the cars are heavy because of the 930 homologation at 1,120 kilograms (2,464 pounds).

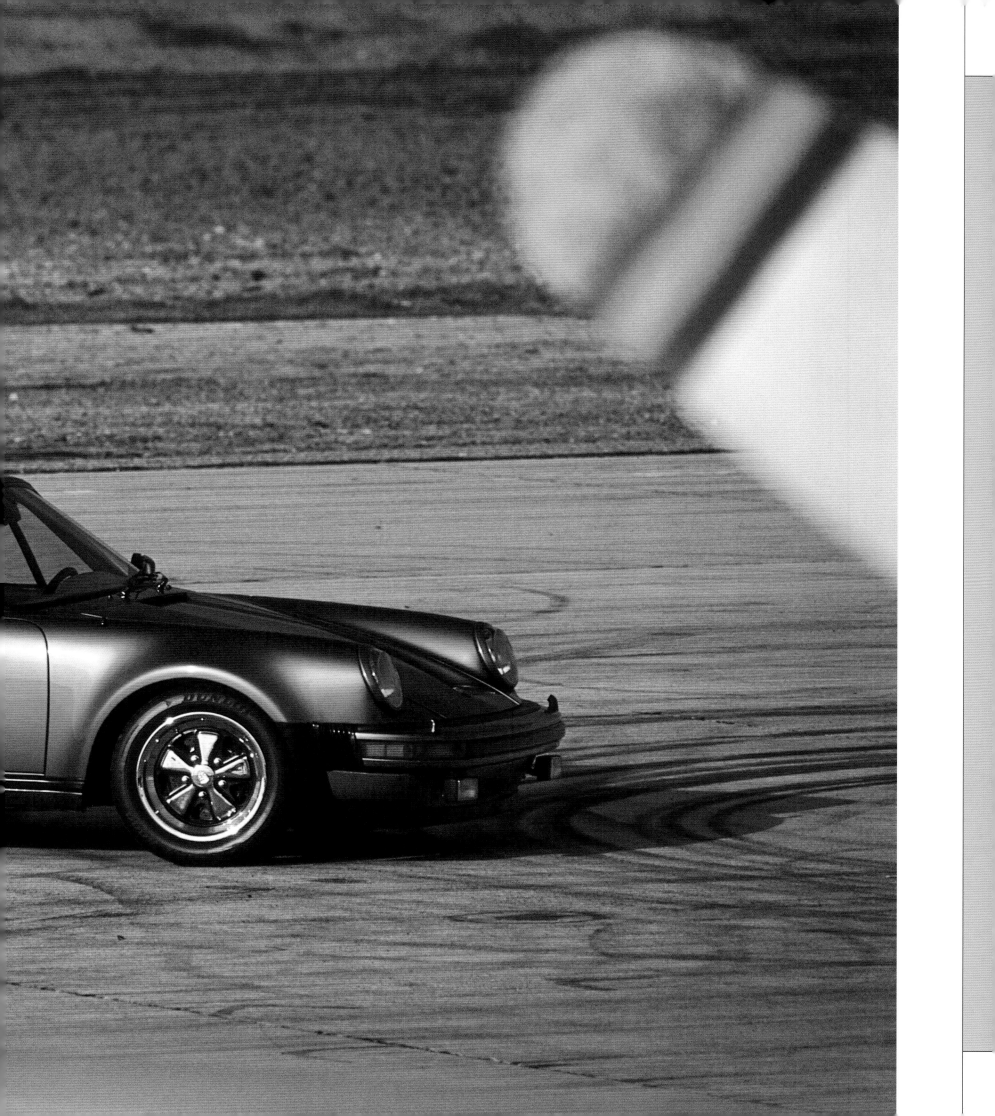

Previous Pages: **1978 930 TURBO**
The new 3.3-liter engine provided U.S. customers with 265 horsepower, but those elsewhere got 300 brake horsepower at 5,500 rpm. U.S. cars had to run on unleaded fuel, and Porsche equipped the engines with EGRs (exhaust gas recirculators) and thermal reactors.

For 1978, Porsche introduced intercooling to its street turbochargers. A new rear wing, the "tea tray," allows additional room for the air-to-air intercooler.

product planners had perceived this market change and had reacted quickly, taking their formerly powerful sporty two-seater into this new direction as "fast personal luxury transportation." With its turbo, Porsche specifically catered to this discriminating customer. For 1977, it broadened its approach. Chassis improvements made the car less physically demanding to drive, easier to steer, brake, and shift; quieter power windows, air conditioning and climate control, automatic speed control, better road and wind noise insulation, and even better theft protection with flush-fitting door lock buttons further coddled buyers who found similar amenities on BMWs and Mercedes-Benz two-doors. Porsche offered some of these improvements as options, others as standard equipment, but they were there.

U.S. buyers had only the 911S (at $14,995, $15,945 for the Targa) and Turbo Carrera to choose from, while the rest of the world still could purchase a base 911 (35,950 deutsche marks for the coupe, 38,450 deutsche marks for the Targa) or a Carrera 3.0 (46,350 deutsche marks coupe and 48,850 Targa) without the turbocharger.

Commensurate with a corporate jet today, the 930 quickly became the ultimate "business express," as well as the ultimate trophy denoting business success.

Porsche launched the Turbos in Europe in 1975 and brought them to the United States in 1976. In the states, Porsche gave them 3.3 liters of displacement and 265 brake horsepower, while the rest of the world enjoyed 300 at 5,500 rpm.

Porsche had sat out of international competition in 1974. It sold Carrera RSR 3.0 models to customers and supported them, but Norbert Singer's efforts at Weissach went into preparing the typ 934 for the following year, when the FIA would introduce the new Group 4 class. Singer also prepared the typ 935 for a Group 5 Special Production Car category, along with a full-on sports-racing prototype, the 936, that bore no relation to either of the "silhouette" category 911-derived racers in Group 4 and 5. The years 1975 and 1976 would prove to be a very exciting time for Porsche racing fans.

Racing again improved the breed. Norbert Singer's protégé, Wolfgang Berger, now working for Singer on racing variations of his production 930, needed to put ever wider and taller tires on racing turbos. This brought 16-inch wheels and tires over to the street 930 Turbo for 1977. The company's first year series production—1,300 cars—qualified the next generation racing Turbo RSR for the FIA's Group 4. Singer's staff created the typ 934, the Group 4 930. This was an unabashed race car that competed with electric windows because the company had assembled the necessary 1,000-plus "homologation" models sold to anxious European and American customers with them as an expected luxury item. (Singer pointed out that the electric drive mechanism weighed less than manual crank systems.) The 934s were 97,000 deutsche mark ($40,000) versions of the

1978 911SC-RS

Produced to meet Group B regulations for the European Rally Series, Porsche lightened the 911SC coupes to 960 kilograms (2,112 pounds).

1978 911SC-RS ROTHMANS

The 3-liter engines, actually 2,994 cc (182.6 cubic inches), develop 255 brake horsepower at 7,000 rpm. Porsche redesigned the SC cylinder head, fitted forged pistons, a more aggressive camshaft, and Bosch mechanical fuel injection.

Of the 20 SC-RS models that Porsche assembled, six went to Rothmans. David Richards in Silverstone, England, prepared the cars by taking them completely apart.

street car but with several massive differences. First, the same 3-liter engine in the 930, complete with Bosch K-Jetronic induction, wrenched out 485 DIN horsepower at 7,000 rpm for this road racer. Torque was 434 DIN ft-lb at 5,400 rpm. Part of what helped this huge power increase was adding an air-to-water intercooler, a first for Porsche, to each bank of three cylinders. (The 1974 auto show prototypes displayed a single large air-to-air intercooler.) This dropped fuel mixture temperature to 120 degrees Fahrenheit from 300. The car weighed just

130 pounds less than the street version, 2,655 pounds instead of 2,785, derived from a complex formula based on its engine displacement and despite its gutted interior and fiberglass panels. Two obvious differences surrounded the wheels and tires. Broad fender flares appeared to be bolted on, Frankenstein-like, to the front and rear wheel arches. These were necessary to accommodate 23.5x10.5-16 front and 25.5x12.5-16 rear Goodyear Bluestreak racing tires. The Sports Car Club of America welcomed the turbocharged 934s into the Trans-Am series, and American racing fans watched closely fought events pitting John Greenwood–modified Corvettes, Chevy Monzas and 454-cubic-inch-displacement Camaros and a shopping cart of FIA Group 3 and 4 Ford Capri 3100s, BMW 3.0CSLs and M1s, against crowds of 934s. It made for exciting events with George Follmer and Hurley Haywood racing to first and second in the points championship.

Porsche's 935, the racing 930 for Group 5, was an even more radical package than its 934. With 590 DIN brake horsepower on tap within a 2,340-pound $75,000 race car, this beast was strictly business. Fiberglass panels replaced steel everywhere possible except the roof. The cockpit, spare to extreme, offered one option never seen on a street car, rear sway bar adjustment that could compensate for front fuel tank load and rear tire wear. Its air-to-air intercooler fit into a rear wing as large as anything Ernst Fuhrmann ever had seen. (The 1974 Turbo RSR had a large flat panel that Fuhrman lamented, calling it an *eindecker*, or monoplane. He ordered it painted flat black to make it less obvious to officials and competitors and less embarrassing to him.) Fuhrmann was relieved when final Group 5 rules forced measurements of the rear wing to fit within the overall dimensions of the car body. Round one went to the FIA. Round two clearly went to Singer and Berger. They interpreted rules to allow them to flatten the front fenders to contours that barely cleared the front tires. They set headlights in the front spoiler and added louvers atop the tires to expel air pressure. All this effort cut drag, reduced lift,

improved driver visibility, and drove the FIA rule makers crazy. With Norbert Singer, they learned they had a maverick on their hands, a creative engineer who would test them repeatedly for years to come. Compared to the 934, with 0-to-60 mile-per-hour times of 5.8 seconds, *Road & Track*, in the same test, got Porsche's 935 to 60 in just 3.3, and on to 100 in 6.1 seconds, four full seconds faster than the 934. Porsche's own tests with the 935s at Paul Ricard topped 194 miles per hour.

Through 1977 and 1978, Ernst Fuhrman, as company spokesman, answered repeated questions about a product lineup that had shifted demonstrably from rear-engine air-cooled sports cars to water-cooled front engine ones. Finally, in early 1978, Fuhrmann categorized the future of the 911. He clarified his comments

David Richards refabricated much of the Porsche factory car to make it easier for his crews to service and repair during the rally season. While competitors ran turbocharged engines, Porsche's drivers enjoyed quicker throttle response and cooler cockpits from their normally aspirated rear-engine placement.

PORSCHE GARAGES AT LE MANS, 1978

Moby Dick, car number 43 at left, and the open prototype 936/78, at right, were still in pieces just hours before the afternoon and evening session began. Both the engine and transmission for Moby Dick were behind the car.

Porsche Archives

1978 935/78 "MOBY DICK"
Through his careful reading of FIA regulations, Norbert Singer noticed that the rules left the shape of the fenders "free" to new designs. The rules also allowed him to add a false roof and door panels over the originals to further streamline the body. This car stunned FIA scrutineers. *Porsche Archives*

in 1991. "In this time," he explained, "we produced I think 45 cars a day. The car was still selling. We still made money from this car. So I set a low limit, at which we no longer make money. I told journalists if ever we go below 25 cars, some number each day, 6,000 a year, we stop. That quieted them." What Fuhrman had stopped already was further development beyond what it took to meet ongoing U.S. emission and safety regulations. The United States still commanded half of 911 sales; therefore half the model's profits came from satisfying American loyalists. The 928 had brought a new audience to Porsche cars, buyers who never had considered any Porsche as a personal luxury vehicle before. The 924 achieved the same at the entry level, bringing a younger crowd to the company. For 1978 Porsche offered loyalists its new 911SC, or Super Carrera. This replaced both the 1977 base 911 and the high-end Carreras, carrying

over the 2.993-cc Carrera engine. Europeans got a 180 DIN brake horsepower version with 195 ft-lb of torque, while new emissions air pumps brought the SAE specifications down to 172 brake horsepower (at 5,500 rpm) and 189 ft-lb torque (at 4,200 rpm; engine speeds were common to both varieties). The additional torque made the car more enjoyable for city drivers used to humiliation at the hands of Corvette owners. Porsche offered the coupe and Targa with either five-speed or Sportomatic transmissions, as well as the Turbo 930.

In a wilder state of tune, Roland Kussmaul created two 911SC entries for the Safari Rally through 3,000 miles of East African deserts and rainforests. Despite brutal terrain that literally broke suspensions, Porsche finished second and fourth.

From this high view, the original doors and original roof (with the curved rear side-window visible inside the race car's elongated version) are apparent. Singer's concept was so brash—and just barely within regulations—that FIA officials compromised, permitting half-covers on the two doors. Testing revealed the need for a higher wing. *Porsche Archives*

Fédération Internationale de l'Automobile (FIA) Appendix J regulations require Group 5 cars to look like the production car on which they're based. Norbert Singer read the rules and found no restriction on what the fenders should look like.

Poor fuel economy that plagued the 1978 models improved for 1979 with ignition timing changes. Styling chief Tony Lapine and his staff advanced their movement toward black trim with mirrors and marker light frames. They shifted the large headlight frames from chrome to body color in their ongoing efforts to blur Butzi Porsche's delineation between function and form. Porsche's styling efforts were subtle and contrasted dramatically with other German tuners for Mercedes-Benz and BMW that moved more radically overboard, painting grilles, badges, wheels, and sometimes tinting window glass to match body color.

Norbert Singer's racing department created the single most radical 911 ever for the 1978. The car was designated as 935/78, but racers and competitors knew it as Moby Dick. It earned the name when Singer first rolled it out for racing journalists to photograph late in the winter. It looked, mostly, like a 911 but it was longer,

Deep inside the fiberglass bodywork, the turbocharged 2.86-liter engine develops 590 horsepower using air-to-water inter-coolers. Norbert Singer's engineers had to thread water-cooling plumbing to the nose of the car and back.

When FIA inspectors came, at Singer's invitation, to preview Porsche's Group 5 entry, they were aghast. Where rules were vague, Singer substantially modified the car, and in areas not addressed by FIA rules, he created his own solutions.

1978 911SC SAFARI RALLY

By this time, Porsche cars had won nearly every major racing competition except one: the East African Safari. Originating in 1953, the event was confined to Kenya by 1978. Competitors raced 5,000 kilometers (3,100 miles) throughout the country.

lower, wider, and wilder than anything anyone was prepared to see. Yet Singer had read his rule books and, once again he interpreted the words in ways that best fit his idea of a winning race car.

"Are you sure you can do this?" Helmuth Bott asked him.

"Well, by the letter, I am quite sure," Singer replied.

The letters said, "The original body shape must be retained, doors, and roof." It also said "fenders were free," meaning they could be redesigned as the constructor needed. That had been the loophole through which Singer had driven the first 935 with its headlights inches above the ground. The latest regulations made other mistakes, left other loopholes, and through these, Singer forced fenders wide enough to accommodate vast fat tires, door panels moved out to meet the fenders, and a new fiberglass roof, fitted outside the original steel roof, that was flatter and led to the longest tail anyone ever had conceived for a 911.

The first race of the season was in Italy, home of millions of loyal Ferraristi. This country's racing pride still smarted from the momentary lapse five years earlier that had allowed Singer to upgrade a production-based RSR into prototype category. This time, Singer felt an ounce of prevention might be worth pounds and pounds of fiberglass. The FIA routinely had offered to preview models. One of those who showed up to examine the 935/78 was long-time Porsche friend and veteran racer Paul Frère.

"Illegal," he said. "You can't do it. The rule book says you have to have the production shape of the door, not these funny . . . . "

Singer undid quick-release fittings.

"No problem. This is only an outside skin. Underneath is the original door." He and his technicians removed extra panels from all over the car.

Monte Carlo winner Björn Waldegaard and his co-driver, Hans Thorszelius, finished fourth overall in this car. The race was held over Easter week, and heavy rains turned east African deserts into mud ponds.

1979 911SC TARGA

Porsche continued to meet the emissions regulations of its customers' home nations by providing six variations of the 3.0-liter SC engine. All of these are rated at 180 horsepower.

When the SC models appeared in 1978, Porsche introduced its rubber-centered clutch disc. Model year 1979 marked the final appearance of the Sportomatic transmission.

"Of course the shape was there," he recalled years later. "And there was no sentence in the rule book about whether you could cover it. It was not mentioned."

The three scrutineers huddled together and concluded that, as it was not strictly illegal, therefore it was legal. Before they left, Singer insisted they approve the car in writing, signing the forms with photos attached.

With 3,211 cc, Hans Mezger's 935/71 engine developed a conservative 750 DIN horsepower at 8,200 rpm. This car weighed just 1,025 kilograms, 2,255 pounds. At Le Mans, it routinely hit 365 kilometers per hour, 228 miles per hour, along Mulsanne. Jürgen Barth, one of the factory's team drivers and head of its customer racing program, was the first to drive the car.

1980 935 K3

Erwin and Manfred Kremer had their first 935 ready for competition in 1979. This car won its class at Le Mans in 1980, taking first in IMSA class and fifth overall. Kremer 935s were so successful that Porsche stopped producing the 935s themselves.

"Oh yes, I remember this car," he said recently. "This was the first race car I ever drove that I held onto the wheel with both hands. With boost all the way up, I think it was more than 900 horsepower. I think 160 kilometers (100 miles per hour) came in six seconds, less maybe. In second gear. Then shift to third and fourth, and it starts all over again each time."

The car never met its expectations. It finished 8th at Le Mans, didn't complete races either at Norisring in Germany or Vallelunga in Italy. In England, at Silverstone, its finest hour, it won easily. Porsche built just two. It would be another several years before copies appeared, created and driven by privateers John Fitzpatrick from England and Gianpiero Moretti from Italy.

Among series production models, things remained more contained and reserved. Factions developed within styling and engineering. The 911 loyalists regretted and resented that design improvements and engineering development stagnated. Wolfgang Möbius, who had designed the 928's body for Lapine's studio, continued to drive a 911 as his chosen company car. Production of the 911SC and Turbo slipped to 9,475 cars. For 1980, U.S.-configured models remained at 180 brake horsepower. The difference between what American customers and the home market got broadened dramatically when stateside buyers noticed a speedometer reading only to 85 miles per hour on their 1980 SCs. They no longer could purchase a Turbo. It made some laugh and others curse.

At the end of model year 1980, production reached 9,943, a slight increase that included the 840 turbos offered to the rest of the world. This put a little more insulation between the 911 and Fuhrmann's 6,000-unit death sentence. However, with advertising and promotion budgets, and engineering and design allocations split three ways, it seemed for many inside the company and to others outside among magazine writers and editors that Ernst Fuhrmann had said one thing but intended another. Porsche's total production of 911s, 930s, 924s, and 928s was 28,622 cars.

There are some that say Ernst Fuhrmann was his own worst enemy. He admitted in an interview in 1991 that he had enemies and he presumed that he had made some of them himself. People criticized him for usurping the role of Ferry Porsche as spokesman for the company at public events. Yet this was part of the job for which Porsche had hired Fuhrmann, and one that all Fuhrmann's successors filled. Those who knew Porsche well described him as introverted and circumspect; he did not enjoy the limelight. But was it to give Fuhrmann room to manage or because he felt pushed out that Ferry moved his offices from the second floor of Werke I to another building some distance away?

Porsche's ability to lead is unquestioned. He brought the 911 into production in 1964. Some say his father never intended to produce a Porsche automobile but this is something Ferry did. He adjudicated the tempestuous family meeting in 1970 that removed in-laws and outlaws from roles within the company save for his own.

The Kremer brothers practiced aerodynamic wind management to a high degree. Strakes along the nose of the car help direct the wind straight over the hood. This maintains downforce from nose to tail. The Kremers faired tiny mirrors into the A-pillars.

That was not the culmination of negotiations by a spineless man. Yet for reasons only he could explain, he had allowed himself to be exiled from his own firm.

In 1971, after Porsche lost development work for Weissach's engineers and designers from Volkswagen's leadership changes, Ernst Fuhrmann went to Detroit to market Weissach's skills and abilities to U.S. carmakers. His last appointment was with Lee Iacocca at Ford Motor Company, and Iacocca was interested. However, by the time Fuhrmann landed in Stuttgart, Iacocca was gone. Henry Ford resented the fact that, while his name was on the building and on most every car that left his plants, the world saw Lee Iacocca. Iacocca had done great work, introducing successful products and giving Mr. Ford the Le Mans racing victories against Ferrari

The BBS extractor wheels suck brake heat out from the wheelwells. Onboard hydraulic jacks raise and lowered the car in seconds, greatly speeding up pit-stop tire changes.

1981 935 KREMER K3

The father and son team, John L. Paul, Sr. and Jr., were among IMSA's fiercest competitors in the early 1980s. Here at Mid-Ohio, a pit-stop flash fuel fire triggered the on-board extinguishing system and covered the windshield. Paul Sr. frantically wiped half of it clear and sent his son back out. John Paul Jr. finished third.

that he wanted so deeply. A few observers of this company's history say Fuhrmann should have taken note.

Early in 1979 Ernst Fuhrmann looked forward to his 60th birthday. As he examined the company that had employed him twice in his life, he glimpsed the future. His three-year-old 924 was successful, turning more than 20,000 copies each year. The two-year-old 928 was earning greater recognition as the high speed grand touring car he had conceived, with production numbers approaching half of the 911 output. For all intents and purposes, the 911 *appeared* alive and well. But it would celebrate its 15th birthday as he enjoyed his 60th. This longevity had matched the 356, and Fuhrmann knew where that long production life had led.

"The new cars, the 924, 928, they were through the program." Fuhrmann recalled. "Work was a little slow. At that time we should have begun a new program. So I went to see Dr. Porsche. I told him I didn't want to work to the end of my life. I would not like to work longer than 65. Since a new program lasts for seven or eight years, I think it is unfair to begin something and leave it uncompleted for my successor. They should do it themselves.

"I said to him, I'm prepared to go any day if you have a new man who could begin again with a new program."

Porsche was not an attractive proposition. It had an angry union assembling its cars. Across town, Mercedes-Benz had made performance a clear orientation. Not only was its 450SLC directly targeted at Porsche's 928 (and vice versa), but its 450SL coupe and roadster were 140-mile-per-hour autobahn left-lane runners. What's more, Mercedes threw a gauntlet to all other carmakers with its 6.9-liter sedan, a throwback to its earlier 300SEL 6.3 super sedans capable of 140+ miles per hour. Total M-B production topped 401,000 cars. Further south, BMW made its racing-developed M1 available to customers who wanted something faster and more exclusive than its user-friendly 633CSi coupes. BMW produced 330,000 cars in 1980.

1981 935 KREMER K3

With adjustable turbo boost, drivers regularly started races with full power hoping to outdistance rivals. Englishman John Fitzpatrick's exhaust typically spat flame on trailing-throttle for the first six to eight laps during any of the IMSA Camel GT endurance races.

1981 911SC

Late afternoon sunlight strikes the nose and reflects off the side of the car, showing every stylish crease and curve of the 911 shape. Because Porsche's boss Ernst Fuhrmann planned to discontinue the 911 in 1982, he allowed very few updates or changes to the car.

Starting with 1980, all U.S. models were "50-state" cars. Lambda-Sonde oxygen sensors and three-way catalytic converters neutralized California's concerns. Porsche replaced the unsuccessful rubber center clutches with spring steel for 1981.

Ferry Porsche contacted Bob Lutz about the chief executive job. Lutz, who had directed operations at Ford of Europe for several years, passed. Ford in Germany was shipping more than twice as many of its compact Fiestas to the United States as Porsche produced in 1980. While he sometimes drove a Porsche, his conversations with Porsche gave him little indication of where the company was going. No new projects meant no new cars for at least five years. Could the 911 survive until 1985 or 1986?

Ernst Fuhrmann went home to Teufenbach before year-end. In his time at Porsche, he developed a legendary engine in the 1950s. He knew that he brought the turbocharger to the street 911. And he believed that he had saved the company in 1971. "The rest of what I did was just giving my engineers and designers the chance to do their own work. Encouraging good people. For me, I had three accomplishments," he said in 1991. "That's enough."

It remained to be seen who had enough courage and imagination to walk into those footsteps. ■

Porsche and Bosch revised their K-Jetronic fuel-injection system with a new cold-start injector. Earlier models sometimes backfired through the air box, immediately stranding the owner.

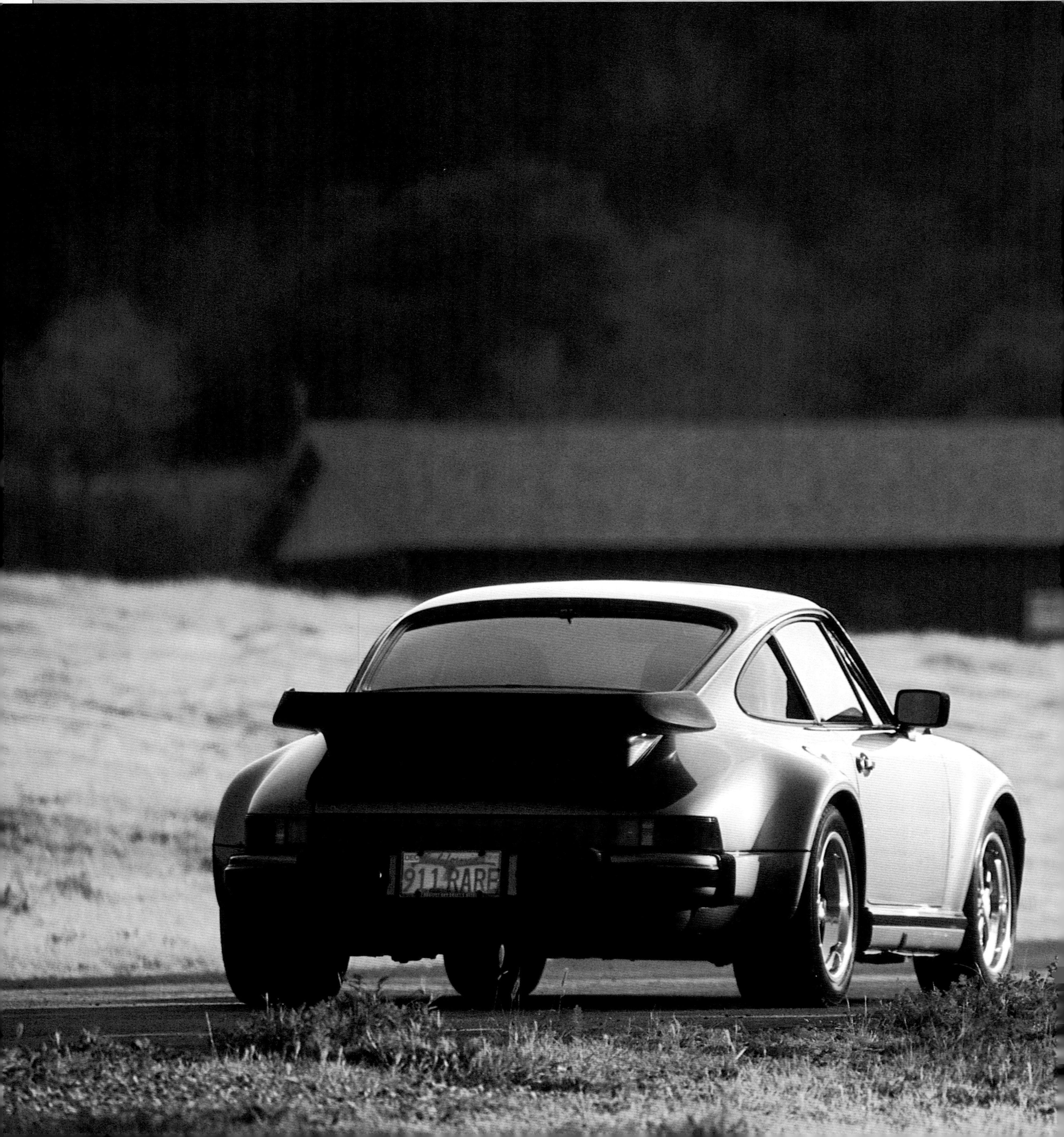
911 RARE

CHAPTER FIVE

A GENERATION ENDS, ANTOTHER BEGINS
1981 – 1989

"Porsche is in the business

of selling memberships in a dream."

Peter Schutz, 2005

"Why do you want me? I don't know the automobile business.
My whole experience has been industrial machinery, diesel
engines, trucks . . . . "

Peter Schutz wondered how Porsche had selected him, the
managing director of Klöckner-Humboldt-Deutz (KHD) diesel
engines, as one of 12 candidates for the job of managing director.
It was April 1980, Schutz had just turned 50, and now he stood on
the terrace of Ferry Porsche's home on a hillside overlooking
Stuttgart. Ferry was there with his four sons, and his sister Louise
Piëch, and her three sons and daughter. They were the 10 owners
of Porsche A.G.

Previous Pages: The mid-1980s marked a turning point for Porsche. The world economy created an exchange rate that allowed Porsche to build new plants, start new racing programs, and conceive new products.

1983 911SC CABRIOLET

Top-down motoring took a long time to reach the 911. It took the arrival of Peter Schutz to reposition 911 development from the "inactive file" to "active, alive, and well."

Schutz recalled his "interview" in the backyard was not going too well. He felt certain his answers weren't what the family hoped to hear. So he imagined what might have been—the job as boss of Porsche—and then he reminded Ferry of his trucking and industrial diesel background.

"No, Herr Schutz, you don't understand our problem," Porsche said. "We have people who know how to design automobiles, how to build them, to sell them and service them. Our problem is that we're not making any money."

Schutz had experience there. He had left his engineering job at Caterpillar because he had ideas to help them make money but management wanted him developing engines. At Cummins, as vice president of sales and marketing, he redefined who their customers were and what they wanted. He still courted America's biggest freight hauling firms to buy the engines, but he instilled a performance philosophy in the individual drivers. Cummins prospered, freight company owners increased their profit, and the drivers earned more money and bigger bonuses. The Teamsters Union asked him to deliver their keynote address at their 1976 national convention. Cummins management questioned this invitation, his techniques, and his motives (without criticizing his results). So he left. At KHD, he improved labor's working conditions through employee empowerment. This increased productivity and raised company profit.

"When we explore the reasons for our poor earnings," Ferry Porsche continued, "we see that people in this organization are simply not working together. We've got manufacturing and sales and engineering all working against one another. We are looking for someone who can get this whole organization unified and working together."

To this day, Peter Schutz can only guess why the 10 owners of Porsche A.G. hired him. They needed someone fluent in German and English (he was born in Berlin in April 1930, and his family fled the Holocaust in March 1939). He was a graduate engineer (mechanical engineering from Illinois Institute of Technology) who had direct experience in sales. He had a track record of improving labor relations in previously troubled companies, the situation Porsche experienced following the Fuhrmann era.

While Schutz had never owned a Porsche, he did his homework before he started. Dealers in the United States and Europe had two consistent complaints: The cars were too expensive, and they had serious quality control problems. To Schutz, this was one issue: No one objects to paying a price for something if it functions perfectly. He heard morale at Porsche was poor because the company planned to discontinue the 911 and push

the 924 and 928. He sensed there was more. He and his wife Sheila got to Zuffenhausen in January 1981. His first weeks were a whirlwind of discovery and action.

"Every Monday, Porsche's top managers have lunch together," Schutz said. "This had been going on forever. So the first Monday I was there, I went to the lunch. It was a mixed bag of engineers, sales people, manufacturing, and I listened to the conversations. After a while, I asked these folks one question: 'What is going on in this company right now that is so exciting that you can hardly wait to come to work?' You could hear a pin drop. I waited a while, then said, 'Okay, everyone, thank you.' Of course, then everyone had a response. 'That's okay. I heard what I needed.'"

Cabriolet models have leather seats as standard equipment. Heated remote-control outside mirrors are part of the package as well.

The cabrio cloth top is operated by hand. A zippered plastic back window was standard, although a heated glass rear window was an option.

1983 930S

Porsche introduced the slant-nose in mid-1981 as an option for the Turbo. Available only through the *Sonderwunsch* (special wishes) program, it offered 935 race car looks for street Turbos.

The next day, Schutz went to Weissach to discuss the company's racing program with Peter Falk, Norbert Singer, and their racing staff and to learn about plans for Le Mans. Their effort, Schutz heard, consisted of three 924 Turbo models.

"What are your chances of winning with these things?" Schutz asked.

"'Herr Schutz, you do not understand,' they told me, 'There is no chance of winning. This is a modified production car. It's good for the sales department, but we are going to be competing against full racing cars, prototypes . . . .'"

Schutz wondered aloud why they were going. He could hear a pin drop.

"Okay, as long as I'm in charge of this organization, we will never go to any race without the objective of winning it." More pins dropped. "Since I do not know how you do this, this meeting is now adjourned. I'll return at 10 o'clock tomorrow morning and you'll give me your plans."

The next morning, everyone in Porsche's competition department, as well as engineers from Bosch, Dunlop, Shell, and Bilstein, filled the conference room. "'There were these 936s in the museum,' they told me, 'retired from racing three years ago. There were turbocharged flat-six engines we developed for America's Indianapolis racing series but we never used. The engines have proven themselves on gasoline in the 935/78 Moby Dick. We could pull the museum cars out, recondition them, install the Indy motors . . . .'

"The excitement in that room," Schutz recalled, "was electric. Word had gotten out. Porsche was going to Le Mans to win. I got phone calls from Jacky Ickx, Derek Bell, and Hurley Haywood, offering their service to bring Porsche the overall win."

He had learned that 911 engine camshaft drive chain tensioners failed. This was the source of Porsche's poor quality reputation. In his first meeting with production engineering, he challenged them. "Do you know how to fix this problem?"

"Oh, yes," he heard them say. "But we're not going to. The car is going out of production. And the repair kits have become a profit source for the company." This struck Schutz as incorrect and shortsighted. Quality problems reflect not only on the existing product but on buyer perceptions in future purchases. A reliable fix would yield plenty of sales as owners remedied the problem once and for all. But it was the first answer that plagued him. Porsche's finance people had shown him that the 911 was Porsche's most profitable car. Most of the 10 owners of the company drove them and seemed, like thousands of others, to love the cars.

Peter Schutz, who had met Helmuth Bott at the Monday lunch, called on the director of engineering the next evening at his office at Weissach.

"When I walked in, I saw a big chart on Mr. Bott's wall, a bar graph. The 928 ran out for four or five years. Along there the 924 became the 944 and it ran out for several years. The 911 stopped in 1981. There was just a tiny little bar and then it quit.

"That was just a few months away. And I thought about everything I had heard. So I walked to Mr. Bott's desk and picked up a crayon marker. I extended the 911 line off the end of the chart. I pushed the line onto the wall, over to the corner, around the corner, and on to the next wall.

"I wrote on his wall with an indelible marker. And I said, 'Mr. Bott, do we understand each other?'

"He was beaming. He said, 'You can do this, Herr Schutz?'

"I can do this, Herr Bott."

Turbo models were not available in the United States due to emissions regulations that Porsche chose not to meet. A gray market sprang up to import these cars privately and modify them to meet U.S. safety and emissions standards.

The 3.3-liter Turbos remained at 300 brake horsepower at 5,500 rpm. The slant nose, fabricated from steel, didn't alter the car's weight but it slightly increased top speeds due to reduced wind resistance.

As Helmuth Bott recalled in an interview in 1991 (a few years before he died in 1994), after Peter Schutz drew on his wall, the question was how to let the world know? Bott had ideas, notes, drawings, and proposals he could never show Ernst Fuhrmann. An open car? All-wheel drive? Ferdinand Piëch had led Audi's engineering staff creating the Quattro. Prototypes of these all-wheel-drive coupes appeared in 1978. In 1980 Audi introduced production models.

For Fuhrmann, the creeping shadow of U.S. regulations prescribed the end of the 911. He would invest no further thought, time, or money. Now Bott walked Schutz down to a garage below his office where he had hidden his prototype cabriolet, a car he called the "speedster." In 1979 Fuhrmann threatened to terminate him if Bott put more effort into it. Under Fuhrmann, no one worked on 911s unless it was crucial.

Thus, Porsche's series production B-Program 1980 and C-Program 1981 models received just minor running changes. Steel spring clutches replaced the failure-prone but gentler operating rubber-centered versions. Bosch and Porsche reprogrammed the K-Jetronic injection's cold-start mixture. Backfires on start-up often destroyed air boxes. These subtle improvements gave no hint of the new indelible marker trail on the Helmuth Bott's office wall. This black line told everyone who saw it that Porsche's 911 had turned a corner and was off on another run.

Frankfurt's biennial auto show came again in September. Porsche had introduced the 901 there in 1963. Now nine shows and 18 years later, it was time to recapture public imagination. Bott and Schutz put all their

1984 CARRERA 3.2 TURBO LOOK

The 3.2-liter Carrera engine uses a 95-mm bore and a 74.4-mm stroke. Bosch added its new Motronic digital motor electronic system to its LEX-Jetronic injection system to help attain 231 horsepower for most buyers. U.S. buyers got 207. New oil-fed chain tensioners finally resolved a long-standing 911 engine problem.

eggs in one basket with a 3.3-liter turbocharged all-wheel-drive cabriolet for the show stand. They would mount it on a mosaic of mirrors to show off the car's underpinnings. They got work started on the cabriolet in March. On April 15, both men saw a white prototype with a red interior. A day later, Bott drove it. Eighteen days later, the board approved development toward a production version.

Schutz knew that Board Chairman Ferry Porsche had taken a small workspace in the parts warehouse in not-so-nearby Ludvigsburg. Across from his own office, Schutz saw accountants working. He moved them and had the space remodeled into a large glass-case lined office for Ferry Porsche.

"It was a lot nicer than mine, and I was very purposeful in doing that. I moved Ferry Porsche into that office. Every morning at nine o'clock he would get there and shortly after that, I would walk across the hallway and we would have coffee together. Everybody in the company knew this was the routine.

"About 90 days after my first Monday lunch with the managers," Schutz recalled, "at another one of those Monday lunches, I asked the same question I had the first day. And everybody burst out laughing!"

At Le Mans in June one of Porsche's museum piece 936s won outright. The second museum car finished in 12th place. It was Porsche's 30th anniversary at Le Mans, and it represented Ickx's fifth win and Bell's second. The two 924 GTP cars finished 7th and 11th overall. Porsche's museum car had conquered new prototypes from Rondeau, Ferrari, Lancia, Lola, and BMW. Schutz mounted the victory stand with Ferry Porsche who at first had hung back.

"He was very shy," Schutz recalled. "He abhorred the spotlight. He didn't want to go up there. But I insisted. 'No, professor, *you* have to play the role here.' The German flag flew over our head. When they played "Deutschland, Deutschland, Über Alles," there were tears on both our cheeks."

In his first six months, Schutz had accomplished Ferry Porsche's mission, to unite the entire organization and get it working together. The wedding ended at Le Mans, where the honeymoon began. It gained momentum at the Frankfurt Auto Show.

Road & Track magazine's cover photo by staffer John Lamm showed Porsche's 911 prototype resting on mirrors. An endless sea of faces stood enraptured by the white cabriolet with its sleek black interior and folded top.

"Porsche has been working for some time on a four-wheel-drive version of the 911," Paul Frère wrote for this cover story in *Road & Track*'s December 1981 issue, "but its appearance at the Frankfurt Auto Show in the form of a 911 roadster came as a surprise." He continued, "For 911 fans the Frankfurt show car was very important, because it signaled just how long a life the 911 still has, one that wouldn't have been as obvious

The M491 Turbo-Look option provides not only fender flares and brake-cooling ducts, it also offers the rear torsion-bar tube and suspension arms of the Turbo. In the United States, with strictly monitored speed limits, Turbos are less useful than in Europe.

Most Turbo-look coupes came with the optional 225/50ZR16 tires on the rear mounted on 8-inch wheels. Front tires are 205/50ZR16s on 7-inch rims. M491 cars also use Turbo brakes and front wheel hubs.

Starting with 1984 models, Porsche replaced the long-standard Fuchs five-spoke wheels with a five-oval-motif wheel soon known as "telephone dials." They were not popular anywhere and this owner abandoned them, as well as the more popular Fuchs, and went with later-model Carrera offset wheels.

at the last Frankfurt show two years ago. Now Porsche is willing to take the time and effort to produce a roadster 911 and redo the model's drivetrain for four-wheel drive."

Schutz continued his morning coffees with Ferry Porsche. "I pumped him. I asked him to tell me the stories. He didn't like talking about the past. He was much more excited about the future." Thinking about the surveys that said Porsches were too costly and suffered quality problems, Schutz wanted to understand this company he now managed.

"Something has been bothering me," he said to Porsche one day. "Whatever got into you to take a Volkswagen Beetle, remove the body, replace it with a streamlined two-seater body, and charge five times as much money for it?

"Without any hesitation, he looked me in the eye and said, 'Herr Schutz, I didn't listen to anybody. I simply built my dream car and thought that others would share my dream.'" It was a dream that Helmuth Bott embraced wholeheartedly.

"Often people think you go in a wrong direction," Bott said, "because you have an air-cooled engine, because you have the engine in the rear, because, because, because . . . . But Porsche always had an outstanding concept, different from others. And that's the key for Porsche, even in the future.

"If you have a water-cooled engine in the front, that's a system everybody can do. Everybody has the parts in stock. Everybody can do it cheaper than we can do it. But the exciting things are sometimes more difficult for the engineers, and in the end, you have advantages the others don't have. And with the advantages you can motivate the customers. That is the secret of Porsche: We do things other people cannot."

Initially, both he and Schutz had hoped to introduce his speedster, the 911 cabriolet, as a 1982 model. However, matters of chassis stiffness and top operation forced them to slip it to 1983, the final year of the 911SC, the last of the third generation cars.

Gerhard Schröder, who designed mechanisms for Butzi Porsche's cabrio concepts in 1963, returned to the assignment. Ferry wanted an electrically operated top. Engineering had a prototype working by March 1982, but its mechanisms needed more work. On the production cabriolet, owners opened or closed the top by hand and zipped a plastic rear window into place. Thinking about it prompted Peter Schutz to laugh.

"My questioning had disclosed that Porsches were too expensive and had too many quality problems. So what we did was we built a convertible, raised the price 20 percent, and created a whole new set of quality problems we never had before. Now we had tops that leaked and tops that whistled and tops that didn't fit. And people ate it up!" The 1983 base 911SC coupe sold for $29,950 in the United States. The cabriolet went for $34,450. (The Targa straddled the middle at $31,450.) The cabriolet weighed 30 pounds less than the Targa and with its top up and windows closed, it provided a better drag coefficient at 0.395 than the 911SC coupe at 0.40. Porsche drivers reached a top speed of 145 miles per hour in a closed soft-top on VW's high-speed Ehra-Lessien test track.

Minimal improvements marked the C-Program 1982 and D-Program 1983 SC models beyond introduction of the cabriolet. These were the last of Fuhrmann's second-generation cars. Increased electrical requirements necessitated a 1,050-watt alternator in 1982, and Lapine's stylists, ever subduing brightwork, painted the Fuchs

The bodywork of the new Carrera models bore very few changes from models 20 years earlier. But new boss Peter Schutz, styling director Tony Lapine, and engineering chief Helmuth Bott had plenty of ideas to make driving more pleasurable and the cars more interesting.

1986 953 PARIS-DAKAR RALLY CAR

For the first time in the six-year-old desert race from Europe to Africa's west coast, Helmuth Bott entered all-wheel-drive Porsches in 1984. Porsche won the 12,000-kilometer (7,500-mile) event. It won again in 1986 with this car.

The Paris-Dakar Rally began in Versailles, south of Paris, in 1986. Cars had to be able to run fast over paved roads as well as desert sands.

alloy wheel centers black. For 1983, the U.S. Department of Transportation (DOT) allowed Porsche to return to 160-mile-per-hour speedometers. Ride-heights that Porsche had raised so U.S. cars met DOT bumper standards, settled back to rest-of-world levels.

For 1984, Porsche introduced the Carrera 3.2, its E-Program third generation 911. The designation came from its engine displacement. The Nikasil cylinders that Porsche used for the 3.0-liter SC engine carried over the same bore at 95 mm. But this new variation adopted the Turbo's longer stroke, 74.4 mm. Total displacement reached 3,164 cc. Bosch's latest L-Jetronic injection system worked with its new Digital Motor Electronics (DME) Motronics 2 engine management system to boost performance, improve fuel economy, and decrease exhaust emissions. Both Carrera 3.2 normally aspirated engines and the 3.3-liter turbocharged engines received new oil-fed camshaft-drive chain tensioners.

Frustrated Americans still could not purchase U.S.-legal Turbos, but by 1984, a booming "gray market" targeted buyers with adequate resources and inadequate patience. The name came from "interpreting" the strict regulations published in black-and-white. A number of mechanics and body-shop operators collaborated on conversions to non-U.S. specification cars acquired used throughout Europe. They fit the cumbersome EPA-mandated exhaust gas recirculators, air pumps, and catalytic converters to the engines. They had to retrofit DOT-required 5-miles-per-hour impact bumpers at the front and 2 1/2-miles-per-hour bumpers on the rear. In addition, side-impact beams were to be welded into the doors. Charges for this work ranged from $6,000 to $20,000 to convert the car, depending on the gullibility of the buyer and honesty of the conversion shop. Sometimes safety work was not done, and many cars ran poorly. Porsche wasn't alone in experiencing shade-tree mechanics and their shady conversions. Ferrari, BMW, and Mercedes-Benz buyers also fell victim to clever get-rich-quick schemes masquerading as DOT and EPA conversion shops.

It was hard to resist temptation. Turbocharged BMW 7-series sedans came in under this smoke screen, badged as 745i models. A few 645i coupe versions filtered into the United States as well. Where Europeans had 500-series Mercedes SLs and SLC models, American buyers only could get 380s, and in 1984 when M-B USA imported the 560s, Europeans still had more power, better performance, and higher fuel economy, further tantalizing those who could not get them.

Throughout this time, Helmuth Bott and his engineering staff were at work on the ultimate not-for-U.S.-consumption Porsche. This began life as an all-wheel-drive model introduced for competition, known as the typ 953 in 1984. By 1986, it was a limited production wonder called the typ 959.

Everything was lightened and/or strengthened. Engineers replaced steel body panels with aluminum, fiberglass, or Kevlar. They used thin Plexiglas for side windows.

In Peter Schutz, Helmuth Bott had a collaborator. Schutz was an engineer who was as interested in the future 911 as Bott was. For him, all-wheel drive belonged under a Porsche 911.

The FIA's new 1982 Gruppe B category offered an umbrella under which to create a racer in advance of series production. Incorporating the old Groups 4 through 7, this category called for closed two-seaters with at least 200 manufactured within 12 months. Ferdinand Piëch's all-wheel-drive Audi Quattros often won European rallies, and they demonstrated the value of this new drive system. Porsche could compete, but the field was crowded with Peugeot's 205 turbo 16s, Toyota's turbo Celicas, Lancia's turbocharged Type 037s, and Ford's RS200 turbos. Homologation requirements meant Porsche had to produce too many of these new all-wheel-drive cars, something to which neither Schutz nor Bott were ready to commit. But desert rallying, with virtually no restrictive regulations, presented clear advantages.

"My racing engineers wanted to do a mid-engine car," Bott recalled. "They wanted to take a car on the base of the 914 and make a race car, as a Gruppe B car." Customer-racing coordinator Jürgen Barth argued that 80 percent of Porsche's customers participated in paved-circuit racing but only 20 percent were rally drivers. Porsche had launched its highly successful Gruppe C racer, the typ 956, winning Le Mans in its debut in 1982, and again in 1983.

"I was fighting against them. I said, 'We do so many mid-engine cars. We cannot learn anything.'" Bott also was concerned about competition. Was anyone else building a mid-engine Gruppe B? If Porsche were alone, would there even be a class? Gruppe B homologation required 200 examples. "If we have to do a car," he continued, "which you have to build 200 times, you can also build 1,000 times. If we *do* build a Gruppe B car, let's have a look at the future of the 911." In early January, Bott formalized his concept on paper. He envisioned a pure competition version and a later series production model utilizing most of the technologies developed for competition but in a customer-friendly package.

Porsche loyalist and Le Mans victor Jacky Ickx had won the 1983 Paris-Dakar Rally driving a factory-prepared Mercedes-Benz 280GE Gelandewagen, more Land Rover than early SUV. "Rally" was a loose term, for this was an implausibly high-speed race through the desert. Ickx always was interested in driving for Porsche, and as the recent winner, he brought valuable experience to Bott's program. Bott had completed his first prototype all-wheel-drive 911 in late 1981. Known as C-20, it was red with a metallic leather interior. He and his staff constantly upgraded it. To prepare for the 1984 event, he took his own red company car to Africa for Ickx to work with.

Quick-release pins allow rapid removal of the rear window, the sole access to some of the car's electronics and engine management system. The 1986 race covered 14,000 kilometers (8,750 miles).

"After the second day, one of the front axles broke," Bott recalled. "The only thing to do was take out the other front axle and to run as a rear-wheel-drive car to the next stop. And that was really a key thing.

"Because, with four-wheel drive, the car handling was perfect. You could exactly drive between the dunes. Left and right, allowing only 15 centimeters (about 6 inches) clearance. And then, when it became the rear-driven car, we had to allow 2 meters left and right. The center of gravity moved around all the time on the sand.

"The next day, we got the front axles and again the car ran perfectly. Jacky Ickx could position the car very much more precisely, very much faster. We thought, if a car is so much better under bad conditions, then you must feel it on the dry road!

"You see," he continued, "our concept with the 911 has always been that it's an all-around car. With very few changes, you can drive a desert rally, and then go to the racetrack at Le Mans . . . to show the people, without changing the concept, this 911 is capable of completely different things.

Group B was an FIA category for international rallies, which Porsche had conquered frequently. New Group-B regulations quickly rendered cars obsolete, so Porsche took the cars it conceived for the series and raced them in the deserts. This car won and its twin came in second.

René Metge and Dominique Lemoyne had 290 mm (11.4 inches) of ground clearance and ran on Michelin 205/18 tires. These tall thin tires cut through or slipped over obstacles on their route. Twin-turbochargers and intercoolers gave them 370 brake horsepower.

Inspired by Helmuth Bott's own "speedster" prototype from 1980, Porsche styling created this 1987 show car based on the 3.2 Carrera chassis. They called it the Club Sport Speedster.

1982 WIND TUNNEL PROTOTYPE 959

In 1982, six years after Dick Soderberg created Moby Dick for Norbert Singer, he applied similar concepts to Porsche's planned supercar by widening front and rear fenders. The stock red doors and roofline hinted at the production body hiding beneath this prototype. *Porsche Archives*

1982 STYLING CONCEPT 959

Dick Soderberg's earliest concept of the typ 959 extended both the nose and winged tail of the 911 considerably farther than the production version. Fender arches were very pronounced as well. *Porsche Archives*

1988 959S U.S. SPORT

Porsche's first pure supercar grew out of a racing application. The FIA's Group B regulations controlled international rally entries, and the FIA required manufacturers to produce 200 closed two-seaters within a 12-month period to qualify a car for competition.

"There is really a very big love from our customers for this 911," Bott explained. "So we thought, let's see if there is anything *against* our building this car for the next 10 years, 15 years. It was a goal, a task much greater than to build a race car."

Bott appointed Manfred Bantle to direct the staff as they stretched every technology available: electronics, tires, suspension hardware, engine fuel delivery, ignition, exhaust, prototype gearboxes. Both men pushed their capabilities. However, Bott's decades at the company had taught him that it was an organization grounded in reality.

"It is always important to not be 1 meter over the ground," Bott said. "You have to stay with your feet on the ground, to think over the things that you can fulfill. Our research department was not looking 20 or 30 years

ahead. In that time, things were changing so quickly. So what we do instead is to look 10 years ahead. And what's possible in the 10 years, we fulfill in 2 years and end up 8 years ahead of the others. And with our small number of production, we are able to do this. These are the secrets."

Bott's concept was visionary. There would be a desert rally car, the typ 959. Bantle and Bott would spin off 20 copies as a roadracing typ 960. Bott's belief that if Porsche could build 200, it could make 1,000, brought in the next level, the typ 961 next-generation Porsche Turbo. (In the ever-fluid universe of Porsche nomenclature, the road racer became the 961 and the Turbo went into development—but never into production—as the typ 965.) The burden weighed heavily on both men. Bantle, in an internal memo that Karl Ludvigsen unearthed, explained that Germany's technical community would accept nothing less than "Typically Porsche perfection of the four-wheel-drive technology." All eyes would watch them as they made choices, decisions, and cars.

Near the end of production, Otis Chandler, a longtime Porsche customer and sometime racer, who by then had a recognized museum, imported this car legally as a museum piece, but it was drivable for "demonstrations." A few others slipped into the country, but only since 2004 has federal legislation allowed the modifications that make these cars road legal in the USA.

Once Porsche's American customers learned of the possibility of a special 320-kilometer-per-hour (200 mile-per-hour) all-wheel-drive model, they wanted to be part of the program as well. U.S. smog and impact safety regulations grew tougher while the car was being developed and Porsche withdrew U.S. availability.

Bantle already had experienced four-wheel drive within Porsche. In the early 1960s, tractor engineer and four-wheel-drive pioneer Harry Ferguson teamed up with English carmakers Allan and Richard Jenson, mating Ferguson's FF system to Jenson's CV8 sports car with its Chrysler 383-cubic-inch V-8. Porsche bought one in 1965, and Bantle had to analyze its engineering and its potential.

Bantle's version, Porsche's 953, went straight to victory in 1984 with René Metge and Dominique Lemoyne finishing the 12,000-kilometer (7,500-mile) event first. Bantle biased the all-wheel drive so that 60 percent went to the rear, 40 percent to the front. Metge and Lemoyne could change the percentages manually and lock the front differential in or out as they chose. The competition department fitted the car bodies with the big Carrera flat wings, and replaced front and rear deck lids and doors with aluminum, fiberglass, or Kevlar panels, and side windows with Plexiglas. They drilled big holes in the thick Kevlar belly pan to shave more weight.

The 1985 race gave Porsche 13,000 kilometers of frustration and failed parts, and left them with three cars that didn't complete the distance. For 1986, Jacky Ickx, now Paris-Dakar team manager, returned to Versailles

for the rally start just as Piëch had arrived at Le Mans in 1970: prepared, equipped, and supported. Three new 959s, with single-turbocharged engines provided their drivers with 370 brake horsepower at 6,500 rpm, capable of pushing the cars to 210 kilometers per hour (about 131 miles per hour) across the fastest sections. An ingenious front axle electronically decreased oil pressure from the drive-clutches during high-speed rear-drive stretches. Yet touching the brakes instantly restored 19 atmospheres—275 psi—of pressure to the clutches to utilize engine braking through the front axles.

Typical of the run, fierce storms and serious injuries cut the starting crowd of 500 entries to 80 finishers. Ickx's teammate René Metge won again as he had in 1984, and Ickx finished 4th. The rules required support personnel to accompany the racers so Ickx's third entry belonged to Roland Kussmaul and Kendrick Ünger, the car's two development engineers from Weissach. They finished 6th overall.

Besides its engineering, the 953's attention-getting appearance and aerodynamic stability were the other factors that contributed to its success. Norbert Singer's racing engineers sometimes were mistrustful of designers and stylists, fearing that aestheticians might adversely affect engineering development. Yet this car, because of Bott's interest in private customer sales for street use—essential for its racing accreditation—had to look less radical than a pure purpose-built racer. This got styling involved very early.

Wolfgang Möbius, Tony Lapine's styling studio manager who had made U.S. safety bumpers attractive, assigned his staffer Dick Soderberg to create the look of the 911 of the future. Soderberg had worked with Norbert Singer on Moby Dick and understood what racing rules allowed. His Gruppe B show car moved

This 2,850-cc (173.9-cubic-inch) flat-six develops 450 horsepower at 6,500 rpm. Two intercooled turbochargers provide the boost to create so much power. The U.S. Sport models accelerate from 0–60 miles per hour in 3.9 seconds.

Above, left: The Sport version incorporates cloth seats, a full roll cage, and five-point seat-belt harnesses. A touring version replaced the cloth with leather, deleted the roll cage, and added air conditioning. The cars sold for 430,000 DM (approximately $260,000) by the time of delivery.

1986 CARRERA 3.2 TARGA

A new Getrag-built G50 five-speed transmission made shifting easier for many customers. Engine output for U.S. customers notched up from 207 to 217 brake horsepower. Engines for the rest of the world still produced 231.

Moby's startling appearance far ahead. Racing regulations and the high costs of new body stamping dies restricted Soderberg. He carried over the existing roof and doors, the same limits the designer had faced with Singer's 1978 rule-bender. Bantle and Bott had hoped the 959 would emerge with no spoilers and wings. But without the new roof that Lapine, Möbius, and Soderberg hoped for, a rear wing was an aerodynamic necessity. Soderberg created a new design icon as his elegantly integrated wing morphed into the widened rear fenders. This structure effectively flattened the roofline by treating detached airflow as if it were still laminar, attached to the car body. He flush-mounted the windshield into the A-pillar, one of several innovations that led to its extremely low drag coefficient at 0.32, compared to the current production Carrera at 0.39. The

1986 930S

The slant-nose Turbos remain a strongly contested matter of taste to this day. For Porsche they were popular and profitable enough that the company made them a regular production option for 1988. Porsche launched the option in March 1987.

pearlescent white painted show car sat on the Porsche show stand at the 50th anniversary Frankfurt show stand in September 1983. It was a teaser, ahead of possible production, representing one more Porsche shot discharged across the bow of its competitors and customers: "Wait for this!" it cried.

It was a tough show with other performance cars competing for attention. Audi had its 200,000–deutsche mark Quattro Sport ($80,000). This was its own Group B homologation production special with its wheelbase shortened almost 32 centimeters (12.6 inches) to reduce weight and enhance maneuverability. Mercedes-Benz tantalized the compact car-commuter with its 185–brake horsepower, Cosworth-engined 2.3-liter, 16-valve, four-door 190E. BMW revised its M1 engine and fitted a 286–brake horsepower version into a more small-family friendly M635CSi. This new M6 concept would become a consistent target to Porsche engineers over the coming years as they conceived and configured their own new models. Saab showed a four-wheel-drive convertible (in white, as Porsche's 911 had been in the previous show). Yet Porsche earned four paragraphs in Doug Nye's show report for *Road & Track*. He summed up the car by saying, "Porsche's Group B program is evidence of its search for the world's most sophisticated high performance all-wheel-drive system."

Countless engineering delays held up introduction beyond its target 1984 and 1985 model years. As Bantle and Bott pushed the envelope, they found the envelope often pushed back. Bott's advanced technology was, in some cases, beyond outside suppliers' capabilities. DuPont reformulated its aramid-fiber Kevlar to work as curved body panels. Bilstein invented electronically controllable shock absorbers that not only dampened road surface undulations but lowered the car as its speed increased, or allowed the driver a manual override. Dunlop created a tire capable of long runs above 200 miles per hour but that also could run flat for 50 miles or so at a much slower speed. WABCO Westinghouse devised an anti-lock braking system (ABS) with the sensitivity to recognize that, by definition, four-wheel drive meant that front axles turned slightly faster than rears, that these characteristics changed in a turn, that all this changed on mixed driving surfaces, and that none of this might require braking. Bosch developed DME Motronic on-board computers capable of monitoring acceleration, braking, steering, traction, and suspension loading every 50 milliseconds, that is, 200 times each second.

Left: Beginning in 1987, Turbos added dual exhaust pipes and larger rear wings to accommodate a bigger intercooler. Worldwide, the Turbos rated 330 brake horsepower, while U.S. customers got engines developing 282 at 5,500 rpm.

Unlike the racing 935s, the steel flat-nose 930s got retracting headlights. Vents along the top are part of the flat-nose aerodynamic racing technology.

Engine complications delayed the car most of all. Moby Dick had introduced water-cooled heads on top of air-cooled cylinder barrels. These achieved legendary reliability in the Group C 956s. Dual overhead camshafts operated four valves per cylinder, driven by, initially, single-row timing chains. Odd, unpredicted torque loads and chain resonances broke the chains. To accommodate double-row chains required redesigning the engine block. Moreover, Paul Hensler's engineers had conceived a progressive water-cooled two-turbocharger system that behaved more like primary and secondary jets in carburetors. At normal engine loads, one turbo accomplished the engine's intake needs. At higher speeds or under stronger acceleration, the second one spooled up. Early prototypes were plumbing-and-ducting nightmares. In street tune, this 2,849-cc engine (with 95-mm bore and 65-mm stroke) developed 450 DIN brake horsepower at 6,500 rpm, and 370 ft-lb of torque at 5,500 rpm. For racing, the target was 600 to 650.

Unfortunately for Porsche, they were not the only automaker in Europe working on the future. Manfred Bantle sometimes encountered delays because his large and small suppliers, working at capacity, were busy developing, testing, and manufacturing for competitors. No one else was targeting ideas so far in the future, and confidentiality agreements kept Porsche's 959 a secret project, but new electronics and materials were giving everyone ideas. These delays forced another crisis on the Bantle/Hensler team. Emissions standards got tougher in Europe for model year 1985. No one worried when the car still was a 1984 racing model. Now as introduction slipped and as Bott and Schutz encouraged development as a road car, emissions standards became a serious concern.

The luster of Group B rallying was wearing off by 1985. The cars, some as light as 1,800 pounds with 600 horsepower, had injured drivers and spectators in high-speed crashes. Porsche 959 participation looked less likely, so its viability as a street hyper-performer drew scrutiny. Peter Schutz and Helmuth Bott believed in the car and what it stated about Porsche technology. Other carmakers produced powerful, fast, sensational automobiles. Ferrari had introduced its 2.8-liter 288 GTO with 400 brake horsepower in a similarly Group B homologation-inspired run of 200 cars. But it offered no advance on technological benchmarks. Jaguar's 12-cylinder XJ-S, introduced in 1981, was maturing sedately by 1985. Lamborghini had a new four-valve head for its wild-looking Countach, but this car always was about looks, not innovation. Aston Martin's Vantage and Volante V-8s were posh GTs offering (in Europe, anyway) adequate power and speed. No competitor had anything close to the end-of-century technology the 959 presented.

1989 911 CARRERA CLUB SPORT
First introduced in 1988, the M637 Club Sport option removes power windows, power seats, sound insulation, radio, rear wiper, air conditioning, and other items to save about 50 kilograms (110 pounds) of weight. Porsche assembled 381 in 1988 and just 97 in 1989.

Bosch's digital engine management system reprogrammed the redline up to 6,840 rpm from 6,250. A short-shift kit made driving more enjoyable.

Buyers could order either a side graphic as the 1973 Carrera RS had or this SC decal arched over the fender. Porsche delivered 1989 models on 205/55VR16 front and 225/50VR16 rear Dunlop D40s on standard 16-inch wheels.

Porsche could afford it. Its 1984 profits had risen by 33 percent over 1983. Schutz saw projections indicating the favorable deutsche mark-to-dollar exchange rate would bring in profits for 1985 up nearly 30 percent over 1984. While this economy was a balloon primed for bursting, few people perceived it as overinflated. In May 1985, Schutz approved a launch at the September Frankfurt show. Helmuth Bott cut a prototype in half and presented it and a whole car to the public. Deliveries would begin in August 1986. It was unfortunate timing. Schutz had watched Porsche's sales in the United States rise to nearly two-thirds of its total output. However, the exchange rate between U.S. dollars that had purchased nearly 3.5 deutsche marks in early 1985 was slipping. By December 1986, the dollar had fallen to two to one. Model year 1986 saw the factory manufacture 52,939 cars, down slightly from the record 54,458 in 1985. The balloon continued to swell.

Porsche regular production models, the 1985 F-program and 1986 G-program cars, included the full line for non-U.S. customers while Americans still could not purchase turbos. Porsche customer service in 1984 had turned the Turbo-Look flared fenders and several mechanical upgrades into a regular production option for Carrera coupes as code M491. This expanded in 1985 and 1986 to include convertibles and Targa models as well. The M506 Turbo slant nose, first offered in 1981 from Customer Service, continued as an option for well-heeled owners outside the United States. (The U.S. DOT had problems with the car's low headlight position. The front-mounted oil coolers caused concerns over fluid leaks after front end collisions. However some factory-built cars did make it in through the gray market.) At Frankfurt, the company announced two versions of the 959, a Sport with a cloth interior (of which it manufactured just 37) and a comfort model with heated seats and leather trim. Each sold for 420,000 deutsche marks, about $140,000 at the time of the Frankfurt show, but prices neared $240,000 as deliveries began. The company requested a 50,000–deutsche mark earnest payment (initially $16,650) from each buyer. This deterred no one. By March 1986, Porsche had accepted 250 deposits, ensuring a full 200-unit sellout by relying on some purchasers to drop out, lose patience, or be disqualified. A reliable cause of disqualification was U.S. residency. After struggling to meet U.S. DOT and EPA safety and emissions standards, Schutz and Bott concluded that they could sell out production in the rest of the world without going through additional delays and expenses to meet U.S. regulations, despite accepting 50 U.S. deposits.

Porsche produced 16 prototypes and 21 pilot production cars in 1985. The tiny shops dedicated to these cars commenced regular production in 1987 and turned out 113 cars, plus 179 more in 1988. Additionally, the factory assembled a final 8 cars in 1992, fabricated from extra parts at a time when Porsche's financial health was not as strong as it was in the early 1980s. With these, total production reached 337.

The desire for 959s in the United States led to some hard work and some heartbreak. Al Holbert, a racer and Porsche dealer in Pennsylvania, collaborated with Peter Schutz's new Porsche A.G.–owned distribution organization called Porsche Cars North America (PCNA). They intended to import about 30 cars. Stripped of all interior appointments, Porsche listed these on shipping carnets and customs manifests as racing cars not legal for public road use. The first eight arrived, and the EPA changed its mind, dashing the hope of the prospective buyers. In the end, Porsche sold about 16 of the cars to U.S. buyers under the restriction that the cars remain outside the United States. At least a dozen of these made their way into the States, not including the single one the EPA and DOT did allow.

Otis Chandler, *Los Angeles Times* newspaper publisher, Porsche 935 racer, and vintage car collector, had established a bona fide museum outside Los Angeles to house his collection. The EPA and DOT granted him a

1989 PANAMERICANA

When Harm Lagaay arrived at Porsche styling he found no new projects underway. He immediately charged up his staff with a styling concept for an 80th birthday gift for Ferry Porsche.

Conceptualizing a new car begins both with designs on paper and with plasticene modeling, the application of a claylike material to a subframe. Pieces such as the engine compartment framework did not often change, so they helped define new shapes.

waiver that allowed him to show the car at the museum or to transport it to shows and exhibitions elsewhere. He took delivery of the first U.S.-legal 959 Sport model in August 1988. As a postscript to the 959 story, a number of the owners spent a decade appealing for waivers to possess and drive their cars legally. In 2001 and 2002, the U.S. Congress enacted two separate pieces of legislation "legalizing" the 959s. San Francisco Bay-area Porsche tuner and racer Bruce Canepa assumed the task of converting engines, bumpers, seat-belt systems, locks, and lights. When Canepa finished the first one, its engine developed closer to the 600-horsepower figure Bott, Bantle, and Schutz had envisioned for the racing versions. The car, designed for the year 2000, remained fresh, current, and blisteringly fast 20 years after its introduction.

Once a concept was approved—in this case, a show car that would be an 80th birthday gift to Ferry Porsche—clay modelers went to work giving Steve Murkett's full-scale drawing a third dimension. Porsche's modelers contribute enormously to the final appearance of the company's cars. *Porsche Archives*

While 959 owners waited for their cars in Europe or elsewhere, U.S. customers once again could purchase turbos, beginning with the 1986 H-Program. Equipped with oxygen sensors and catalytic converters as well as Bosch's latest Motronic system, it sold for $48,000 in the United States, compared to the Carrera coupe at $31,950. The Turbo, with 282 horsepower at 5,500 rpm and 287 ft-lb of torque at 4,000 rpm, now put smiles on Porsche owners' faces around the world. Normally aspirated cars received the new easier-shifting Getrag G50 five-speed transmission.

Porsche's J-Program production cars for 1987 model year saw improvement. The cabriolets received Ferry Porsche's long-awaited power top. Porsche offered the Turbo in both cabrio and Targa body styles, and it made the M506 slant nose into a full factory option as the 930S model. Turbos outside the United States developed 330 brake horsepower. But power was not the only thing on which U.S. buyers felt shorted. The exchange rate had fallen by half in two years; by late 1987, the dollar bought just 1.8 deutsche marks. Prices rose to

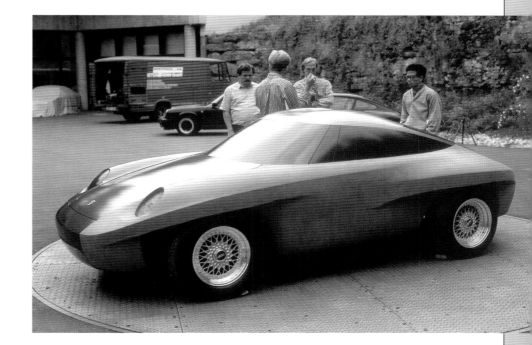

accommodate the devaluation. Porsche's total production dropped to 48,520 cars, and U.S. sales slipped to below half, at 23,632 units. The balloon burst and the world financial outlook grew bleak on October 19, 1987. The Dow Jones Industrial Average plummeted 508 points and lost almost 23 percent of its value that day. The *Wall Street Journal* quoted a retired stockbroker, "All those guys with 65 credit cards and Porsches who think they are geniuses at 25, now they see what's happened!" The whiplash and fallout from this loss hammered Ferrari as well. Sales of its newly introduced 471 brake horsepower F40, a thinly disguised race car, plummeted to just double digits. This delayed its introduction to the U.S. markets until 1989 and provoked huge price markups. Porsche's J.S. sales throughout all of 1988 reached only 15,737 cars. Peter Schutz cut production severely.

Outside the design center in Weissach, styling chief Harm Lagaay, with his hand to his mouth, looks over Steve Murkett's plasticene styling model of the Panamericana. The turntable allows designers and executives to see all angles of a styling prototype that may not run. At right is designer Pinky Lai. *Porsche Archives*

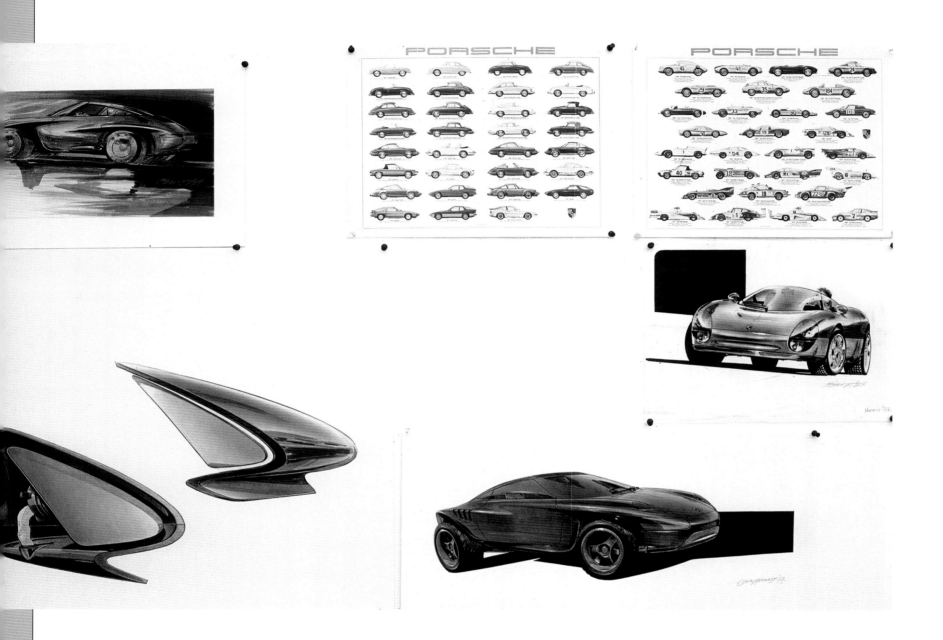

HISTORY IS INSPIRATION

Porsche's own design and racing history are never far from the minds of its modern-day designers and stylists. As concepts came together for the Panamericana show car, the legacy always remained within easy view.
Porsche Archives

The 1988 K-Program models returned to Fuchs wheels from the "telephone dial" style that arrived in most world markets when this third generation appeared in 1984. Engine output from the 3.2-liter remained at 231 DIN brake horsepower at 5,900 rpm and 209 ft-lb of torque at 4,800 for all non-U.S. markets. In the States, buyers got 207 SAE brake horsepower and 192 ft-lb at identical engine speeds. For buyers everywhere, Porsche created a very-limited edition Club Sport model, removing 110 pounds of air conditioning, power window and seat mechanisms, insulation, and undercoating while raising the red line to 6,850 rpm. While Porsche never published horsepower figures, reliable estimates place output at 255 DIN brake horsepower and approximately 234 SAE. The company produced 381 examples in 1987 but only 97 in 1989, fewer than

a dozen of which made it to U.S. buyers. But few people were buying Porsches anywhere in the world. Peter Schutz began interrupting production for a week or more each month. This kept the employees on payroll and the company alive.

Model year 1989 witnessed the end of the 911's third generation. Turbos, now priced at $70,975 because of a devalued dollar, received the new G50 five-speed transmission already in the Carreras. The company introduced a 911 Speedster, inspired by the earlier 356 version from the mid-1950s. The factory manufactured 2,065 of these open two-seaters. About 823 of these $65,480 models reached the United States. In the States however, sales continued their near-death spiral with dealers moving only 9,479 cars that year.

1989 SHOW CAR STYLING CONCEPTS
It all starts like this. When styling chief Harm Lagaay arrived at Porsche in 1989, he found no new projects underway. He quickly assigned his staff to dream, to invent. Steve Murkett came up with the X-Country, a dune buggy–inspired 911. *Porsche Archives*

1989 911 SPEEDSTER

Inspired by the 1955 Speedsters, Helmuth Bott had created his own in 1983. By 1986, he had convinced Tony Lapine and Peter Schutz to bring the Speedster concept back—based on his car—as a limited production run for 1989.

Derived from the 911 cabriolet body, Porsche assembled between 1,930 and 1,940 Speedsters on Turbo-Look wide bodies. Records indicate that another 160 to 170 emerged from Zuffenhausen assembly on standard narrow-fender cabriolet bodies.

Neither Bott nor Schutz were there to see the Speedster. Helmuth Bott took the brunt of criticism for the 959's failure to make money. According to historian Karl Ludvigsen, supervisory board member Ferdinand Piëch learned that each 959 cost the company 1,300,000 deutsche marks. In 1988 dollars, this was about $720,000, about three times its delivery price. Peter Schutz shared in the responsibility for high costs and overruns. The blame was not universal but it reverberated from several of the company's 10 owners and some outside stockholders who had watched their share value drop 30 percent as effects of the 1987 market crash ricocheted around the world.

For most of 1987, Schutz's wife Sheila had lived in Florida, establishing her own business restoring, renovating, and reselling homes. While she visited him regularly that year, she had found Germany's male-dominated business society uninviting to an independent outsider with ambition. Schutz had endured a rough year, missed his wife, and reckoned that his waning popularity might encourage Porsche to release his contract a year early. This coincided with Porsche's supervisory board's growing desire to replace him.

The fiberglass cover resembled a racing piece with its two simplified headrest forms. It hid a simple top (that was not simple to erect) and large storage.

1986 911 CARRERA 3.2

The 911's replacement was in the wings awaiting formal introduction. For 25 years, this shape had captivated driving and performance enthusiasts. It spawned a loyal following that keeps more pre-1990 model Porsches on the road than any other make.

In early December, it accepted his resignation and by mid-January, Peter Schutz had left the building, the country, and the continent.

Summing up costs and values of the 959 is difficult. Piëch's figures, even weighed most conservatively, suggest the car cost twice what it recouped in sales revenues. Other sources more recently offer a longer view. The expertise in these new systems that the 959 demonstrated has brought research and development contracts to Weissach worth perhaps twice the car's development costs. Engineering accomplishments on that car formed the foundation of Porsche's fourth generation 911s, the 964. That same work moved Porsche into a position where its fifth generation models advanced far enough beyond their competitors

that they set the 911 as their target for their own new products. Those now compete against Porsche's sixth generation.

Helmuth Bott, cast adrift by an abrupt and dramatic change of management, hung around until late 1988 to see off the last 959s. Then he retired at age 63. He had tamed the handling of the 356s at one end of his career at Porsche, and at the other end he established a new automotive category with his 959. It became the ultimate target, the Super Car. ▤

This marks the end of several eras—in personnel, in products, and in thinking. The new 911 body would resemble this shape, but engineering and aerodynamic considerations would modify it dramatically.

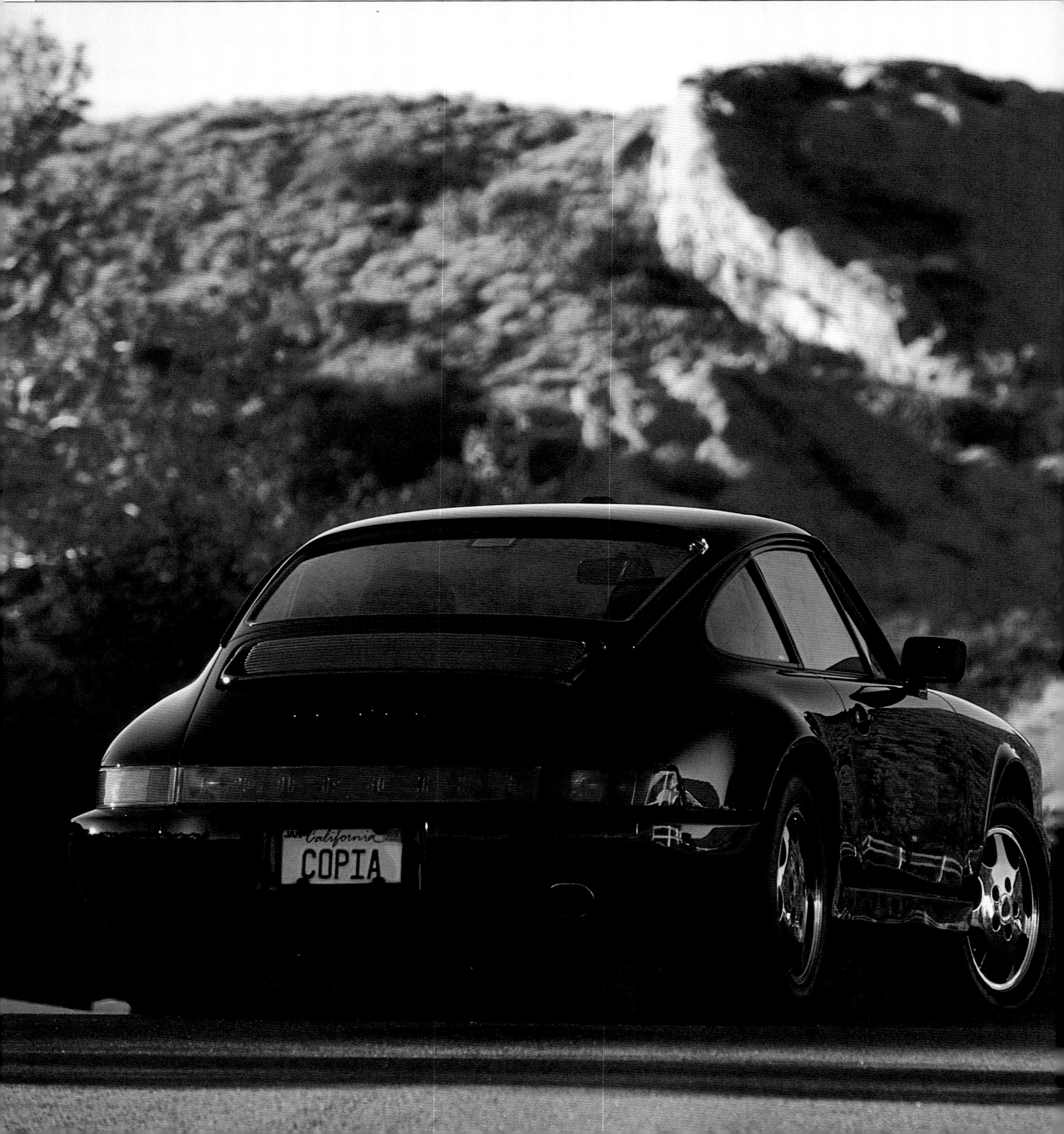
California
COPIA

CHAPTER SIX

PORSCHE'S THIRD GENERATION— THE 964

1989 – 1994

"We have here the 911 for the next 25 years, the concept that will help our favorite model to reach its 50th anniversary."

Heinz Branitzki, 964 introduction press kit

By the late 1980s, few people inside Porsche or elsewhere in the auto industry underestimated the threat from Japanese carmakers. Honda Motor Company had startled the automotive world by introducing sedans it priced at $27,000 from its new Acura luxury car division (in the USA) in 1986. Several years later Honda stunned journalists and sports car enthusiasts with the striking looking NSX street-racer. This mid-engine 2,977-cc dual-overhead camshaft, four-valve-per-cylinder V-6 engine developed 270 brake horsepower through innovative variable valve timing and lift control. (Back in early 1972, American manufacturers changed gross horsepower readings made at the flywheel with only fuel,

water, and oil pumps running off V-belts, to net ratings derived with all accessories and a full exhaust system mounted on the engine. This net result, roughly 80 percent of gross output, was within 0.14 percent of DIN results. Over the ensuing decade, manufacturers internationally agreed to drop SAE and DIN attribution on published outputs.) The sleek 3,098-pound aluminum-bodied car, suspended on titanium A-arms, developed a coefficient of drag of just 0.32, the same as Porsche's 959. Acura sold these 165-mile-per-hour machines for $62,000 in the United States.

Decades earlier, in 1962, Honda had decided to compete in Formula One, at about the time that Porsche withdrew to concentrate on the 901/911. The Japanese carmaker won its first race in Mexico City in 1965. While it sat out most of 1966 developing a new engine and chassis, it took its second victory at Monza in 1967 in front of Ferrari's home fans. Yet Honda's engineers scarcely were done challenging established automakers.

FINISHING THE FRONT END OF THE 964

One of the styling, structural, and engineering goals with the front end of the next-generation 911, the typ 964, was to better integrate the energy-absorbing bumpers into the appearance of the car. *Porsche Archives*

Previous pages: **1990 CARRERA 4**
It was known as the new 911. Internally, Porsche called it the typ 964. It took all-wheel drive from desert racing and from its own rarified supercars and offered the feature to every customer.

For the 1968 races, company founder Soichiro Honda set his designers to work creating an air-cooled Formula One engine "to gain a foothold in the passenger-car market." He was convinced "that world-class cars must be powered by air-cooled engines." This engine raced once, the project languished, and Honda returned to manufacturing efficient, economical, water-cooled, front-engine, front-wheel-drive cars.

Then in 1983, as it returned to Formula One, Honda launched the idea of an underseat, mid-engine, rear-wheel-drive sports car, the NSX, or New Sports car Experimental. The company had running prototypes by 1986. In February 1989, as Acura unveiled the car at the Chicago Auto Show, Formula One driver Ayrton Senna, in Japan at that time testing for McLaren, drove a fourth-generation development NSX. "I feel it's a little fragile," he told engineers, as reported in Honda's official history of the car. "Even though the car was designed," their history continued, "for a level of rigidity equaling that of a Porsche or Ferrari," Senna's comments compelled engineers to raise their objectives by 50 percent. For their next test, they ran in Porsche's backyard at the Nürburgring for three weeks to reach their goal. During media launches in June, American and European journalists concluded: "This car will change the standard for modern sports cars."

For Porsche engineers and racers like Jürgen Barth and Roland Kussmaul who had advocated a mid-engine Group B concept, this kind of acclaim to a latecomer had to hurt. While the car's configuration clearly targeted Ferrari's $72,000, four-year-old, 260-horsepower 328 GTB, it also aimed squarely at Lamborghini's 255-horsepower, $58,000, eight-year old Jalpa. The NSX moved onto Weissach's radar screens.

Honda wasn't alone among Japanese carmakers challenging the status quo. Nissan had not stood still. Its attractive 300ZX improved in two ways in 1989. Nissan introduced a 2+2 model that rivaled Porsche's 944S2, the 928, and 911 models at a fraction of the price. The 300ZX delivered 222 horsepower against the 911's 247 and the 944S2 model's 208. Nissan's 300-horsepower Turbo, at only $33,000, came close to Porsche's latest Euro-specification 330–brake horsepower Turbo (at $71,000) and beat the U.S. version that got along with 282.

Weissach's Manfred Bantle and Fritz Bezner, his production car counterpart, had not been resting either. As Honda's board approved its NSX, so Porsche's board launched the next production series, the typ 964 normally

The appearance remains faithful to 911 enthusiasts. The new 3.6-liter engine utilizes two spark plugs per cylinder to improve combustion. This offers 250 brake horsepower to buyers worldwide.

1990 930S CABRIOLET

As Porsche customers learned that there would be no Turbo in the new 964 series, serious enthusiasts rushed to get "the last Turbo" that would be available for the foreseeable future. *This* was the final 930S on this platform.

aspirated cars and typ 965 Turbos. Initially, these two lines were to debut in late 1988 as 1989 models. They would carry over 959 innovations including self-leveling suspensions, ABS brake systems, and all-wheel drive.

In 1991, Helmuth Bott recalled that back in 1984 three possibilities for the next 911 seemed logical to him. One carried over the Carrera 3.2 configuration while offering a 964 all-wheel drive as a new model. The second scenario gave the 3.2 body a facelift and mounted it on both rear-wheel-drive and all-wheel-drive running gear. Lastly, they discussed designing and engineering a unitized body in which the body served the function of chassis. This would appear in two- and four-wheel-drive configurations.

At this point, Porsche enjoyed the advantageous exchange rate of nearly 3.5 deutsche marks to $1. Bott installed a wind tunnel at Weissach. Wendelin Wiedeking, a young production engineer who arrived in 1983, earned the assignment to supervise construction of a new paint shop. He then designed and directed construction of Porsche's new body shop. The company accomplished these expensive improvements out of cash reserves without borrowing a single deutsche mark.

Based on such financial strength and the attractive drawings for the company's new 959, the board selected Bott's third option to devise an updated body form with new function as well. But the board allowed stylists

The project started life when a New Yorker ordered a Carrera 3.2 with a leather dash. That request led him into the wonders of Rolf Sprenger's *Sonderwunsch*, or special wish program, where virtually anything is possible—from hundreds of leather trim items to hundreds of extra horsepower.

Porsche used this 220-mile-per-hour speedometer only on the 959s before using it on this unique Turbo. The light-emitting-diode boost gauge comes from 935s, though they are usually not equipped with a digital clock in the center. Porsche supplied variable boost on this car.

Tony Lapine, Wolfgang Möbius, and Dick Soderberg only to *update* the body. They could not change it as radically as Soderberg had done with the 959. Fenders and headlights remained sacrosanct, as was that big expensive roof panel. While the company had the resources to underwrite something more radical, it chose to acknowledge those loyalists who would allow change, but not too much of it.

Bott's *Lastenheft*, the car's concept specification book, set a new target. Ironically, this category was something that aerodynamic engineer Tilman Brodbeck had heard from his friend in Volkswagen's wind tunnel more than a decade before: Porsche's aerodynamic drag was far out of line even with lesser-performing sedans. Ford's sleek Scorpio four-door (its first all-wheel drive and Europe's first mass-market car with ABS) had established a new benchmark with a drag coefficient of 0.29, followed by Audi's shapely 100 models at 0.30. Porsche's 0.395 embarrassed engineers and stylists alike. Soderberg's 959 had reached 0.31 drag coefficient, so achieving Bott's goal of 0.32 seemed reasonable. To accomplish this, Soderberg and Möbius fine tuned front valances, flush mounted front bumpers, and fitted a belly pan under the nose of the car that shielded the area around the new front differential and driveshaft tunnel.

At the rear, engineers and stylists jointly created an electrically operated rear spoiler providing less obvious lift control. At speeds above 80 kilometers (50 miles per hour) the spoiler emerged from the rear deck lid and reduced rear lift to zero, an effect that far surpassed Brodbeck's original Bürzel.

As the 964's new drivetrain came together, Bott and Bezner configured its weight balance and front-rear torque split differently from either the 959 rally or road versions. The 964 settled at 59-percent rear weight bias and 69-percent power allocation while 31 percent of the power went to the front end that bore 41 percent of the weight. Bott's goal was "to provide our customers handling characteristics that felt familiar to them, and were similar to rear-drive 911s, but with the benefit of additional traction in poor conditions."

The commitment to all-wheel drive created what Porsche engineers now call a target-conflict, a good-news-bad-news challenge that arises from choices they make. In this case, the front differential forced Bezner and Bott to abandon Porsche's dependable torsion bars as rear springs. The driveshaft forward from the engine would have gone directly through the transverse tube that housed the torsion bars. But this change created other problems because that tube had added considerable stiffness to the cars. The new rear suspension was a compromise that became one of the 964's weaknesses.

Another target-conflict arose when engine chief Paul Hensler committed to using dual spark plugs for ignition. He intended to use this technology to meet California's ever-tightening nitrogen-oxide emission standards. Twin ignition would burn the fuel more efficiently from idle up to the high ranges. This would leave less unburned matter for catalysts to incinerate, and it would increase power. However, two spark plug holes in the air-cooled heads left less room for fins. To better transfer cylinder head heat to the heavily finned cylinders, engineers eliminated the head gasket between them. This eventually led to leakage problems that subsequent

Changes and modifications ranged from a thinner fiberglass flat nose to the BBS extractor wheels. When Rolf Sprenger completed the car, his options list ran to 28 pages. He estimated horsepower at close to 500.

1991 CARRERA 4 RS LIGHTWEIGHT

This is another special Porsche customer product, although this one came from Jürgen Barth's customer racing department. While it was conceived as a racer, no road course series existed for all-wheel drive at that time.

engineers had to solve. The process of automobile design frequently is one wherein one solution creates a problem that brings another solution, which causes a new problem. Moving the 964 engine through this process delayed model introduction until mid-model year 1989.

New computers, electronics, other features, and their wiring, added more than 500 pounds (240 kilograms) of weight to the new model. It was almost 20 percent heavier than the 3.2 Carrera, at about 3,200 pounds (or 1,455 kilograms). To meet their performance targets, Bezner, Bott, and Hensler tried a new 3,506-cc engine achieved by increasing the bore 2 mm to 100. But even this did not move the all-wheel-drive version as quickly

as the current model, let alone meet their goals. Lengthening the stroke by 2 mm gave them 76.4 mm, for total displacement of 3,600 cc exactly. These engines routinely developed 250 brake horsepower at 6,800 rpm with 229 ft-lb of torque at 4,800. That was good enough to initiate production, and marketing named this new product the Carrera 4, or C4. Its rear-wheel-drive version was the Carrera 2, or C2, which followed in early 1990.

The efforts and delays took the car over its budget. The tardy introduction did not help a company now disadvantaged by an exchange rate, by the departure of its chief executive officer, and by the elevation of the pfennig-wise business manager Heinz Branitzki to Schutz's former role.

The 964 proved to be much like what journalists, enthusiasts, and Porsche's engineers expected, but it was less than engineering and styling had hoped, and it cost much more than most people knew. Commonality in parts, the number of items that Porsche shared between the 3.2 Carrera or the new 944 Turbo and the 964, was so limited that when Wendelin Wiedeking examined parts lists, development costs, and production revenues, he concluded that no one had monitored Porsche's engineering. Karl Ludvigsen reported that Wiedeking accused Helmuth Bott of destroying the company through his fiscal practices. When Wiedeking concluded that no one at Porsche cared about his discoveries, he left. But so did Bott a few months later, just before the 964 Carrera 4 introduction and two years before his scheduled retirement.

By the time the car appeared, the deutsche mark-to-dollar exchange put the new Carrera 4 at $69,500 in the United States, against 114,500 deutsche marks throughout Germany. The L-Program 1990 964C2 appeared

without the C4 front driveshafts and differentials. This saved 220 pounds, 100 kilograms, and increased the trunk capacity. The C2 debuted in coupe form at 103,500 deutsche marks, and $58,500 in the United States. Prices climbed to 120,100 deutsche marks for the C2 cabrio, $67,890 in the States, against 131,100 deutsche marks or $72,830 for the C4 cabrio. If the 964C4 had been the indulged child of Weissach's engineering department, those involved in creating a new all-wheel-drive Turbo as the 965 were among Porsche's defeated and disappointed.

Branitzki's promotion brought death sentences for some projects, including variations on the 928 that styling and engineering had advanced, such as a cabriolet and a four-seater. Sales of the 928 had shrunk almost to boutique levels and further development was no longer supportable against diminishing revenues. The 965 Turbo, however, made it through Branitzki's initial project slaughter.

The wide white whale-tail and flared wheel arches recall a 1978 rally special 911SC-RS. While those models competed internationally, these unusual lightweights went on to serve a different purpose. They taught Porsche the marketing value of extremely limited production vehicles.

Porsche Club Sports and Speedsters—with production runs in the hundreds in 1989—had nothing on these cars. Fewer than two dozen appeared, and these cars convinced Porsche that well-heeled enthusiasts would be attracted to ultra-limited-edition models.

One of the two variable-traction controllers is visible through the steering wheel. One adjusted fore-aft power distribution, and the other shifted traction from left to right. It's possible to put all the power to a single front or rear wheel, or evenly to all four.

Stylist Tony Hatter had watched Walter Möbius and Dick Soderberg craft smart and aggressive shapes for the 959. Hatter adopted the rear cooling slots, the front end and headlights, and the integrated rear wing into his own concept for the next generation Turbo.

As Bott and Bezner worked on the 965, they experienced similar cooling and horsepower output problems that plagued them with 964 engines. This prompted Bott and Manfred Bantle, who had developed the racing 959s, to contemplate alternatives. They considered developing a V-6 version of Porsche's latest V-8 Indy engine, with four valves per cylinder and dual-overhead camshafts, or even detuning a version of that V-8. Each of these solutions was viable but also expensive and time-consuming. By late summer 1988, water-cooling the flat-six had become the favorite solution.

By this time, former managing director Peter Schutz had gone home, styling chief Tony Lapine, in a dispute with management while recuperating from heart troubles, was asked to stay at home, and former chief

engineer Helmuth Bott had left for home. Dutchman Harm Lagaay, who had designed Porsche's 924 with Dick Soderberg, had left for a job at Ford, and then he had gone to BMW. There he supervised design of the company's controversial but innovative Z-1 two-seater. He returned now as Lapine's replacement. BMW's Ulrich Bez, who had left Porsche 10 years earlier to work in engineering at BMW Technik, had directed development of the Z-1. He returned to Porsche in September 1988 to succeed Bott.

As personnel changed, ideas and variations swirled around. The logic of water-cooling either a flat-six or V-8 gained some ground though Bez recognized this would take years, not months, to fully develop. To energize customers who loved the Turbos in an overall market that demanded resuscitation, Bez and Branitzki concluded that enthusiasts could be well served if Porsche installed the 3.3-liter 930 Turbo engine in the new all-wheel-drive 965 as a 1991 model. Engineering then could move ahead on one V-8 with normal aspiration and another

1991 TURBO

Porsche had in mind an entirely different looking Turbo for the new series. Known internally as the typ 965, it uses styling cues that include the rear wing from the 959. Budget considerations dictated a different direction.

While the 3.6-liter Carrera 2 and 4 engines used dual spark plugs, the 3.3-liter Turbo retains single-plug ignition. The village of Gmünd, Austria, home of Porsche cars, made a suitable location to photograph one of the town's offspring.

with turbochargers. They could investigate larger 3.6-, 4.0-, or 4.2-liter displacements they might use in the 965 for 1993 or 1994, as well as for a new car line, a four-door designated the typ 989, a seemingly logical step in view of products Bez and Lagaay had developed for BMW.

By mid-November, perspectives shifted. Porsche would introduce a rear-drive-only 965 that looked less sensational than Hatter's concept, while his fully fashioned version would begin production with twin turbochargers similar to the 959. Within a month, however, the 965 body in all its variations died. "We had to redo it completely," Hatter recalled, "take off all the aggressive looking hoops and things and make it a reasonable car."

That reasonable car came about as Fritz Bezner and Ulrich Bez struggled to fill the gap created by discontinuing the 930S. They carried over its 3,299-cc engine into a rear-wheel-drive 964 body with production starting in May 1990 for introduction as a 1991 model. This package, incorporating pieces of a former option "Sportkit," boosted output to 320 brake horsepower at 5,750 rpm with 332 ft-lb of torque at 4,500 rpm.

Two other target-conflicts appeared, but together they resulted in a performance record for the new car. The United States now legislated corporate average fuel economy, CAFE. This system allowed large companies to develop and produce less efficient gas-guzzlers so long as they also sold fuel-efficient models

After a one-year absence, the Turbo returns on the new Carrera 2 chassis. A larger intercooler helps the 3.3-liter engine develop 320 horsepower at 5,750 rpm. Initially, the Turbo was available only in Europe.

This car rides on 17-inch Carrera Cup wheels using 205/50ZR17 Bridgestones on the front and 255/45ZRs on 9-inch-wide wheels on the rear. With torque of 332 ft-lbs at 4,500 rpm, acceleration is exhilarating.

1992 AMERICA ROADSTER

This is essentially a Carrera 2 cabriolet with Turbo-Look fenders and wheels. This model incorporates the Turbo's suspension, brakes, and 17-inch wheels and tires. But it uses the C2's 3.6-liter normally aspirated engine. Porsche produced just 250 of these.

that lowered company-wide averages to reach federal targets. For smaller companies, this represented another obstacle for their engineers to hurdle. One fundamental technique to decrease consumption used slightly higher gear ratios to reduce engine speeds while maintaining road velocity. This method also benefited Swiss customers, who encountered roadside microphones monitoring the country's strict noise standards. Slower revving engines ran more quietly. Yet, since gearing changes had no effect on peak engine speed, longer gears yielded higher velocities in every gear. This especially was the case in fifth, where German and English magazines testing the new turbos each reached 171 miles per hour. As these governmental regulatory dramas played out between design, engineering, and production offices at Porsche, a smaller project in the competition department took form that would invite its own U.S. scrutiny.

In late 1988, Customer Sports Department Manager Jürgen Barth proposed to competition director Peter Falk the idea of building two or three rear-wheel-drive 964 RSR racers using 3.4-liter engines to enter in the

1992 CARRERA CUP

Porsche produced 45 of these for a race series that never came together. Andial in Southern California converted 25 of these to full competition specifications but then refitted airbags, standard seats, power windows, and fog lights to most of them after the series collapsed.

This car is now a lively competitor in Carrera Cup and Porsche Owner's Club events. It is one of very few survivors from the model run.

24-hour endurance race at Nürburgring. Porsche sales were seriously depressed due to the world exchange rates. This affected customer race cars sales as well, and Barth sought a project to develop. Years earlier, Norbert Singer had created a graphic presentation clearly demonstrating that when Porsche raced, sales increased. With that ammunition, Barth got a tentative approval for that idea and a second project as well. His back-up plan was to create a strictly customer car on the new platform but one that would use up some exotic spare parts Weissach had sitting around.

Typically, when Porsche builds a new-technology race car, it doesn't merely construct the few examples that other competitors and the public see. For the 1986 Paris-Dakar 953s, Porsche had assembled three cars.

Yet there were about 30 sets of all-wheel-drive running gear. With its high clearance, the 953 strictly was an off-road works entry. But Barth envisioned constructing perhaps half-a-dozen new cars with lower ground clearance, possibly for circuit racing.

Barth had been at Porsche as it created the 1973 911RS Carrera 2.7s and successive 2.8 and 3.0 RSR versions. He knew all about Ferdinand Piëch's 911Rs. These cars had fit rules, skirted them, or existed entirely outside of them. Existing competition regulations meant there wasn't anywhere for this all-wheel-drive racer to compete; however Barth had watched Porsche's influence operate in the past. He knew if the company pushed it, venues and series would open up. However, these were different times, better times, and worse times. It was the accident of timing that made this car interesting, its story relevant, and its lessons important.

In the United States and throughout the world, those who weathered the 1987 stock market crash without needing bankruptcy protection looked for new ways to work their money. Successful businessmen always have collected trophies and though Porsche's dealers had trouble selling cars for $60,000, "investors" with no racing interest or experience were buying 908s for $400,000 one week and selling them for $700,000 a week later. Prices, if not values, were soaring. On golf courses and in gym locker rooms, speculators showed snapshots of their latest investments instead of bragging over recent stock transactions. Legitimate racing cars, even those with no competition history, became the new platinum commodity.

One more element made Barth's idea timely. In Washington, the EPA and DOT had clamped down on the gray market auto industry in 1987, enforcing rules they previously had treated less vigilantly. Red flags went up because an increasing number of 1973 RS 2.7s came into the country as race cars. These didn't look like race cars, they seemed to have full interiors, they had trunks, and not every one had a roll bar. This had tripped up PCNA's efforts to import 959s and got red flags waving around the sight of any Porsche. As Californian Kerry Morse put it recently, "You can't bring a car into the United States with a 17-digit serial number, a roll bar, and air-conditioning and call it a race car. The folks at the EPA and DOT are not stupid." Unwittingly, however, they contributed to the racing car investment frenzy.

Morse knew the federal agency people well, having owned, raced, imported, and brokered countless modern and historic racing cars throughout his career. He had witnessed the recent price jumps and understood the two significant features that motivated speculators: These cars were purpose-built with ultralimited production that easily could be verified and as such, they were importable. Kerry Morse also knew Jürgen Barth, visiting

This was the last of the Cup cars that Porsche produced and Andial converted. Its comfortable interior and electric windows seem out of character with its race car nature, but the ill-fated U.S. series required the cars to be equipped this completely.

him on every trip to Germany and frequently staying at Jürgen's home. On a trip in mid-1989, Morse asked his host what was new.

Barth explained his idea to gut the 964's interior and body of all possible excess weight, install 953 running gear, and, in essence create a 964RS. Morse asked how large a run Barth was considering. Six, eight, twelve? Morse immediately committed to take the first one. Neither of them had a solid idea of its price, but Barth estimated it might be 200,000 deutsche marks, about $110,000 at the time. With a solid order, both men knew it was easier to move a project forward.

Helmut Flegl, at that time number two in engineering behind new director Ulrich Bez, got involved and questioned the project in early July. As codeveloper of the new 964 Carrera Cup model with Roland Kussmaul,

Flegl wondered where this 964RS was to fit in competition. Barth answered each inquiry and pressed ahead, ultimately removing close to 350 kilograms, 770 pounds, of weight from the cars. He replaced doors and front and rear deck lids with thin aluminum, and side windows with Plexiglas. A roll bar clung to the sterile interior that was set off by two large dials on the instrument panel. Porsche racers recognized these as turbo boost controls on 935s. But this engine was normally aspirated, not one fitted with twin turbochargers. For this car, now called the Carrera 4 Leichtbau, or C4 Lightweight, these two matching knurled knobs controlled front-to-rear and left-to-right differential bias. Barth fitted a stainless-steel dual exhaust system that delivered a stunningly loud 107 decibels at 4,500 rpm, making it one of the loudest Porsche race cars ever. There was no engine noise protection, no air filter, and no heater fan. Modified electronics and the improved exhaust increased engine output to 265 horsepower, up from the production stock 250. It got a single-plate sintered-metal clutch, short-ratio five-speed transmission, and an ultralightweight flywheel "for racing purposes." It made a potent package at about 2,430 pounds, about 1,105 kilograms. Visually the car appeared stock and quite tame. It ran on stock-width tires and wheels, sixes in front, eights in the rear. It had neither flares nor modified bodywork. Barth had gotten some things accomplished in

1993 3.8 RSR SUPERCUP

Porsche conceived these cars for the European BPR series. They quickly became the foundation of the single-make Supercup series that developed as a support race to Formula One Grand Prix event weekends.

making his unusual car. Flegl and others in management vetoed others. All this work took months. As the first one neared completion, it got one other essential specification that Morse recommended and Barth pushed through.

"After the situation with dozens of 1973 Carrera RS 2.7s with their full serial numbers, and the 959 debacle," Morse explained, "almost anything Porsche did was going to get serious scrutiny from U.S. EPA and DOT. Race cars have six-digit serial numbers. These cars could not come into the United States with a serial number beginning WP0ZZ. Barth pushed hard for it and he got it done. He started with 964001 rather than 964101 so the cars would seem more like factory works cars than customer series."

Word spread quickly through the small world of Porsche race car devotees—this was something that might not ever race but it would be rare and it was available. The run expanded to 21 cars and sold out quickly. The first car went to a collector in the United States. The initial four emerged between September and November 1990, as 1991 model year editions. Zuffenhausen delivered raw body-in-white shells to Weissach, which painted them in the race department and installed their modified engines and running gear. Internal politics drove the price upward from Barth's hoped-for 225,000 deutsche marks to 285,000, as some decision makers saw an opportunity to let this odd marketplace pay extra for its exclusiveness. Cars went to England, Japan, France, several came to the United States, and others remained in Germany . Because the EPA and DOT decided only to admit these cars as racers following individual inspection of each one, U.S. buyers had to take delivery at the factory, adding another 39,000 deutsche marks in value-added tax (VAT) to their purchase price. They could recover this upon leaving Germany with the car, but suddenly these cars cost more than $200,000. This figure was hard to swallow when any one of 70 starting-flag-ready 964 Carrera Cup cars—for which a series in Europe and the United States. already existed—sold for 123,000 deutsche marks, or $73,650. Some people wondered aloud if 953 running gear was worth the extra $120,000. C4 Lightweight deliveries continued through 1991, but the collector car world was approaching critical mass.

Porsche fitted a race-reconfigured ABS system and 18-inch Pirelli 235/40 tires on the front and 285/35s on the rear. Handling and braking are exceptional. Paul Frère reported a brake force of 1.4g decelerating from 120 kilometers per hour (75 miles per hour) in one of his tests.

One of the RSR's more startling visual cues is its elaborate fiberglass rear wing. Weissach fabricators formed the doors and front hood from thin aluminum. Porsche sold these cars ready to race for 270,000 DM, about $160,000 at the time.

When the balloon burst in 1992, its fallout scattered everywhere. Prices for Ferrari 250 GTOs had reached $25 million, figures formerly reserved for Monet oil paintings or medium-sized islands in the South Pacific. Porsche 908s changed hands for $1 million and deals for 917Ks approached $5 million. Prices had swollen to four times life size just as the sharpest speculators jumped to the next trend. This left hundreds of amateur players holding cars attached to ruinous loans. It affected racing dramatically; the 24 Hours of Le Mans, which typically counted

50 to 60 entries through the 1980s, had just 28 cars start in June 1992. Barth had to send letters to buyers reminding them of their commitments.

The last car left Weissach in late 1992. The project made money as Jürgen Barth's projects virtually always had done. It had cost Porsche nothing extra to delete sound insulation or to add running gear and a fixed rear wing that it already had in stock. The legacy of the C4 Lightweight would live on, reiterating as it had done, that special limited editions, including the 1973 RS or even the 1989 Speedsters, had strong appeal to loyal enthusiasts. Perhaps not at the nearly 30 percent exclusivity markup that some in Porsche's management cynically had applied, but Porsche now knew that its customers would dig deeply in order to be the only one in town with something unique. It was a lesson Porsche would neither forget nor ignore.

Overshadowing such racing-oriented limited production, the company manufactured 20,666 C2 and C4 models in 1990. M-Program 1991 models assembled starting in February 1991 provided both driver and passenger with air bag restraints. The same economy that affected Barth's C4 Lightweights tripped up sales of production cars in 1991. C2 and C4 sales suffered additional impact from the growing sales of the competitively priced Honda/Acura NSX and the nearly half-priced Nissan 300ZX. Zuffenhausen manufactured just 13,816 cars including its 944S2 and 928S4 models, but these included two new models that already reflected lessons of Barth's limited editions and of those that came before.

The new Turbo appeared in model year 1991 in Europe at 183,600 deutsche marks, the equivalent of $122,400, and in 1992 in the United States, where it sold for a less-profitable $95,000. However the Turbo body adorned a limited production cabriolet Turbo-Look, as Porsche called it in Europe. For the United States, it became the America Roadster, a model recalling the ultra limited production road car–race car from mid-1952. To encourage sales in the States, Porsche priced the car $11,000 lower than it did for European markets. In Germany it sold for 169,300 deutsche marks (nearly $106,000) against $94,960 (or 151,935 deutsche marks, for comparison) in the United States. Porsche kept this model in production for two years.

Along with this wide-body C2 cabriolet, Porsche introduced three variations of a 964RS, though none of these was anything like Barth's C4 Lightweight. Like the America Roadster, these ran on C2 chassis. The road, or touring version with simple interior and no sound insulation weighed 2,690 pounds, or 1,223 kilograms. Its engine developed 260 horsepower at 6,100 rpm. This model used the same Freudenberg dual-mass flywheel that Porsche introduced in 1990 on C2s to reduce drivetrain vibration. A basic version 964RS used a lighter flywheel and spring-dampened clutch. The third version, the Sport, provided a sintered-metal solid-disc clutch. Porsche manufactured 1,053 of all three versions in 1991 and another 1,345 in 1992. None of these 145,450–deutsche mark ($91,000) models was available in the United States. American buyers enjoyed another happy instance of reverse discrimination with the 1992 and 1993 911RS America coupes. Very similar to the Touring European 964RS, Porsche sold this model in the United States for $53,900, a substantial savings (86,240 deutsche marks) over the home market version. In fact, this came in almost $10,000 less than the C2.

Even these two special models were not enough to stem the outgoing tide of cash-holding Porsche buyers. Production throughout 1992 dipped to 9,747 C2 and C4 models, and 3,298 Turbos. Porsche had manufactured

Weissach engineers bored out the 3.6-liter engine cylinders another 2 mm to 102 mm but kept the stroke at 76.4 mm. This yielded 3,746 cc (228.5 cubic inches) total displacement. The engine develops 325 brake horsepower at 6,900 rpm.

1993 AMERICA ROADSTER GS

The America Roadster was another limited run of 250 cars commemorating a dual-purpose model that Porsche introduced in 1953. Turbo-Look cabriolets typically got the C2 3.6-liter engine. While this car looks fairly routine, there is almost nothing typical about it.

1,058 of the Turbo-Look cabrio or America Roadster models in 1992, but only another 321 in 1993. For 1993, as Porsche introduced its new 3.6-liter Turbo, it added the flared bodywork as an option to C4 models, and for that year and the next it offered a C2-based speedster. Through 1993 and 1994, Porsche assembled only 904 of these Speedsters, of a planned run of 3,000, all built on the C2 cabrio's narrow body. Rolf Sprenger's *Sonderwuncsh* department, Porsche's Special Wishes division, created about 20 Turbo-look speedsters, reminiscent of those produced in 1989.

The factory created its own most special wish in 1993 with the introduction of the limited edition Turbo S. Originally slated for a production run of 50, Zuffenhausen ultimately assembled 80 of these 3.3-liter 381-horsepower marvels. Fitted *without* airbags, air conditioning, power windows, power seats, power steering, or rear window wiper, but with thinner side glass and carbon fiber front and rear deck lids, the car weighed about 2,820 pounds (1,288 kilograms). This was 420 pounds (190 kilograms) less than the standard Turbo. These special editions were not cheap, costing buyers 295,000 deutsche marks at the factory, about $175,000. For U.S. customers, Porsche created a version called the Turbo S2 in a regularly equipped Turbo body. This incorporated an engine the company advertised as developing 322 brake horsepower but which was the 381-horsepower S powerplant. The International Motor Sport Association (IMSA) had created a new Supercar series, and Porsche used the TS2 to qualify entries for this competition. Street cars could hit 60 miles per hour in 4.8 seconds, reach a top speed of 178 miles per hour, and in the United States, they sold for $119,950.

Fitted with the RS 3.8-liter flat-six, the owner, a loyal Porsche customer, also received a racing-prepared Tiptronic transmission and racing anti-lock braking system (ABS) with adjustable sensitivity. Two-tone, custom-fitted competition seats sit in a fully finished leather and carpeted interior.

While its performance capabilities are spectacular, one of this car's more interesting features is its removable hardtop roof with working electric sunroof. The bi-plane elevating rear spoiler is unique to this car, though both of these unusual features led to new production developments.

1994 SPEEDSTER

The next-generation Speedster came from standard C2 cabriolet bodies, not the wider Turbo-Look option that characterized the 1989 models. It was designated as regular production option M503.

Porsche originally planned to assemble and sell 3,000 of the new Speedsters. Demand proved to be nowhere near that great. The company manufactured only 771 in 1993 and just 154 in 1994.

Both C2 and C4 lines offered a new transmission, introduced in 1990, called the Tiptronic. Porsche developed this four-speed gearbox jointly with ZF. Porsche was using its innovative PDK double-clutch transmission in 956s for development and racing. Helmuth Bott had husbanded this development, and he had enough faith in it that he urged its adoption in the 959. He also hoped to see it, or something similar, in production 911s. By 1986 however, a hoped-for partnership with Audi had evaporated. They had considered using it for their new V-8 sedan, but now this left Porsche to face development costs alone. As they worked with ZF on a new system, their priorities became clear. While this transmission would shift automatically, it had to respond to the way Porsche drivers operate their cars, and this might be very different from how BMW, Audi, or Chevrolet drivers control theirs. In addition to that, engineers wanted a manual shift function that would override the gearbox automatic characteristics, yet would automatically avoid damaging the engine or gearbox.

As with the 1989 version, the twin-hump fiberglass piece serves as a tonneau cover for the low-profile convertible top. It also protects a large storage area behind the front seats.

1994 TURBO S

This special-order Turbo weighs 1,293 kilograms (2,844 pounds), which is about 190 kilograms (420 pounds) lighter than regular production Turbo models. Engineer/racer Roland Kussmaul, in charge of development, lowered the chassis 38 mm (1.5 inches), which further stiffened the ride and enhanced handling.

Four years of work went into developing and testing this transmission and when it first appeared, enthusiast magazines eagerly awaited the chance to test it and criticize it. Instead, they found it provided acceleration and top speeds within very few percentage points of the manual box and fuel economy in the same tight range. The Tiptronic quickly found an audience and nearly one in every three C2 and C4 buyers paid the extra 6,000 deutsche marks in Germany or $2,950 in the United States for the new transmission.

Still it was a very tough time at Porsche. A number of dynamic new leaders arrived at the company on the eve of the 964 introduction. Heinz Branitzki, the cautious accountant in charge of the company, hailed this new car as "the 911 for the next 25 years." In a tight economy, Branitzki no doubt hoped this was the case. He had

Weissach engineers fitted the 3.3-liter engine with larger valves, more aggressive valve timing, and a larger turbocharger. Their improvements boosted power output from the stock 315 to 381 brake horsepower at 6,000 rpm.

Of the 80 individual Turbo S cars produced, Porsche assembled 39 with this updated slant-nose front. Cooling air intakes in the front bumper and rear fenders are visual cues to the rarity of this model.

watched development cost reports float across his desk. By that, he also meant that he could not envision engineers or designers needing to do much more work to the car during its second quarter-century. Less than a year later, he had retired after the annual shareholder's meeting in March 1990. Arno Bohn, a man from the computer industry, replaced him. Yet Bohn would be out after just 30 tumultuous months, during which time he battled business, the economy, and the board. He left on September 30, 1992.

Into Bohn's footsteps marched a man of proven abilities. Wendelin Wiedeking had constructed a paint shop and a body fabrication plant. He had left in 1988 feeling frustrated by management indifference to runaway development costs. Then he returned as board member for production in July 1991.

Few people who had arrived in 1988 or 1989 were in love with the 964. Ulrich Bez and Harm Lagaay, both coming from BMW, had led that company into the 1990s before joining Porsche. BMW introduced a 7-series

sedan with a massive 5-liter, 296-horsepower V-12 in 1988 and would bring out its startling 8-series coupe with the V-12 engine in 1990. In 1991 it would introduce a high-performance 5-series sedan, the 310–brake horsepower M5. For many buyers, these cars would forever redefine what kind of daily drive to work they would accept.

When Bez and Lagaay arrived at Porsche, they looked around. They could see that they had their work cut out for them.

"I was not someone who was afraid of changing the 911," Harm Lagaay recalled in January 2005, several months after retiring as head of Porsche's design department. "On the contrary, I was absolutely convinced that it had to change radically. So the 993 was the first step. We started the 993 immediately after I arrived." ▤

To get the power to the ground and keep the car on the ground, Porsche fitted 18-inch Speedline Cup Design three-piece wheels with 235/40s on the front and 265/35s on the rear. With a 290-kilometer-per-hour (180-mile-per-hour) top speed capability, one German magazine described the car's performance as "an eruption of primeval violence."

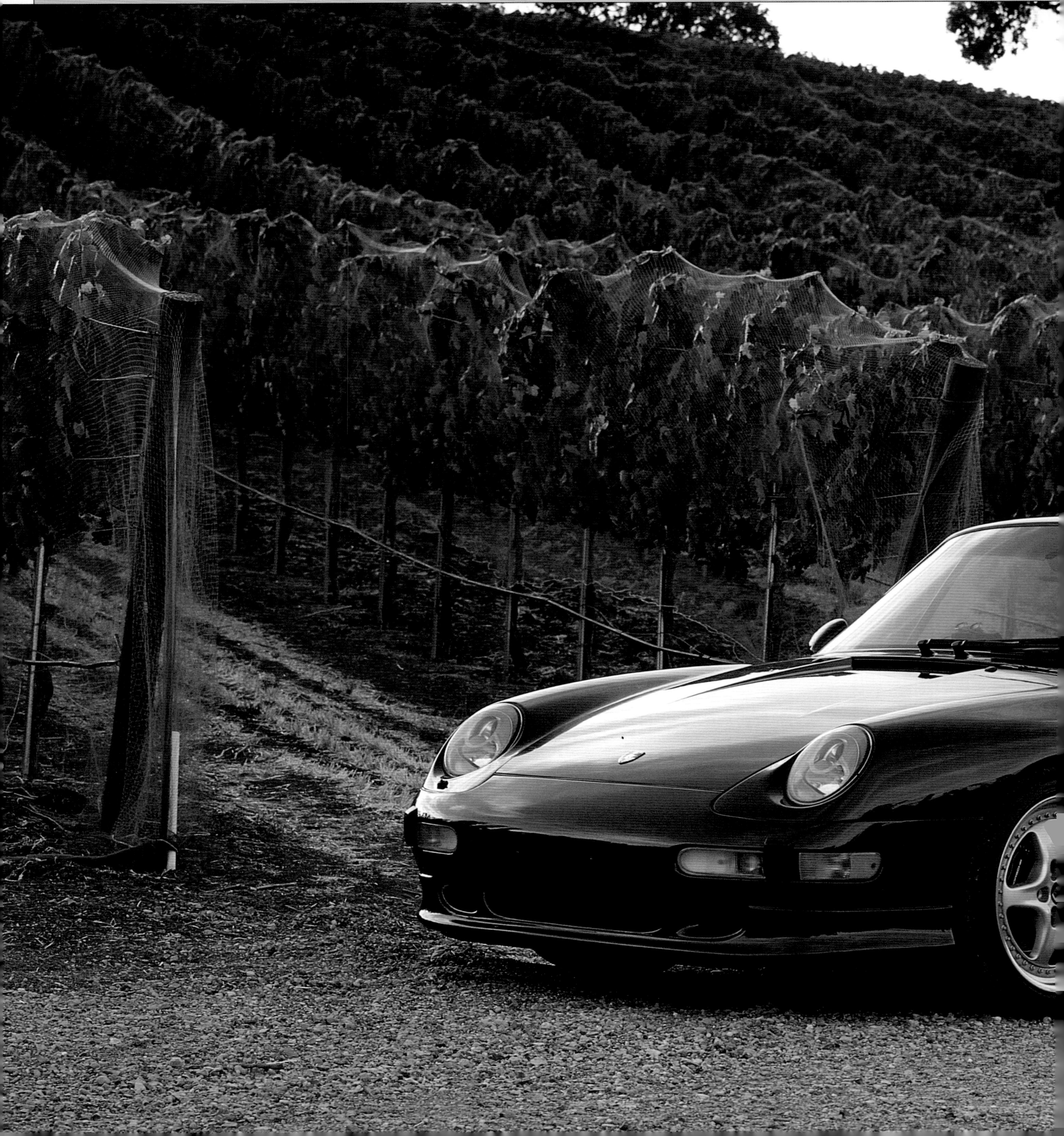

CHAPTER SEVEN

THE FOURTH GENERATION— THE 993

1994 – 1998

"A new 911—Look!

White smoke above Weissach."

Kevin Smith, *Car and Driver*, January 1994

"We started the 993 immediately after I arrived," Harm Lagaay explained. Lagaay had retired from Porsche during the summer of 2004, settling in a beautiful lakeside resort community west of Munich. He recalled that when he arrived in late 1989, there was nothing going on in Porsche's advanced design studios. This is not surprising in view of former chairman Heinz Branitzki's often-repeated mantra that the 964 was the 911 for the next 25 years. The new car offered innovations over the previous 3.2 Carrera and styling had subtly modified its appearance. However, the engineering and design compromises forced on them had made it less of a success than the creative minds at Weissach had hoped.

Previous pages: The 993 redesign was so extensive that Porsche carried over just the 964 roof for the new coupes and its front trunk lid for coupes and cabrios for the next-generation car. New front and rear suspension improved handling and reduce weight and noise. Aerodynamic teardrop outside mirrors replace the large rectangles of the 964.

With fresh eyes, he and Ulrich Bez, Helmuth Bott's replacement as technical director and Lagaay's former colleague at BMW, perceived the flaws. Their mission came from the supervisory board: "Get it right," was how Lagaay remembered it.

"The 911 concept, that's the first issue." Lagaay continued. "How you go and treat it, how successful you can be to get it moving and keep it moving continuously, that's the job. The third thing is the result of these components, the phenomenon, the car, the 911. Not only is it a sports car in its own right, in its own way, but it also is a segment in the automotive world which is extremely attractive. You build a car for that amount of money. You make it unique. You keep it unique, and that's why people drive it. They compare themselves with it, because it's a successful thing."

The 911/964 was not so successful a thing when Lagaay arrived. He had been away from Porsche for nearly 12 years. Between 1977 and mid-1985 he designed at Ford under Uwe Bahnsen, Patrick LeCamel, and finally Andy Jacobson. Then he supervised design at BMW for the next four years. Lagaay had experienced how other studios worked, the systems and processes they used for design review and project direction, and in his mind and on paper he continually evolved a plan for the day when he would run his own operation. He did not expect it to be Porsche but when Bez called him, he arrived prepared.

He brought with him Pinky Lai, a designer he first had worked with at Ford and whom he'd taken with him to BMW. He soon hired Grant Larson, and then added Mathias Kulla. He looked at the staff he inherited and plucked Tony Hatter from some less-interesting, less-challenging assignments. The staff began sketching concepts for the next 911 immediately.

"With the 964," Hatter explained, "the 911 had kind of gotten out of balance, with its big fat bumpers in the front way up in the air and the rear end hanging down. We addressed the complete proportional balance of the car. That was the main goal."

1995 CARRERA 993 CABRIOLET
The new 911 arrived with improvements to its 3.6-liter engine management system. It now delivered 272 brake horsepower to buyers worldwide. Porsche introduced a six-speed manual transmission and a new Tiptronic S with gear-change switches on the steering wheel.

While Hatter and his colleagues worked under Lagaay examining forms and proportions, Bez queried his engineering staff about what the 911 should be. Peter Falk, the venerable competition director with decades of experience in both racing car and series production model development, embraced the assignment. He came up with the concept that crystallized what Bez was seeking. Falk used the word "*Wendigheit*," meaning "agility or nimbleness." He prepared a 20-page paper that examined the word from its Latin language roots up through Porsche's next-edition 911 targets. For him, these included the Acura/Honda NSX and their current Carrera 2. (He did not add the Carrera 4, which everyone agreed had gone too far toward understeer in taming the tail-happiness of earlier 911s.) He contrasted maneuverability with agility, concluding that agility had more to

do with responsiveness while maneuverability referred, in his mind, to controllability in direction change. He acknowledged that any successful car could have one or the other characteristic or both. As Falk revisited earlier 911s, he recognized agility had been disciplined out of the 964s. That extended even to its appearance.

"The car got kind of tail heavy through the 964," Tony Hatter explained. "We addressed that. We stayed a long time with theoretical surfaces and edges. Rather than rounding off the fenders, there were a lot of sharp edges for a while. We made sure that the front and rear balanced out. It was a big proportional exercise. When you look at the original 911, you see a lot of that balance."

The new Cup Design wheels, 7x16 in front and 9x16 in rear, pull brake heat from the rotors at high speed. Tires are 205/55VR up front and 245/45ZR at the back. The rear suspension abandons the long-lived semi-trailing arms for a new multi-link system.

1995 993 CARRERA CUP/SUPERCUP SERIES PACE CAR

Porsche produced 35 of these 3.8-liter racers to continue the Formula One support series. Lightened to 1,100 kilograms (2,425 pounds), the new cars were more stiffly sprung than 964 versions and had adjustable anti-sway bars and shock absorbers.

Lagaay recalled a Porsche tradition of creating a special car for Ferry Porsche's significant birthdays. To get the design moving and to stimulate outside reaction, Lagaay selected a staff stylist Steve Murkett's radical concept of a Porsche dune buggy. The 1989 Panamericana, presented to Ferry for his 80th birthday, supposedly was not one of Ferry's favorite gifts, nor was it one of the design staff's prettiest automobiles. It did provide hints of the forms that would emerge from Lagaay's department.

Hatter, who had worked with Dick Soderberg on the 965 Turbo body, first adopted some of the shapes and air inlets from that project. Some features of the 965's front end already had gone into the 944-replacement known as the 968 that still was in development. Lagaay gave some thought at that point to linking the designs closely, an idea that reached maturity in Porsche's next generation 911.

Hatter painstakingly fine-tuned his design, working to make this new Porsche very much a Porsche. "I think there's no doubt about it that we spend a lot more time on *that* aspect of the car," he said. "We really work surfacing to perfection. You can't do it in an afternoon or a week. The models tend to mature over time as you work on them.

"I always like to compare the forms to muscles, forms with a lot of surface tension in them, not just rounded biological forms. They have a definite tension to them, a definite structure. There are no shapes or forms on the cars that don't have to be there. The bulges, that's where the wheels are. You can see where the people sit. It's such a tightly packaged vehicle that it's like a trained athletic shape."

Beneath that athletic shape, engineers worked equally hard to resolve the complaints over the C4 handling. There was rear suspension noise on both rear and all-wheel-drive models. They also worked to provide their customers with more horsepower but wondered if they could achieve that goal without redefining the air-cooled 911.

The engineers addressing engine questions reviewed the 964/965 proposals for water-cooled engines either in flat-six, V-6, or V-8 configurations. Porsche was developing a V-8 for its proposed 989 four-door sedan model. The current Indianapolis V-8 for Quaker State and Foster's Lager, the typ 2708, offered ideas as well. They worked up concepts and numbers for a normally aspirated 2.5-liter V-6 that might provide 220 brake horsepower, and a turbocharged 3.3-liter V-8 could offer as much as 408 brake horsepower and Turbo and normal versions in between. Each of these was too costly to the board so engineering returned to the 3.6-liter flat-six of the 964 with 100-mm bore and 76.4-mm stroke.

For the first years of this car's life, it served as the series pace car for Supercup events. In 2003, the car retired to a more active role as participant in a variety of regional and Porsche Owner's Club–sponsored events.

With the proper gearing, these cars can reach 174 miles per hour. The 3,746-cc (228.5-cubic-inch) engine develops 305 horsepower at 6,500 rpm. While Pirelli was a Supercup series sponsor, the current owner had different preferences.

As Herbert Ampferer examined the engine, he set targets. He aimed to rid the crankshaft of the torsional vibration damper that the 3.6-liter engine required for smooth running. He and his staff accomplished that challenge, and in the heads they incorporated self-adjusting hydraulically operated valves and reduced the valvetrain weight. They revised the entire exhaust system. When it entered production, it developed 272 brake horsepower at 6,100 rpm and 243 ft-lb of torque at 5,000 rpm, and it was quieter than any 911 engine before it.

To get that power to the ground, to meet and exceed U.S. and Rest-of-World (RoW) fuel economy standards and expectations, and to further reduce engine noise, engineers added a sixth gear to the G50 transmission. They had introduced this five-speed gearbox in the 3.2 Carreras in the 1987 model year and carried it through the 964s. First gear was lower now, while sixth permitted the car a maximum 168 miles (269 kilometers) per hour at 6,700 rpm.

Work that Tony Hatter and the design department's production engineers did to "work surfacing to perfection," aided in achieving that top speed. The new body produced a coefficient of drag of 0.33 for the wider-body 993. This was barely 0.01 higher than the slimmer, trimmer 964.

Body engineers glued the windshield in place. This change measurably increased the car's torsional stiffness, improving handling as a side benefit. There were bigger changes under the skin. Short of time and resources to solve the problem completely, engineers had mounted the 964's rear suspension directly to the car body. This had allowed road noises and suspension noise and movement to transfer into the passenger compartment. Fritz Bezner and project manager Bernd Kahnau had hoped to pick up the rear suspension of the 965 Turbo that would have used parallel wishbones. The board vetoed this for costs, although Ulrich Bez argued effectively that the new car needed a better rear suspension if it were to improve. Bezner created a system using a lower wishbone and a wishbone-like pair of converging links on top. He devised this novel configuration to accommodate a rear-wheel steering system similar to what Honda offered in 1986 and 1987 on its Prelude 4WS all-wheel-steering models. While Porsche chose not to go that direction, it adapted the 928's "Weissach" rear axle geometry that countered the effects leading to oversteer, rear axle squat on acceleration, and rear end lift on braking. Bezner mounted all the components on a subframe of Vacural, a heat-treatable alloy die cast with thin-walled stiffening webs providing exceptional strength. This technology soon surrounded front driveshafts for Carrera 4 versions as well. But for the rear suspension, this configuration required no upgrades or modification for competition Carrera Cup cars. Outside suppliers assembled the entire subframe, delivering it intact to Zuffenhausen assembly.

Where all-wheel drive had been Helmuth Bott's priority with the 964C4, Ulrich Bez and his successor, Horst Marchart, recast the concept to provide superior handling. A viscous coupling at the nose of the transaxle connected a torque tube to a much smaller exposed front differential that split power to each front wheel. This configuration replaced the computer-controlled differentials and heavy planetary gears that made the 964's system work. This new combination cut the weight in half as well, down to 50 kilograms (110 pounds) which aided in obtaining Falk's target of agility.

One of the design criteria that Tony Hatter faced when he started the 993 was that the car, whatever it looked like, had to be less expensive and less time-consuming to manufacture. Ulrich Bez had impatiently urged engineers and designers to complete this new car in a short time. His intolerance for delays incited a lobby against Bez. They dissuaded management from renewing his contract. He left in the fall of 1991, though by this time he already had driven a 993 prototype.

While Harm Lagaay got Steve Murkett to work on a Panamericana show car, he started several teams to work on the next-generation 911, the 993. Lagaay began hiring interior designers to style, detail, and coordinate interior colors and textures. *Porsche Archives*

1995 911 GT2

Unlike previous models, Porsche introduced its Turbo 993 in the same year as its normally aspirated cars. This allowed Weissach's racing engineers to create a racing version designated the GT2, which was intended for competition in BPR events in Europe and IMSA races in the United States.

Porsche produced 43 of these cars in 1995. Lightened to 1,100 kilograms (2,425 pounds) and fitted with the twin-turbocharged 3.6-liter engine, racing versions develop a minimum of 480 brake horsepower at 6,200 rpm. Base price was 251,000 DM ($182,000) in ready-to-race form.

Hatter, one of those whom Bez and Lagaay pressed to meet persistent deadlines, soon got his own 993 prototype experience.

"These things happen, every now and then. And every now and then . . . is good enough," he explained by way of introduction.

"It was a ride in one of the first prototype 993s. It was dark. Someone called me to come to the test track. We were working impossibly long hours in those days. This was the headlight test car, and it pulled in. It was this really nasty, ropey-looking matte-black thing. I opened the door to jump in, but I had to take the computers and printers and readouts and put them on my lap. As I was fitting on my crash helmet, the driver took off.

Because there are no lights on the test track, I couldn't see anything. Of course, the test driver knew where he was going, so he went fast. Very fast. It was absolutely terrifying."

Wendelin Wiedeking had been at Porsche for several months by this time, dedicated to streamlining procedures and reducing costs. He knew of Toyota Motor Company's legendary efficiency and its faith in the Japanese philosophy characterized by the word, *kaizen*, or "continuous improvement." Another Japanese legend, *Shin-Gijutsu*, the company founded by two former Toyota executives teaching "new technology," came to Zuffenhausen. Its founders forced Wiedeking himself to take a power saw to parts shelves that stood 3 meters, or 10 feet, tall after shouting in Japanese, "We said 'Bring us to the factory. This is a warehouse!'" Wiedeking managed to reduce assembly floor inventories from 28 days on hand to supplies for just 30 minutes. Instituting just-in-time inventory delivery required hard work between Porsche and its suppliers. Wiedeking

Dave Maraj of Champion Racing in Pompano Beach, Florida, acquired this GT2 in 1995 and raced it through the rest of the year. In March 1996, with Hans Stuck and Bill Adam driving, the car won its GTS1 class and finished sixth overall in the 12 Hours of Sebring. Adam, a loyal Los Angeles Raiders football fan, added a Raiders sticker to the back window for luck.

1995 GEMBALLA CABRIOLET

Opening in 1979 as an interior and audio shop, Gemballa, in Leonberg, Germany, near Zuffenhausen, began to offer aerodynamic upgrade kits for Porsches in 1981. Within a few years, the company added mechanical modifications as well.

Uwe Gemballa's modifications range from mild to wild, starting with subtle aerodynamic chin spoilers and modest rear-brake cooling vents. At greater extremes, Gemballa creates gullwing-style doors, Plexiglas-covered headlights, and turbocharger upgrades in 50-horsepower increments from 450 to 650.

and his lieutenants forced these smaller companies to rethink their own traditional techniques or lose business to an organization more adaptable. Many suppliers became subassemblers who delivered, for example, complete rear suspension subframes on an as-needed basis, just in time for mounting onto the unibody.

On the eve of the 993 launch, Porsche was in the midst of its biggest change in its history. It also was moribund. Sales revenue through 1992–1993 totaled a perilous 1.9 billion deutsche marks, about $1.2 billion. Zuffenhausen had manufactured just 8,341 C2, C4, and Turbo models, barely 1,188 of the 968 coupes and cabriolets, and only 119 of the 928S4 models. When Wiedeking's accountants finished their sums, the company had lost 253 million deutsche marks, $160 million, a record for a fiscal year. Ferry Porsche's concerns over the 15 million–deutsche mark investment before the 901 launch surely seemed grave in 1963. However, Ulrich Bez and Arno Bohn, both now departed, had administered a 500 million–deutsche mark ($310 million) commitment to the company's new anchor product.

Porsche assembled 2,374 of the new coupes and 22 cabriolets before New Year's Day, 1994. Called the 911 Carrera in two-wheel-drive configuration, the company considered these to be 1994 model year cars for Europe. In the United States, impatient journalists and buyers got coupes and cabriolets starting in April, though Porsche badged these as 1995 S-program models for American audiences.

"That cabrio was tricky," Tony Hatter recalled. "The first cabriolet that Porsche did was the G model (the 1983 911SC). Then they used the same roof on the 964. I never liked the look of the early cabriolets. The classical 911 shape is the coupe. With the 993, we tried to get some form into the roof. It was the first time, I think, that we tackled the roof."

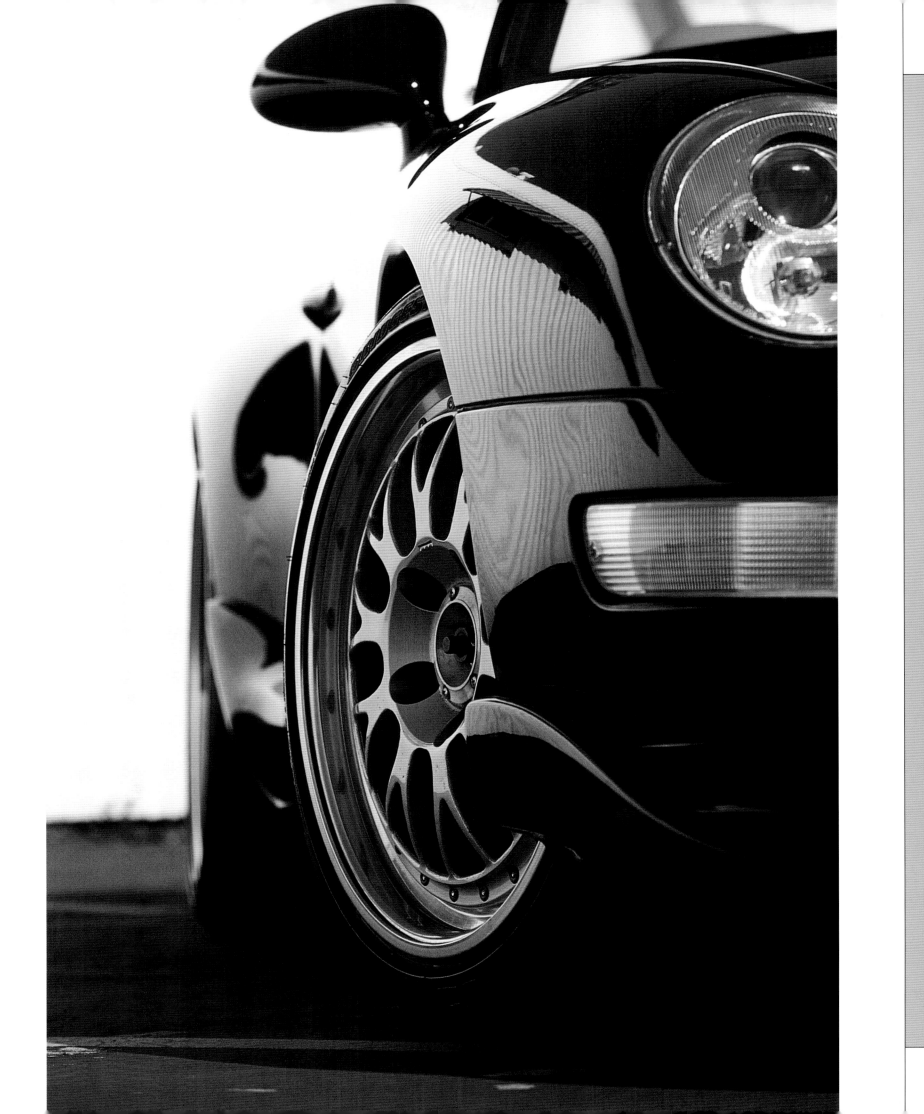

1996 911GT1/96

After McLaren's win at Le Mans in 1995 with its F1-GTR, Porsche's loyal racing customers demanded a more effective tool for competition than the heavier and less-powerful GT2s. Norbert Singer and Herbert Ampferer responded with the GT1, derived from the production 993. FIA rules required that any racer qualified for U.S. or European events must be created from a street-legal automobile that customers could purchase.

Wide mirrors on both sides scarcely provide a full rear view. Massive air-induction channels to the engine make any kind of rear window impossible. Porsche manufactured 30 customer racing versions of the car, selling for 1.58 million DM ($1 million). This copy went to Roock Racing.

Porsche won Le Mans in 1996 with one of its two factory-entered GT1 racers. That quickly inspired orders from 30 racing teams that wanted their own cars. Depending on gearing, acceleration was startling, with 0 to 100 miles per hour taking just 6.1 seconds and top speeds ranging from 280 to 350 kilometers per hour (174 to 220 miles per hour).

The much-improved Carrera 4 appeared in the midyear as a 1995 model. Those hungering for a turbocharged 911 made do with 964 carryovers through 1994 until the new 3.6-liter twin-turbo version appeared with the Carrera 4. This was no accident of timing as this new powerhouse arrived with four-wheel drive and the new six-speed transmission.

The 993 was a big success. The factory manufactured 7,865 coupes and 7,074 cabriolets as well as 100 new 305-horsepower 993 Carrera Cup cars to compete in the ongoing series in Europe and the United States. Magazine reviewers judged it was what they had hoped the 964 would be. However, the 993 was even better because, due to Bez's relentlessness and Wiedeking's watchfulness, Porsche introduced the cars at a $5,000-lower base price. By the end of 1994's fiscal year, accountants had stowed their red pencils.

On the heels of Jürgen Barth's frustrating efforts with the 964 Carrera 4 Lightweight, he and new motor-sports director Max Welti hunted for a more international form of competition than the Carrera Cups events. They created a 911S LM, based on the 964 with twin turbochargers, for Le Mans in 1993. Barth had helped establish Porsche's reputation for customer race cars: They delivered tested, proven automobiles that did not break. After an accident put the car out of the race, a French team purchased it and campaigned it vigorously through 1994 with considerable success.

One single factor helped Porsche define the car, helped it achieve success, and helped initiate a resurgent interest in Gran Turismo, GT-class racing for closed cars. Through the early 1990s, as the economy ground to a halt, the Fédération Internationale des Automobiles ended the Group C series. With just 28 cars starting at Le Mans in 1992, indications were that times would get worse before they improved for expensive prototype

This is Porsche's first mid-engine 911. In race tune, the fully water-cooled 3.2-liter flat-six develops 590 horsepower at 7,200 rpm with FIA-mandated air-intake restrictor plates. Unrestricted engines tested well above 800 brake horsepower. Engineers stuffed the turbochargers deeply into recesses ahead of the rear tires.

acers. But almost every country had its own rules for GT cars, each slightly different and rendering it a gamble to produce a car for one series or another. Jürgen Barth raised the issue with two colleagues, Patrick Peter, who organized the Tour de France, and Stéfane Ratel, owner of the Venturi company, a firm with serious racing ambitions. Together these three men created the BPR series, using the first initials of their last names. They established rules that made sense to competitors.

Porsche produced cars to meet these criteria starting with the 1993 Carrera RS 3.8, based on the 964 rear-wheel-drive platform. Engineers achieved this new designation by enlarging cylinder bore to 102 mm from 100, while holding stroke unchanged at 76.4 mm. This increased overall capacity to 3,746 cc. At 6,500 rpm, these engines, capably managed by Bosch's new Motronic 2.10 system, developed 300 brake horsepower at 6,500 rpm, and 265 ft-lb of torque at 5,250 rpm. An adjustable roll bar allowed competitors to tune the chassis for individual venues. Weissach fitted aluminum doors and front deck lids, and formed the rear deck lid and spoiler in fiberglass. Porsche charged 225,000 deutsche marks for the cars, ($140,625) and buyers in Europe could run them on the streets with optional radios and airbag, or compete with an available roll cage and fire extinguisher system. This homologation package helped legalize the real racer, the 3.8RSR, a car welcomed in BPR's GT3 and GT4 categories. The all-out machine, with no airbag or radio options, sold for 270,000 deutsche marks ($160,450) and offered center lock wheels, built-in pneumatic jacks, and supplemental brake cooling. The 3.8 engine developed, conservatively, 325 brake horsepower at 6,900 rpm. In 1993 and 1994, the RSRs proved their worth and justified their prices by taking overall victories in Spain, Belgium, and Japan, and a class victory at Le Mans in 1993, with regular class wins throughout 1994. The cars did not break.

Ferry Porsche's delight here is obvious. This was his first look at the interior of the 911GT1/96, the car that represented Porsche's return to serious endurance racing. *Porsche Archives*

For street racers seeking staggering performance, Porsche waited until mid-model year 1995 to introduce its next 993 Turbo. With the 959, Porsche set a precedent, later loosely enforced, that any series production model providing more than 400 horsepower would be all-wheel drive. With 408 brake horsepower coupled to front-driven wheels as well as the adapted Weissach-rear axle suspension, these 3.6-liter automobiles provided memorable performance and handling. Magazines typically reached 100 kilometers per hour (62 miles per hour) in 4.4 seconds and the turbos topped out at 290 kilometers (180 miles) per hour. Porsche produced 2,457 during 1995 (not including 9 early production cars done before the Christmas holidays in 1994). These sold for 212,040 deutsche marks ($151,000) in Germany but only $99,000 in the United States.

Competition at this extreme of the automotive spectrum had intensified in 1995. Aston Martin's $240,000 Virage still boasted 325 brake horsepower and a top speed near 180 miles (290 kilometers) per hour. BMW's 850CSi could squeeze smaller adults behind the driver and passenger, it delivered 340 brake horsepower for $101,000 in the United States, and BMW chose to speed-govern it to a relatively sedate 155 miles (250 kilometers) per hour. Ferrari's new F355 delivered 375 brake horsepower at 8,250 rpm from a 3.4-liter V-8. The United States price was $127,185. But Ferrari's bench marker was its outrageous F50, boasting 517 brake horsepower from 4.6 liters. It advertised a top speed in excess of 200 miles per hour (320 kilometers per hour) and commanded a price tag in the United States above $480,000. Lamborghini's exotic Diablo, with 485 horsepower since 1991, soldiered on at a $250,000-suggested retail price and a 185-mile-per-hour (nearly 300 kilometers per hour) top speed, while offering an optional rear wing for another $5,000. (That reduced

speed by 5 miles per hour but turned heads rapidly.) Mercedes-Benz had introduced its V-12-engined 600SL in 1993. This 6-liter engine delivered 389 horsepower in a sleekly stylish body for $120,000. The troubled economy of 1991 and 1992 was robust by 1995.

There is a figure of speech that applies more accurately to a whispered challenge in novelist W. P. Kinsella's famous baseball fantasy, *Shoeless Joe*, and a film called *Field of Dreams*. It applies to Porsche:

"If you build it, they will come." Jürgen Barth, Roland Kussmaul, and others within the Customer Sports Department at Weissach knew that Porsche's 959 had proved that customers would ante up as needed for Peter Falk's agility and Herbert Ampferer's engines. As a result, the 1994 911S LM quickly begat a new series, the GT2, configured to fit within the Barth/Peter/Ratel series category. BPR rules required manufacturers to produce 25 cars in each year they hoped to compete. Customer Sports quickly sold 45 of the 993 GT2s before introduction, following that with 43 in 1995 and 14 in 1996. Of these, Weissach equipped 21 for road use.

Aluminum doors and front deck lids, paper-thin side and rear windows, and a ruthless removal of everything not needed for racing from the interior and elsewhere, brought the car's weight down to 1,112 kilograms (2,447 pounds) for racing. Road car customers got a 1,295-kilogram (2,850-pound) version and had to get by with 430 brake horsepower for their 276,000 deutsche marks, or $200,000. Racers invested 248,500 deutsche marks ($180,000) on a no-frills model, and got 480 brake horsepower. Fully optioned, race-equipped GT2s priced out nearer 335,000 deutsche marks, about $242,600.

To reassert its road-going benchmark, Porsche introduced a stronger Turbo S in 1997. With 430 brake horsepower advertised, the company claimed it would reach 300 kilometers per hour, or 188 miles per hour. In Germany, the S sold for 235,000 deutsche marks, or $130,000. When U.S. buyers could get them in 1998, Porsche reversed previous practices so Americans paid $155,000 for the exclusive model, limited Porsche claimed, to just 199 cars.

Then, just when buyers could imagine no more, Kussmaul and Customer Sports raised the bar, issuing 25 GT2s for 1998 with electronics devised from its Formula One effort with Techniques Avant Garde (TAG). This pushed engine output to 450 brake horsepower at 6,000 rpm with 430 ft-lb of torque in 4,500 rpm. Customers could order airbags, electric windows, and air conditioning, but in a repudiation of earlier policy, they could not get all-wheel drive, as this feature did not appear in its homologation papers.

As its category name implies, GT2 was not the premier classification on BPR's competition program. That was GT1. In this group Porsche found daunting challenges from former Formula One ally, McLaren's Gordon Murray with his carbon-fiber-chassis F1-GTRs (which had won Le Mans in June 1995), and from perpetual competitor Ferrari, with its new V-12-engined 333SPs. While Porsche had a solid lock on GT2 and GT3 class wins, those who had been around in the days of Peter Schutz remembered his dictum in 1980: "We won't go anywhere that we do not intend to win outright."

Rules for GT1 required the manufacturer to offer road versions for sale, though it seemed a single issue would do. Norbert Singer knew the 911GT2 needed better aerodynamics, greater downforce, and more horsepower to compete. Rules mandated a flat bottom from the nose of the car to the rear axle. From there back, the flat base could rise to form one or more venturi to help hold the car down (but that would not run full-length providing vacuum-cleaner like suction). There was one way Singer and Herbert Ampferer figured this could work. They had to mount the engine backward ahead of the rear axle. GT1 could use longer wheelbases, and Singer stretched the GT2's from 89.4 inches (2,270 mm) to 98.4 inches (2,499 mm).

1996 911GT1/96 ROAD VERSION
When the company rolled out "customer" GT1 models, it required owners to take Porsche-supervised driving instruction before delivering the vehicles. At one of the car's introductions, building illumination and the headlights of another car transformed the GT1 into an earthbound spaceship. *Porsche Archives*

1997 911GT1/97 ROAD VERSION

To make the GT1 legal as a race car, Porsche had to produce road-going versions that customers could purchase. Designer Tony Hatter redid his front fenders and doors for the 1997 versions. This road car streaked past a field of wild mustard. *Porsche Archives*

1997 CARRERA S

The VarioRam induction system first introduced in racing became standard in 1996 and continued on from there with the 3.6-liter flat-six. The engine now develops 285 brake horsepower at 6,300 rpm. The wider-body S variants sacrificed some top-speed potential due to slight additional wind resistance from the wider rear fenders.

Engineer Horst Reitter, working with Singer, developed package specifications that included all the necessary mechanicals. Reitter also called for incorporating the production car's front end; it had passed both U.S. and German crash tests, necessary for the single road car's homologation. Using the production front end allowed Weissach to fit the 993 instrument panel as well. The supervisory board already had given the project a provisional okay, but one condition of final approval was clear: The car had to be "identifiable as a 911 at first glance."

"Initially, my job was to keep the cars looking like 911 Porsches," Tony Hatter recalled. "With Norbert Singer and his team, looking back now, it was a great time. But it was a very intense few years, those GT1 years.

"Mr. Singer was very disappointed when he found out that he had to work with the design department. Disappointment is the wrong word," Hatter continued, "but respect for the designers, at least initially, was not there. But then he found out that we worked with the newest technology in the automotive world, which the racing department didn't have. We could build cars digitally. We offered him a system where he could create shapes and forms and cars, and mill them out in zero time.

"He was very skeptical at first. He's a man with a lot of hands-on experience, and here, he couldn't touch anything. He couldn't do anything. He'd walk away. I'd do something on the screen while he was away."

Hatter lengthened the 993 and widened it to accommodate racing tires. Computer aided systems made this easier, quicker, and smarter than Singer's collaboration with Dick Soderberg on the 1978 935/78 Moby Dick. The board gave the go-ahead in late July 1995. It was Porsche's first mid-engined 911, targeted at mid-engine cars from McLaren, Ferrari, Nissan, Toyota, and others.

Between July and the following January, few individuals in the competition department or in Tony Hatter's design studio got much sleep. To fit the production nose over a racing suspension required Horst Reitter to modify his ideas. Herbert Ampferer revised the engines that had propelled the 962 coupes to victories throughout 1994. He used their 95-mm bore (shared with the 959) with 74.4-mm stroke for a 3,164-cc engine. He water-cooled the entire package, going the next step beyond both 959s and 962s, with only their water-cooled heads. Porsche completed a road-going version first for homologation requirements fitted with a tame 3.3-liter Carrera engine tuned to develop 300 brake horsepower. Because it had the production instrument panel, it and the race cars all started similarly to any 911, with a key on the left of the steering wheel.

Work advanced on the race cars. Jürgen Barth drove the first one on March 14. Through the rest of the month, Weissach mechanics worked frantically. That was when Tony Hatter got another phone call.

"It was the roll-out of the GT1 car," he explained. "I think it was Roland Kussmaul, and we pushed the car out at about 11 o'clock one cold night. We were getting the car ready for [the April trials at] Le Mans. It was the first time out of the workshops for that one, as it had just been put together. Kussmaul started it up and drove it out. Everybody ran out behind. It was freezing cold. And Kussmaul drove it off into the distance. You could hear it moving around the track. He brought it back in again to where we all were standing.

"They had gotten some lights out there, ready for it. Kussmaul turned it off and there was smoke coming from everywhere. It was absolutely surreal. They took off the front and rear, checked everything out. Roland was still sitting in there. They saw that everything was okay, put it all back together again, and sent him out."

1997 TURBO S

This variation started life in Europe as a Turbo model with a tuning kit. The kit increased output to 430 brake horsepower at 5,750 rpm. For home markets, Porsche offered it through Porsche *Exclusiv*. U.S. customers acquired them through Porsche Cars North America dealers as the Turbo S.

The viscous coupling driving the front axle allowed Porsche engineers to turbocharge the C4 all-wheel-drive chassis. This essentially reincarnated the road-going capabilities of the 959 from a decade before at a much lower price.

Subtle air intakes in the rear fenders and rear wing bring additional air into the engine compartment, helping to eke out an extra 16 horsepower. The factory announced the car's top speed at 300 kilometers per hour (186 miles per hour).

"The next time he came past, the car made this really unearthly 'woooouuuuuum' sound. I stood there thinking, Jesus Christ! I had something to do with this car. It was utterly unreal, like a close encounter of the third kind."

In typical Norbert Singer fashion, he and his staff exhaustively tested the new car, running more than 1,200 miles in one five-day test alone. When chassis 001 and 002 reached Le Mans in June, Porsche was ready. At the checkered flag, chassis 002, with Bob Wollek, Thierry Boutsen, and Hans Stuck sharing driving duties, had finished second overall and first in GT1 class, behind Reinhold Joest, driving a Porsche-engined open sports racer.

"Less than 48 hours after Le Mans," Jürgen Barth recalled, "we had gotten 10 calls, orders for street cars. By Friday, we had close to 40 orders and they only slowed down when we told them they got a car with 300 horsepower, not the Le Mans engine!"

Weighing just 2,328 pounds (1,058 kilograms) and running with 600 brake horsepower, the race car's acceleration was astonishing. From a standstill it reached 130 miles per hour (210 kilometers per hour) in 9.8 seconds, using gearing for a top speed of 174 miles (280 kilometers) per hour. Longer Le Mans ratios allowed top speeds near 235 miles per hour, or 375 kilometers per hour.

In each of the remaining three BPR events, in England at Brands Hatch, in Belgium at Spa, and in China at Zuhaï, one or the other car won outright. By year end, Weissach got to work manufacturing to fill the almost-30 solid orders for road and racing versions of the car known as GT1/96. Zuffenhausen set a price of $1,000,000, just shy of 1.6 million deutsche marks. Road cars got 544-brake horsepower engines, not the Carrera engines, and sold for about $890,000, nearly 1.4 million deutsche marks. As Paul Frère wrote in *Road & Track*, private individuals will buy the GT1 "for the pleasure of driving the closest possible thing to a full-blooded, very high performance racing car."

Through 1996, more mundane series production T-Program 993 road cars offered buyers 285 brake horsepower at 6,100 rpm. This increase in output, from 272 in 1995, resulted from Porsche's introduction of its

Above: Any surface that wasn't leather got covered in carbon fiber. White-faced instruments were part of the series specifications. PCNA limited production for U.S. customers to just 199 cars.

Above, left: Cars sold at the factory for 235,000 DM, while PCNA's dealers charged $155,000 for high-speed exclusivity. At 60 percent of the price of a 959 and providing full United States safety and emissions certification from the start—as well as performance that matched the earlier supercar—this Turbo S was a relative bargain.

1997 CARRERA TARGA

Webasto International, an outside steel and roof-system supplier headquartered in Munich, manufactured and assembled the entire roof, delivering it to Zuffenhausen assembly for installation on top of a 993 reinforced cabriolet body. The panel over the driver and passenger slides back and beneath the rear window. A retractable shade blocks direct sunlight on hot days.

Harm Lagaay had conceived the idea of a sliding roof while he was a staff stylist designing the 924 in the mid-1970s. Technology wasn't ready at the time, and projected costs made it too expensive. But the timing was right by the early 1990s.

remarkable VarioRam intake system that first appeared on the 1995 European-market-only Carrera RS and Club Sport models. This system incorporated two intake pipes for every cylinder. The longer one, tuned for maximum midrange torque, fed fuel and air until the shorter one opened at about 4,400 rpm. Exposed by a sliding sleeve, this pipe affected the horsepower developed at medium and higher engine speeds. As if that were not sophisticated enough, the system opened again at about 5,800 rpm to provide a large cross tube for the highest engine ranges. This sophisticated system not only evened out delivery of horsepower and torque, it also added measurably to the driver's listening enjoyment as engine tones changed in each new induction path.

Tony Hatter and design chief Harm Lagaay created a new Targa using an innovative sliding glass roof that opened a large portion of the cabin to the skies. Lagaay had developed this idea in 1977 for as part of the 924 concepts he designed. The 993 configuration followed Wendelin Wiedeking's practice in which outside suppliers delivered subassemblies ready for installation. Zuffenhausen assemblers fitted the roof system onto specially reinforced cabriolet bodies and welded side rails and front and rear mounts into place.

Porsche's increasing fiscal well-being enabled the company to expand a practice it understood well now, offering special bodies for special interests. The return of the Turbo and designer Tony Hatter's gently exaggerated shapes found a huge appeal among the company's product planners. They mated the Turbo body,

its brakes and large wheels, to Porsche's all-wheel-drive chassis with the normally aspirated engine as the new Carrera 4S, introducing it in 1995 as a 1996 model. World-market cars also used Turbo springs and shock absorbers although Weissach engineers, recognizing the poorer condition of U.S. roads, fitted softer suspensions for American buyers. For 1997, Porsche offered the rear-wheel drive in the Turbo-Look body as well, called the Carrera S.

In the rarified stratosphere in which Porsche GT1 road cars and racers operated, the company found itself in an unexpected crossfire. McLaren naturally had improved its F1-GTR as well as its own million-dollar, three-seater road car. Now, however, neighboring Mercedes-Benz made Barth and Singer's successful GT1s

With each passing year of the 993 series, Porsche introduces additional interesting and exciting models. This all-glass-roof Targa initially appeared in 1996. Styling chief Harm Lagaay derived its roofline from Steve Murkett's controversial Panamericana show car created for Ferry Porsche's 80th birthday.

1998 CARRERA S

Both Carrera S two-wheel-drive models and the C4S all-wheel-drive version could be ordered with or without the Turbo rear wing. The wider Turbo body and running gear greatly improve handling, with or without the wing. As with standard C2 and C4 bodies, at higher speeds the retractable spoiler emerges from the rear deck.

their own target for the 1997 racing season. M-B announced plans to compete in the GT series, then annexed by the FIA as an 11-race event under its sanction and incorporated onto its calendar. Mercedes unveiled its V-12 6-liter CLK-GTR. Whatever Wendelin Wiedeking's plans had been for the company's GT1 prior to Mercedes' announcement, he supported Norbert Singer and Horst Marchart. Having sold 30 cars to customers, Porsche could not now abandon them. As Singer sought to develop a competitive evolution, he and Tony Hatter made enough changes that they had to create a new road car as well. This would pick up styling cues of the new production models nearing completion in the design department. Porsche committed to the full 11-race FIA series.

The GT1s did not distinguish themselves through 1997 against the Mercedes-Benz. Singer, Barth, and their customers knew what it would take to get back into the game: a new chassis of carbon-fiber that would save the extra 200 pounds (90 kilograms) which everyone felt the car had to shed. Wiedeking's cost-saving efforts

coalesced, benefiting a series production run of 993s that captured customers' imagination. The company and its chief executive were in a position to renew the Porsche's commitment to customer racers.

There would be a GT1/98. With support from the company's highest officials, Norbert Singer and Tony Hatter, Horst Reitter, and Herbert Ampferer, and dozens of other engineers and mechanics had a new assignment.

"While all the guys were working through all the new production car challenges," Tony Hatter explained with a laugh, "I got lost in the racing department with various hybrids based on the 993. First, this was based on the 993, and then, still based on the 993, but with the new headlights. It was a bit of a mess." He laughed as he recalled some of the efforts. "But those were the things we had to work with.

"And in the end, of course, we made one car without anything to do with a 911, and we still stuck the new headlights on it. Strange when you think about it." ▦

As the 993 series drew to a close, Porsche had a full range of 911 models on the road. The company used the series to establish a pattern of new developments and product introductions that would continue with the coming generations of 996 and 997 models.

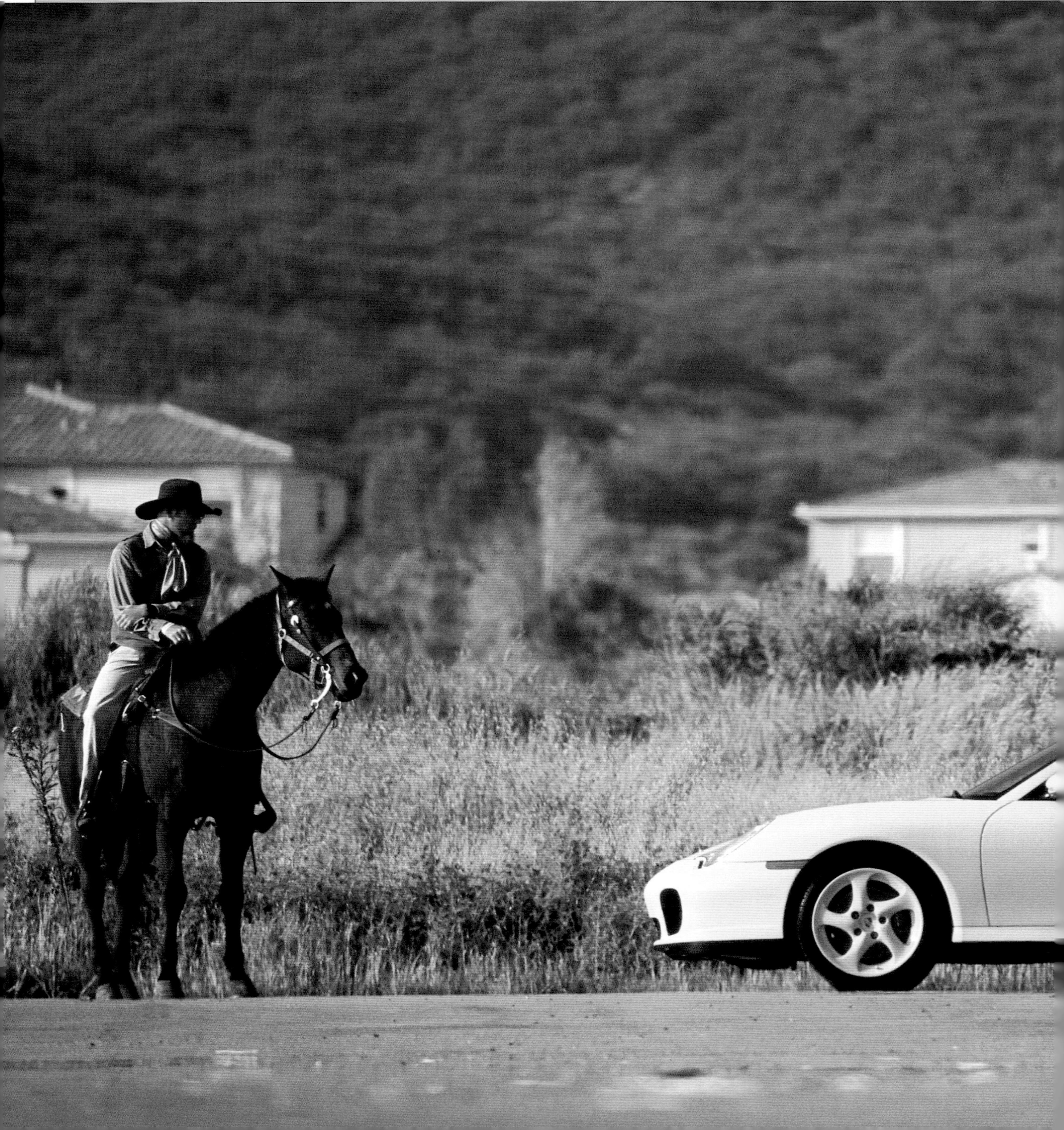

CHAPTER EIGHT

PORSCHE'S FIFTH GENERATION— THE 996 1999 – 2004

"This magic concept came
of making two cars with one face.
And, if you're a designer, when you hear that
for the first time, your heart stops."

Harm Lagaay, January 2005

"The 993 was hardly finished and we had a new mission."
Harm Lagaay raised his eyebrows as he recalled the inception of
another new car in 1991. This was still three years before the
"new Model 993" even would be introduced. "And it had a very
short life time. People don't realize that. They think, 'Oh, the 993;
it was there for 10 years!' Not true. Four. Four very short years. It
wasn't even that successful.

"If you look at the sales figures," he continued, "it went up, and
then whoop, back down again. The reason was that it obviously
captivated the right people. They looked at it and said 'Ahhh, this
is exactly what I want. A little improvement. But not too much.'

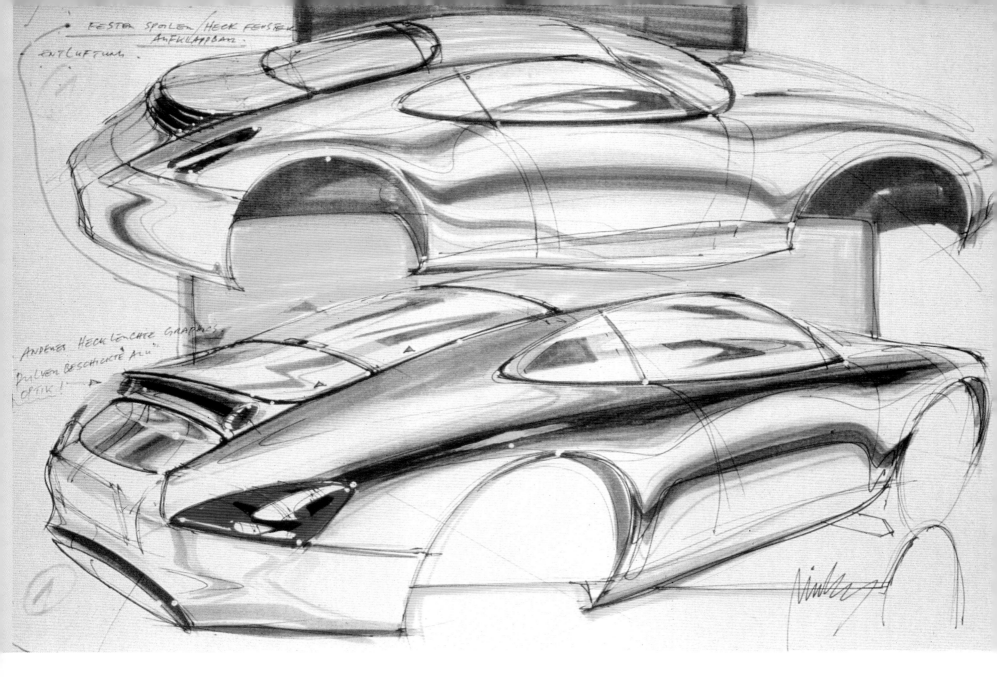

Pinky Lai worked alongside Grant Larson as they developed the bodies for both the 996 and the 986 (Boxster). *Porsche Archives*

Opposite: PINKY LAI'S 996 REAR DESIGN Once Porsche launched the Boxster to great acclaim at the Detroit International Auto Show, design chief Harm Lagaay got styling additional resources; Pinky Lai's sketch of the 996 rear view showed a new retractable rear wing. *Porsche Archives*

"We had to enlarge the studios," Harm Lagaay explained, "because we had to have a pair of cars together all the time. A Boxster and a 911 next to each other. One proposal, one team, two cars. And in the next studio, another proposal, two cars side by side. And the next. Always the pair, side by side. Because if you change something on one, you have to change it on the other. Because the front ends are the same and the doors are where the rear end meets the front. If you change the design of the 911 and the Boxster is in the other studio, you can't just say, 'Oh well, that's what they're doing but I'll do this.' No! You have two designers and all the time they have to do teamwork. Because on the Boxster the doors resolve one problem and on the 911 it is another way."

The chief designer's job has two important facets. One is determining the right people for the right job. Each of Lagaay's staff had strengths and weaknesses, and he asked himself where to put them and how best to structure the teams that would compete for the final design. The second element is that the boss must know

"This magic concept came
of making two cars with one face.
And, if you're a designer, when you hear that
for the first time, your heart stops."

Harm Lagaay, January 2005

"The 993 was hardly finished and we had a new mission."
Harm Lagaay raised his eyebrows as he recalled the inception of
another new car in 1991. This was still three years before the
"new Model 993" even would be introduced. "And it had a very
short life time. People don't realize that. They think, 'Oh, the 993;
it was there for 10 years!' Not true. Four. Four very short years. It
wasn't even that successful.

"If you look at the sales figures," he continued, "it went up, and
then whoop, back down again. The reason was that it obviously
captivated the right people. They looked at it and said 'Ahhh, this
is exactly what I want. A little improvement. But not too much.'

Previous pages: Eighteen-inch wheels beneath those carbon-fiber fenders allowed Kussmaul to fit enormous 380-mm (14.96-inch) diameter front-brake rotors, while he used 355s (13.97 inches) in the rear. RSR models weigh about 1,110 kilograms (2,442 pounds).

They bought it. But then you can't rely only on that category of Porsche buyers, and the company realized that. So that's where the big changes came from.

"And the 996 was just a result of many changes that came before. Before this car, we did a couple of things, explored other possibilities. Till this magic concept came of making two cars with one face, with one front end.

"That is, for a designer . . . if you hear it for the first time, your heart stops. You think, 'Oh, ohhhh, NO!' You get a shock and you think, 'No, that cannot work!' And it certainly wasn't easy." Lagaay paused. His eyes appeared focused far beyond the walls of his shop. "It was a struggle . . . . It was very difficult.

"There is no equal in design and car layout strategy to what we did with the Boxster and the 911. No one else in automotive history, not even today, has performed that concept. It is a typical Porsche solution. Pragmatic. Functional. You get two different characters with a reasonable amount of research and development investment, and you get two cars."

Shortly after Ulrich Bez left in January 1991, Porsche's supervisory board put to death the 989 four-door that he had adopted and championed. Arno Bohn, in charge of the company and the other four-door cheerleader, quickly changed course. The sedan had acknowledged that Porsche's entire lineup was dated and going obsolete. But its development costs and the fact that the dealer network hadn't embraced it cast its fate. The 968, as a third generation 924, had been around 15 years, as had the luxurious but expensive and unpopular 928. The 993 advancing through production

FIRST PROTOTYPE 996

Designer Pinky Lai labored on his drawing board and in a wind tunnel to create a car body without a wing because initial budget limitations prohibited a movable rear spoiler on the 996. Meanwhile, engineering simply added a 930 Turbo wing and some other black bodywork onto their first mechanical prototype of the water-cooled 911 in September 1994. *Porsche Archives*

development would push the company forward, reminding customers, enthusiasts, racers, and journalists that Porsche was not, once again, nearly dead. However, the variability of international currency exchange and world politics had priced the 911 beyond the reach of many new customers. Horst Marchart, Bez's successor, knew that Porsche needed a new entry-level car, and he needed a new 911. Both cars had to be affordable to manufacture and to purchase.

For decades, many of Porsche's competitors had projected a family "face" on their vehicles. Aston Martins carried over the scalloped-corner rectangular grille that David Brown introduced on the DB3 in 1957 and DB4 in 1958. Jaguar's 1950s vertical oval subsided into a horizontal with the 1963 XK-E. This motif, with and without its chrome waterfall, carried on into its mid-1990s models. Pininfarina dictated the Ferrari's signature appearance so the company's wedged F40 and F50 models advanced a design heritage. Honda, Toyota, and Nissan each had established a familiar face and profile. Both BMW and Mercedes-Benz

had forged unmistakable identities. But no one yet had mounted the same front end, the same face, on two separate models.

This offered obvious production economies. The cars would share headlights, fog lamps, and turn signals. Wiring harnesses designed for one car would service the other. Brake cooling ducts would be interchangeable. But those were small considerations. The enormous cost of crash safety and testing could be halved. This was Marchart's concept in October 1991 for corporate identity and frugality. In late February 1992, the board approved the idea.

In March 1996, Porsche's test drivers took 996 prototype number 1-14.9 to Vizzola, Italy, for wet-track road-holding development and evaluation. They painted the body black as it grew closer to production shapes and decked it with body-disguise cladding. *Porsche Archives*

FESTER SPOILER / HECK FENSER
ANFKLAPPBAR
ENTLUFTUNG

ANDERES HECKLENCHTE GRAPHIC'S
Pulver Beschichte Alu
OPTIK!

Pinky Lai worked alongside Grant Larson as they developed the bodies for both the 996 and the 986 (Boxster). *Porsche Archives*

Opposite: PINKY LAI'S 996 REAR DESIGN Once Porsche launched the Boxster to great acclaim at the Detroit International Auto Show, design chief Harm Lagaay got styling additional resources; Pinky Lai's sketch of the 996 rear view showed a new retractable rear wing. *Porsche Archives*

"We had to enlarge the studios," Harm Lagaay explained, "because we had to have a pair of cars together all the time. A Boxster and a 911 next to each other. One proposal, one team, two cars. And in the next studio, another proposal, two cars side by side. And the next. Always the pair, side by side. Because if you change something on one, you have to change it on the other. Because the front ends are the same and the doors are where the rear end meets the front. If you change the design of the 911 and the Boxster is in the other studio, you can't just say, 'Oh well, that's what they're doing but I'll do this.' No! You have two designers and all the time they have to do teamwork. Because on the Boxster the doors resolve one problem and on the 911 it is another way."

The chief designer's job has two important facets. One is determining the right people for the right job. Each of Lagaay's staff had strengths and weaknesses, and he asked himself where to put them and how best to structure the teams that would compete for the final design. The second element is that the boss must know

2000 CARRERA CABRIOLET

The 996 coupes first appeared in Europe as 1998 models and in the U.S. as 1999s. It had been a challenging development process incorporating a new fully water-cooled, 3.4-liter, 300–brake horsepower flat-six engine, along with a new body, suspension, and running gear. Cabriolets debuted worldwide as 1999 models.

what he wants. From Erwin Komenda through Butzi Porsche and Tony Lapine to Harm Lagaay, the job requires the manager to understand their designers' proposals, their vision, and to help them execute it. Without playing favorites, he helps their colleagues as well so each proposal reaches the same level. At some point, the chief designer sets these proposals on a stage, introduces them to the board, and finally says, "But my choice is that one."

Lagaay made that choice, selecting and recommending the work of Pinky Lai on the new 996 and Grant Larson who had shared the studio and concept on the 986 Boxster.

"I was not the only guy who worked on the 996," Pinky Lai said. "It was a really big team. Everybody was asked to get into the idea making. It was not just a new engine, not just a new package. It was a new ball game.

"Every possible worst case happened that year," he explained. "Sales were lowest that year [1992]. Personnel reduction cut the workforce, even in the studio. Budget restrictions were extremely tight. We were not allowed to put a moving spoiler on this car. We had a very high aerodynamic target to achieve, but we are not supposed to use a moving spoiler.

"Everybody knows a little bit about car silhouettes, what the rear end must be like if you want a certain downforce. You have to have a tail that is really up there. We spent thousands of hours in the wind tunnel. And still we couldn't achieve any kind of side silhouette that was recognizable as, or that you could call anything close to, a 911. It was like everybody tried to stay away from that kind of challenge."

Porsche lengthened the wheelbase 81 mm (3.2 inches) to 2,350 mm (92.5 inches). Because Porsche developed this new 911/996 and the 986 Boxster simultaneously and side-by-side, both cars share a MacPherson strut front suspension system. The new 911 got a new Getrag six-speed manual or a Tiptronic five-speed automatic transmission.

2001 996 TURBO

Introduced in Europe as a 2000 model, North American customers got the new Twin-Turbo as a 2001 model. It uses a water-cooled version of the 3.6-liter engine derived from the 1998 Le Mans—winning GT1.

Grant Larson, who designed the 986 Boxster alongside Lai as part of the winning design team, added his own thoughts.

"I did not work on the 911. I was working on the Boxster. It was a parallel thing. That was a tough battle. It was all about cost, all cost-intensive. Porsche wasn't particularly healthy at that time and the 'no-move-able-spoiler' had to do with reducing these costs and simplifying things. But this low back-end just wasn't going to be aerodynamically efficient."

Porsche's 1955 550-Spyder and its 1960 RS60 racers inspired Larson's work on the 986 Boxster. In June 1992, Lagaay proposed building Larson's concept for the January 1993 Detroit International Auto Show. Bohn and the board gave the go-ahead. The car was one of the hits of the show. The reaction from journalists and the public had huge impact on the design studio where Pinky Lai labored to force aerodynamics onto the 911 without making it appear as though it had slipped on a bustle. The Detroit show also introduced Porsche's new boss, Wendelin Wiedeking, who shared in the limelight just as his own ideas were reaching designers, engineers, suppliers, and customers.

"We were just about to scrap the whole model, very close to that point." Pinky Lai remembered. "We could not make anything work. At the same time, the only good thing we experienced was the launching of the Boxster show car. That really gave us one shot of revitalizing the morale and our motivation. 'Hey, something is happening at the show in Detroit!'

"We were doing a lot of back-and-forth long distance telephoning. Harm was at the show and I was in the studio working with Eberhard Brose, my modeler.

"'We really have to break the barrier,' I said. 'Forget about the cost issues; go for elegance, for the coke-bottle shape.'

"Before the Boxster show car, the body sides pitched straight forward, almost too traditional, like a traditional 911 door section. And right after the market reaction to the Boxster, that really was where the so-called 'little revolution' started. We started breaking all the rules.

"I asked Harm to give us another couple of days before we scrapped the design. We had a full-size clay model and we'd been going in and out of the wind tunnel just because of the spoiler business. At the end of the second day, I came up with a half of a moving 'lip'. Just one of the grilles in the engine cover, the very last end, in fact.

With 415 horsepower on tap and all-wheel drive to deliver that potential to the pavement, Porsche re-engineered the front-drive viscous-clutch system. Relocating it to the front differential allowed engineers to develop a Tiptronic S transmission capable of the torque and horsepower. Porsche Stability Management, PSM, a blend of traction control and anti-lock brakes, is standard equipment.

The Turbo body is typically wider than the normally aspirated models. In this case, styling and engineering add an extra 65 mm (2.6 inches) at the rear to accommodate 295/30ZR18 tires, while the front runs on 225/40ZR18s. The six-speed manual Getrag gearbox is actuated by a cable linkage.

2002 CARRERA

Porsche stylist Pinky Lai, who had spent months in the wind tunnel at the beginning of 996 design, returned to fine-tune his work for the 2002 facelift. He slightly reshaped the front wheel arches and added small flexible spoilers in front of the front tires, which reduced lift 25 percent in front and 40 percent in the rear.

"We ran a couple of tests in the wind tunnel and it really brought us closer to the aerodynamic target. So we called a meeting of the Big Platform board. They were watching over all the finances and technical matters. We said, 'There's no way we can come up with a decent rear end for the new 911 if we don't get some extra money to invest in that small moving lip there.'

"They gave us just a little finger! We put a whole arm on it, a whole moving spoiler. And we were back in business again. Up till then, it was really sleepless nights the whole time!"

One of the greatest front design influences also was one of the car's largest engineering challenges: the transition from air-cooled engines to water cooling. The 911 now needed radiators. Horst Marchart's concept of two cars with one face embraced two model lines with one engine family.

"Water cooling allowed us to get higher performance because of the better cooling of the cylinder head," Stefan Knirsch explained. Knirsch joined Porsche in 1996, as these new engines were in preproduction phases. He was the troubleshooter at the start of production for both Boxster and the 996. "The robustness of these heads against knocking is much better, so our ignition angle is earlier. This helped in fuel economy, and it helped power output.

"The only drawback was additional mass," he added, "the 20 liters of water and all the parts. But it made sense for a sports car with a high power output and good fuel consumption. You need low temperatures of the components, of the cylinder head, and of the block to get a high output and good fuel economy." Pinky Lai's 996 body forms had elevated the tail to try to achieve aerodynamic efficiency. This provided the engine engineers additional space to house their somewhat larger engine.

The new engine, with 96-mm bore and 78-mm stroke, displaced a total of 3,387 cc. No longer needing cooling fins made four-valve cylinder heads more easily achievable, so the design engineers returned to a single spark plug for ignition. Also gone was the 911's long devotion to dry-sump lubrication as the new engine, destined for road use only, did not need it, nor was Marchart willing to carry over the leaks the system permitted. The new engine developed 296 brake horsepower at 6,800 rpm and 258 ft-lb of torque at 4,600 rpm. Engineers tuned intake and exhaust manifolds not only for flow efficiency but for the sound they produced as well. As Karl Ludvigsen reported, "Acoustics contribute substantially to the positioning of the car in the market, to product identity, and to customer acceptance." Water cooling, while further quieting the mechanical noises of the engine, improved heating and defrosting capabilities.

Porsche and Getrag designed a new six-speed transmission to handle not only the new 996's power but much more, a sensible move considering the variations that grew from this introductory model. The Tiptronic S transmission offered five speeds.

Through 1993 and 1994, as Wendelin Wiedeking implemented *kaizen* and *shin-gujutsu* policies, factory productivity increased, costs dropped, profits increased, and confidence in Porsche's future grew. Assembly-line personnel, formerly masters of their own trade, moved beyond past jacks-of-all-trades status to become masters of many disciplines in assembling the cars. Some 18 months before 996 production started, Zuffenhausen began assembling the new cars between regular runs of 993s whose demand was tapering off. Wiedeking accepted that manufacturing could slow now so that it would not when sales demand required full speed.

The Carrera engine grew from 3.4 liters to 3.6 liters. Engineers lengthened the stroke to 82.2 mm, while leaving the bore unchanged at 96.0. Utilizing the new VarioCam Plus valve system, these improvements increased horsepower from 300 to 320 at 6,800 rpm.

The change from rod-activated gear change to the new cable-actuated shift linkage results in shorter throws and easier shifting. The 2002 models also incorporate the onboard computer with LCD display.

Coupe production commenced in early fall 1997 as a 1998 model for Europe with cabrios beginning slightly later. This way workers streamlined procedures on one car at a time. Porsche delayed U.S. launch to mid-April 1998 and PCNA introduced both models together. The company promoted the new model throughout Europe and the United States, where owners of 928s received invitations to come test-drive "the valid alternative" to their car. Marketing urged 968 owners to "move up to the 996." BMW and Mercedes-Benz customers who had visited dealer showrooms but not bought a 993 found brochures in their mailboxes that talked about the "new size" Porsche 911 Carrera.

Porsche had added 3.2 inches, or 81.3 mm, to the wheelbase, at 92.6 inches or 2,352 mm. Overall length stretched 6.8 inches (173 mm) to 174.5 inches or 4,432 mm. Engineers had expanded front and rear wheel track by nearly 2 inches, about 50 mm, and the body grew an inch (25.4 mm) wider, to 69.5 inches, or 1,765 mm, overall. In a nod to owners and customers who had widened as well, this new car offered 1.2 inches (30.5 mm) more front seating width as well. Interior storage space increased by 14 percent, and the front trunk gained 6 percent more capacity.

"The 996," project manager Bernd Kahnau recalled several years later, "was the car for everyone who wanted to drive a sports car but who didn't always want to hear every sports car noise. We went a long way in that direction."

Porsche took a gamble with its Boxster and 996. Giving the two cars the same front end validated Horst Marchart's engineering, design, and financial estimates. Yet the timing of the introductions broadcast an unintended message to many enthusiasts and journalists. The 996 was the company's new premier product but it appeared a knockoff of the entry-level car's appearance. Writers and reviewers lambasted it as a car for Mattel's Barbie doll, labeling it the awkward offspring of the Boxster and the discontinued 928. One comment that may have stung came from the father of the 911's *formsprache*, form language, Butzi Porsche himself, when he declared that the shape of the new headlights was "incomprehensible." In reality, they were another economic solution.

"Having round headlamps was not being typically Porsche any more," Harm Lagaay explained. "I told the board of directors that we cannot distinguish ourselves anymore just with our headlamp design. Those days are over. We have to have the overall sculpture of the car much more as an identity than just a couple of headlamps, and so having the module was a typical Porsche decision. They said, we need to be able to mount the headlamp in 20 seconds. Push it in, fix it in place. Just 20 seconds for the complete installation. So we came up with these five functions in one piece: Main beam, dipped beam, fog lamp, turn signal, light washer. It was a typical business decision.

"Everybody loved us in the production plants. The comptroller loved us. The engineers loved it," Lagaay continued. "Only the people who thought it looked too milky did not love it. Today, lights function at the back

The mid-project-run facelift gave the 996s new headlights similar to those that Pinky Lai designed for the 2000/2001 Turbos. Front air intakes increase airflow to the cooling radiators by 15 percent. The bi-xenon headlights, formerly standard on the Turbo, now appear on the Carrera models as well.

Racing engineer Roland Kussmaul began developing the GT3R models in the fall of 1998 as soon as GT3 production models were approved. The RS model uses carbon-fiber body panels for doors, hood, front and rear deck lids, and fenders. The large rear wing is adjustable.

With about 450 horsepower available at 8,200 rpm, the cars are capable of 320 kilometers per hour (200 miles per hour) with the proper gearing. The slippery body shape really helps to reach and maintain those speeds. With no turbochargers to help muffle engine noise, Roland Kussmaul called this one of the loudest race cars Porsche has ever built.

of the fixture, and there is a clear lens over the top. But in those days, they brought all the light technology to the front of the headlamp, and all the gluing was at the front as well. So looking on top of the light, it's not clear, it's a bit milky. And you have this set-back orange blinker. Well, that's how this fried egg comparison came about. It had nothing to do with the shape but with the fact that it was too milky."

In other terms, those of performance, handling, interior comfort, or sophistication of development, the 996 provided abundant satisfaction and earned praise. Acceleration to 60 miles per hour came in 4.6 seconds, to 100 in another 7. Its top speed floated around 174 miles per hour (280 kilometers per hour) depending on who tested and where. Its drag coefficient of 0.30 was another favorable result of Lai's design work and patient wind tunnel efforts. Base priced in Germany at 135,610 deutsche marks (about $75,000) at the exchange rate, PCNA suggested the retail price in the United States for a base model was $67,880, though options often added $5,000 to $10,000 to the price.

2003 40th ANNIVERSARY 911

Porsche polished the 18-inch wheels and the exhaust tips for 40-year commemorative models. The engine for these cars is a special 345-horsepower version of the 3.6-liter water-cooled flat-six mated to the mechanical limited-slip differential.

This aluminum 911 logo sits on the rear deck lid. In the interior, dark gray heated leather sport seats are set off with aluminum trim, and a numbered anniversary plaque is affixed to the center console. Porsche Stability Management and the sport suspension complete the handling package.

at 6,000 rpm. It took an updated version of the GT3's VarioCam valve system, called VarioCam Plus, to make it work. This offered either 3 mm or 10 mm of valve lift, and it varied lift timing from early to late, depending on driving demands. As if that weren't enough, Porsche's drivetrain engineers, who had strengthened the Tiptronic so that C4 drivers could use it, enhanced it so Turbo owners could now enjoy the automatic. Magazines testing the Turbo saw top speeds in excess of 190 miles per hour (305 kilometers per hour) and cars reached 60 miles per hour from a standstill in 4 seconds or less. At about $116,000 in the United States, it notched in about $7,500 less than Ferrari's F360 Modena with 400 horsepower and rear-wheel drive, and at half the price of Lamborghini's near-classic Diablo SV, which still out-powered it with 530 horsepower.

In 2002, Porsche returned its Turbo-Look C4S concept to the market place along with the 996's long-planned facelift. This provided the simpler new Turbo headlamps throughout the entire 996 lineup, and gave buyers a slightly more muscular sculpting of the body. The facelift also elevated performance, as engineering lengthened piston stroke from 76 mm to 82.8 mm. This expanded total displacement to 3,596 cc and introduced VarioCam Plus throughout the 996 lineup. Put all together, this engine with its new induction provided 320 brake horsepower at 6,800 rpm and 273 ft-lb of torque at 4,250 rpm.

Porsche revised the Targa for 2002. Reliability problems and warranty claims against jammed glass roofs led engineers to rethink the complex system. The lift caused by sustained high speed driving stressed the welds of the roof members mounted on top of the reinforced cabriolet body. For the 996, body engineers devised a new system. An assembly line robot inserted the new roof (also produced by convertible top–maker CTS) in through the windshield of a strengthened, modified, and decapitated coupe body before welding it into place. Any lift characteristics helped to seal the seams more tightly.

Automobile companies do not work in a vacuum. But they do operate in a time warp, conceiving, developing, and testing cars years before their introductory dates. By the time any criticism of the 996, its headlights, or its appearance reached Weissach, project managers Bernd Kahnau and August Achleitner, and design chief Harm Lagaay already had resolved the problems in "facelifts" that were in development as next generation models moved across drawing boards.

"There is something which people outside the automobile business don't realize," Harm Lagaay said. "What you read in the papers and magazines, and what people are talking about, they are physically what our cars are at that moment. But we are already going ahead, so whatever turmoil may have been going on 'outside', we already are on the move. Our next mission is starting, and no matter how bad the figures or the comments or the stories may have been, I only could say, 'Well, all right. Let's get back to work. We have to go on.'

"Porsche is recognized, apart from the fact that by now everybody knows the 911, which makes it easier, by its own form language. In German, it's *formsprache*. And this form language is shaped in a different way from other cars. There are people who say that Porsches are round. They are not round. We have very sharp edges and sharp radii and tight lines. There is a lot of time spent to achieve this visual identity, a lot of modeling experience and expertise to have this soft shape structured. This is the most difficult. You can make a soft shape with larger radii or softer transitions. But if they are chaotic, if they are not structured well, then it looks like a mess. At Porsche, you have to be in total command of that shape that is recognizable as a Porsche. Another step forward, it moves its boundaries again."

The *formsprache*, or form language, that Pinky Lai and modeler Eberhard Brose created for the 996 made adaptation easier for GT1 race car stylist Tony Hatter, as he endeavored to design a successor. He first had to fit a 26.4-gallon fuel bladder behind the cockpit, which forced him, Norbert Singer, and Horst Reitter to lengthen the wheelbase from 2,499 mm, or 98.4 inches, to 2,870 mm or 113 inches. At that point, it was a new car. So Hatter and the racing engineers started from scratch, developing the body and carbon fiber tub entirely on

To commemorate 40 years, Porsche produced 1,963 of these anniversary coupes. Available only in GT silver, the cars use Turbo-style front air intakes as well as silver air-intake grilles and sill trim.

Front wheels measure 18x8 mounted with 225/40ZR tires. The C4S uses Turbo brakes with their distinctive red rotors. The front spoiler is unique to this model.

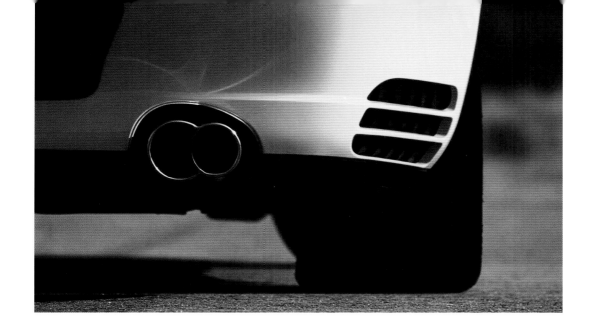

Rear tires, 295/30VR18s, ride on 11-inch-wide wheels. The C4S also utilizes the Turbo suspension with slightly different shock valving to account for weight differences between the slightly heavier Turbo and the C4S.

Porsche *Exclusiv* produces an encyclopedic catalog of custom parts for every Porsche model. Body colors repeated inside the car on center consoles, sport seatbacks, and in leather stitching or upholstery piping are just a few of many dozens of possibilities to personalize a car. Both seats are fully adjustable with driver's-side memory.

computer screens and never producing a full-scale studio model. Hatter's computer design mirrored work he and racing engineers did with scale models in the wind tunnel.

Singer and Reitter moved the driver to the right side in this version to better suit most of the world's racing courses. Hatter slightly enlarged the new 996 headlamps to accommodate extra lighting. The family resemblance remained and the form language was preserved, but this definitely was a race car. Revisions to the engine left it with 95.5-mm bore and 74.4-mm stroke, for 3,198-cc total displacement. It developed 550 brake horsepower at 7,200 rpm with 465 ft-lb torque at 5,000. The 1998 season was one of frustration, finishing perpetually behind new 1998 model Mercedes-Benz CLKs, except at one event, the 24 Hours of Le Mans.

The Turbo-Look bodywork stretched 58 mm (2.3 inches) wider than the standard C4 that it replaced. Above 120 kilometers per hour (75 miles per hour), the rear spoiler emerges from the special glass-reinforced-plastic rear deck lid.

Toyota, Nissan, Ferrari, McLaren, and of course Mercedes-Benz each presented well-supported teams and new cars to challenge the three GT1/98s from Weissach. At 4 p.m. on Sunday, June 7, Porsche's entries finished first and second. It was a significant victory, coming as Karl Ludvigsen pointed out, one day before the 50th anniversary of Porsche's first road car certification in Austria in 1948. The next day, participants in the otherwise undistinguished racing season learned they would not have a second year to campaign the car. Wendelin Wiedeking announced a new Porsche-Volkswagen collaboration. Porsche's 1 billion–deutsche mark commitment would expand the company's product line into a direction few immediately could understand. It would add a new factory and fuel a firestorm of criticism that would take years to extinguish. The size of the investment that Porsche's board had planned to bring the Cayenne utility vehicle to market left no money for motor sports beyond existing commitments for clearly production-based 911s.

Sixteen months earlier, in February 1997, Roland Kussmaul began development of the new series 996 Supercup GT3 models. Porsche had contracted with FIA to run these 50-mile match races at all European Formula One Grand Prix meetings through 1999. These Cup cars, selling for 185,000 deutsche marks ($103,000 at the factory) ran engines that blended the old dry-sump cast-aluminum block with full water cooling and four-valve heads. They developed 360 brake horsepower at 7,250 rpm with 265 ft-lb of torque at 6,000 rpm. Since the first days in 1993, this series had run on unleaded gasoline to demonstrate Porsche's ecological responsibility. Catalytic converters remained on the equipment list for the 996GT3 Cup cars. The 1998 models utilized Pinky Lai's understated rear wings that performed well but offered insufficient adjustment. The specification and series continued through 1999, when civilians could buy a road version of the GT3—for 179,500 deutsche marks, or $102,500. Those who had lamented that the 996s looked tame compared to the

2004 911GT2

Generally spoken of in near-reverential tones, the 477–brake horsepower GT2 is a thinly disguised race car clad in a fine suit for public display. As a rear-drive-only model lacking Porsche Stability Management, driving the car hard and fast is not recommended to those faint of heart or short of skill.

The GT2 weighs 100 kilograms (220 pounds) less than the Turbo and is capable of a 312-kilometer-per-hour (195-mile-per-hour) top speed. To keep the car on the road, Porsche mounted 315/30ZR18 rear tires on 12-inch-wide wheels. The front 235/40ZRs ride on 18x8.5 wheels.

wilder 993 C4S variations fell silent on seeing, and then driving, the 360-horsepower, road-going GT3. If they attended races, they had something to scream about with the new GT3R models. These commanded nearly double the price of the street cars, at 359,200 deutsche marks, nearly $200,000. They were 2,760-pound (255 kilogram), 420–brake horsepower, no-compromise race cars. The 2001 GT3RS gained another 30 horsepower and delivered good competition to BMW Motorsports aggressive V-8-powered M3s. For Cup contestants, 2001 models offered a larger, adjustable rear wing and 370 brake horsepower.

For Porsche owners desiring more power for their road cars, the company offered two answers. One it delivered off-handedly and under its breath. The other came with a wave to dealer's showrooms. Its unofficial suggestion led

enthusiasts down the road to Pfaffenhausen to visit Alois Ruf. For nearly 25 years Ruf had satisfied the fire in the belly of Porsche performance customers by igniting one in Porsche's performance. As early as 1977, he had energized the 911SC's 180 horsepower to 215. The Turbos, which he modified at the rate of 150 to 200 per year, enjoyed similar power increases as well as suspension modifications that matched handling to engine output. Before Porsche offered a five-speed transmission for its turbos, Ruf collaborated with Getrag for his own.

Ruf let his engines and engineering do the talking, however. On their exteriors, the cars bore only subtle modification. By the mid-1980s, he was manufacturing his own automobiles, 10 to 20 per year, under the Ruf name with subtle badges. These cars bore a strong resemblance to Porsche's own.

Porsche's composite ceramic brakes are standard, along with dozens of other changes reducing weight and incorporating elements desirable for race cars. The six-speed manual transmission uses steel synchronizer rings, a change that would appear model-wide with the 997.

Alois Ruf's shops at Pfaffenhausen south of Stuttgart have turned out understated über-performers for more than 20 years. His high-quality workmanship is very much Porsche-like, and his speeds are often faster. This RGT RS pays homage to the Carrera RS of 1973 and the IROC RS of 1974.

Every detail of a Ruf is worked to perfection, including the gearshift knob.

Unlike Porsche's own production Turbo, Ruf revisited the styling of the 1973 and 1974 models with their characteristic ducktail rear spoiler. He also managed to pull another 154 kilograms (338 pounds) out of the car, bringing his model to just 1,230 kilograms (2,705 pounds).

By the end of the 1980s, there were few performance enthusiasts, whether they drove Porsches, sailed 12-meter yachts, skied double-black-diamond runs, or flew fighter jets, who hadn't heard of Ruf. His legendary CTR, a 3.4-liter, 469-brake horsepower Turbo coupe, had won *Road & Track* magazine's top-speed comparison test, staged at VW's EHRA-Lessien facility. The car, dubbed *Yellow Bird* for its brilliant chrome paint, ran 211.5 miles per hour, or 338.4 kilometers per hour. Name-awareness came nearly as rapidly. Ruf followed with 964 variations and then 993 modifications, and by 2002, his 996-derived RUF RGTRS boasted 550 horsepower at 6,000 rpm and top speeds beyond 210 miles per hour. Ruf produced about 2 of his own cars per month and continued modifying 8 to 10 more for customers. His cars, with his own suspension, drivetrain, engine, and braking engineering and improvements, generally provided nearly one-third more power, and often gave buyers all-wheel drive and an extra forward gear in advance of Zuffenhausen models. They sold for about a third more, as well.

Ruf offered this limited-run automobile in any of the vivid colors in which the original IROC racers competed. The price was around 152,000 Euros, or about $176,000.

Ruf met all of Germany's rigid requirements to become a manufacturer in his own right years ago. For 2004, 35 cars left his factory wearing Ruf badges. These particular lightweights use Porsche's 3.6-liter normally aspirated engine, but Ruf's modifications brought output up 15 horsepower from the Porsche GT3's 380 to 395.

2004 911GT3

The reconfigured engine allows speeds up to 8,100 rpm in the first four gears of the six-speed gear box. Priced at $99,900 (approximately 90,000 Euros at the time), the GT3 was one of the high-performance world's better deals. Porsche quotes a top speed of 190 miles per hour (304 kilometers per hour).

It's the perfect car for those moments when the road ahead is clear and dry and all the police are off-duty. While buyers in the rest of the world could acquire the GT3 starting in 1999, U.S. customers had to wait until 2004.

For those who wanted a Weissach-modified Turbo, Porsche cooperated with its own 996-derived GT2. As with the 993 versions, this few-frills car appeared in rear-wheel-drive configuration only, and its 3.6-liter twin-turbocharged engine developed 462 brake horsepower at 5,700 rpm along with 457 ft-lb of torque at as low as 3,500 rpm. Because of changes in racing categories—and competitors, because the Porsche would run against V-10 Vipers and V-8 Corvettes with at least twice the displacement—the company chose to render the car as a street racer with a fully carpeted interior. Weissach and its customer racing sales director Hartmut Kristen looked

to produce 400 to 500 of the cars, selling for a very respectable 339,000 deutsche marks at the factory, or $185,000 in the United States. Porsche had assimilated the lesson of Jürgen Barth's 964 Carrera 4 Lightweights: For an automobile that looks and performs similar to a race car, and offers proven exclusivity, there is a sure market.

Through the six years from the 966's introduction in 1999 to the last of the 996 Turbo coupes and cabriolets in 2005, the car evolved. It survived near cancellation in a wind tunnel in January 1997 as Harm Lagaay and Wendelin Wiedeking prepared to unveil the Boxster in Detroit. The 996 emerged, thrived, and surged ahead. The facelift and performance models that appeared in 2002 invigorated it. It is the best-selling 911 of all, with more than 170,000 delivered. It opened new audiences and new eyes to Porsche's products, pulling loyalists out of BMW 3- and 6-series coupes and Mercedes-Benz SLs. In the United States, it enthralled corporate captains of both sexes who had favored pickup trucks and big sedans alike. It captivated them, humbled them, and then inspired them to take driving courses. A lot of 996s crossed Zuffenhausen's transoms, Germany's borders, and the Pacific and Atlantic Oceans. This was a car that easily engaged first-time Porsche buyers. It had brought Porsche a long way from the moment of Pinky Lai's "little revolution."

"It was really tough," Lai recalled, "especially when we had a show car getting good reception, good response at Detroit. Then at home, you have so much homework, regulations, and cost restrictions to take care of. We were really fighting all fronts with cost people, with technical guys. It was really a tough job.

"The only good thing was the end. The emotion was what won out. Basically, sticking to what the car really was all about, that was what actually took place." ▤

The elevated rear wing did not rise any farther, but owners could adjust it through three settings to modify the handling for their track-day outings. Porsche attached lightened pistons and connecting rods to an eight-bearing crankshaft.

Above, left: A caliper for Porsche's composite carbon brakes, its PCCB option, peeks through the 18-inch wheel. Such stopping power is not an unwise choice for a 1,383-kilogram (3,043-pound) car with 380 horsepower.

CHAPTER NINE

THE SIXTH GENERATION— THE 997

2004 – TODAY

"The sports car is an athlete.

An athlete is not a body builder.

The Porsche 911 is an athlete."

Luc Donckerwölke, Chief Designer, Lamborghini S.p.A.,
December 2004

"The main product of this new line, the *lead* model of the 997, was the convertible," August Achleitner said, "and not the coupe." Achleitner was Porsche's director of product line management for the Carrera. Before this, he was responsible for new vehicle concepts and packaging for all Porsche vehicles from 1989 through 2000. The 997 was largely his creation. "We didn't talk about this, but now you know it. This strategy came from the engineers' point of view. The convertible is the more difficult car because of the stiffness that is necessary. Your work is easier when you consider some of these special parts, some of the reinforcements right from the beginning." In the past, Porsche had

Previous pages: The Bose audio system adjusts itself for optimum sound with the top up or down. The front-to-rear speaker balance shifts forward, and bass and treble increase with the top down.

2005 911/997 CARRERA S

While the onboard navigation system wouldn't pinpoint the location of local police, it would tell the cockpit occupants where they are and how to get where they're going. The screen also hosts an optional Sports Chrono package that records lap times around the Nürburgring, around Road America, or around the usual loop from home to office and back.

made its coupes first and then, after they were finished, engineers started on open cars. With the 997, Achleitner's team developed both simultaneously.

Wolfgang Dürheimer, Porsche's vice president for research and development, explained the advantages the 997 derived from Achleitner's simultaneous effort. Developing the cabrios had provided Weissach's engineers some unexpected benefits as they worked through the target-conflicts. These are the good-news-bad-news dilemmas that arise when one decision revealed two or three more questions, challenges, or choices.

"It was clear for us, right from the beginning, that we will have a coupe and a convertible. That was more or less the same with the 996. But this time we did it in a very concentrated fashion. So all the derivatives that the 997 will see, the Targa, the all-wheel drives, the various GT models and others, all these we took into consideration right from the beginning.

"It makes life a bit harder to consider all these variants from the start. But it makes things easier at the end. It's classical front loading. It takes a little bit more time thinking about things before you can weld the first parts. But some of what we tried to improve on the cabriolet brought us some very good aspects on the coupe as well.

All Carrera S models came standard with a new Porsche Active Suspension Management (PASM) system that allows drivers to switch from sport to touring or normal mode with the press of a button. It was an option on base Carreras.

"As you can imagine, to make a coupe quite stiff is not too difficult, because you have a closed car with a roof. But if you want to have a stiff body on a cabriolet, it's a little bit more difficult. We initiated this so-called third load path in terms of passive safety. It's an upper load path that can take forces of an accident through the upper door section into the back of the car."

This new load path relied on a strong beam inside the sheet metal that extended across the top of each door starting at the base of the A-pillar at the instrument panel. When Porsche drivers opened the door, they saw a three-corner aluminum piece in the B-pillar. Th s was the point at which the door beam connected,

The 3.8-liter Carrera S is the hotter of two 997 models and represents the first time since the 1970s that Porsche has offered two engine levels simultaneously. With 355 brake horsepower, the S model jumped 30 horsepower ahead of the standard 3.6-liter Carrera model with 325 horsepower.

making a very rigid torsional-, bending-, and stiff-load passage from the front fenders to the rear of the car. One of its purposes was passenger compartment integrity in a front, side, or rear end crash. It kept the compartment from folding in on itself, as can happen in other open cars in high speed accidents. It provided the new 997 cabriolet with five percent greater torsional stiffness and nine percent more flexing stiffness than the 996 cabrio.

"This system helped the coupe a lot even though it has a roof," Dürheimer continued, "because the body along the windowsill line got the same very strong reinforcement. This was an idea we had at the very beginning, thinking about the convertible and how we can make it more rigid. This is the profit of making the cabriolet and the coupe at the same time."

The 911 presents a hard legacy to follow up. Its heritage offers as many challenges as it provides guidelines. For more than 40 years now, Porsche has produced this two-door automobile. Its characteristic front fenders

still retain a form that, as Ferry Porsche first dictated to Erwin Komenda, allows the driver to see where the front wheels are located. The 911 carries on Butzi Porsche's iconic angled-down roofline. It still defines itself with the rear engine that has dictated the car's shape, its form, its handling, its sound, and its appeal.

"Designing to fit the 911 heritage is a big challenge," Grant Larson said. Working together, he and Mathias Kulla penned the lines that make the 997 coupes and cabriolets seem so Porsche-like. "There isn't any target really. We all just set our personal goals to improve our car. While it's a sports car, there's also that strong daily-use quotient. Your margin is greatly narrowed, because you're doing something special for a very special company. My goal," Larson continued, "was to tighten everything up, to make the car look more technical, more precise, more agile. There were things that I wanted to work with, things that Pinky Lai had started with the 996, the resolution of some lines, to tighten the waist, widen the hips." The work he and Kulla did literally

Grant Larson's first sketches of the car show it with large wheels. Project chief August Achleitner decided to go ahead with optional 19-inch wheels, and this choice led to hundreds of other changes, modifications, and redesigns from the 996 and from the original concept for this car.

defined the car. While their later tweaks with engineering also enhanced aerodynamics, reducing the drag coefficient from 0.30 for the 996 to 0.28 for the new coupe, the original concept was more revolutionary.

"Grant Larson made his first sketches with taller, wider tires," August Achleitner explained. "It became clear that this choice had wide-ranging ramifications." The tires intensified loads under cornering, acceleration, and braking so greatly that they literally destroyed the first running prototypes in 2001. It forced body, chassis, and suspension engineers to redesign much more of the car than they anticipated. Starting with the unibody of the 996, they developed techniques to weld and glue components. These methods increased body rigidity by 8 percent. Additional reinforcement and adhesives resulted in a 40 percent improvement in chassis stiffness.

Achleitner was one of several engineers boasting that the new 997 was 80 percent changed from the 996. More than half of that was beneath the surface. Not a single suspension piece was interchangeable. While this conflicted with Wendelin Wiedeking's often-repeated goal of commonality of parts, many of these new pieces were simpler to manufacture and easier to install. Above all, Wiedeking, who frequently is named Germany's Best Business Manager and often heads the ranking of world's best, understands that his company's target is the best sports car possible. The 20 percent that remained unchanged included very expensive elements, such as the roof panel and the 3.6-liter engine block, as well as the interior rear seats, and the 3.6-engine crankshaft and its pistons.

The 19-inch wheels forced power train engineers to rework gearboxes. The larger rolling circumference required shorter final drive gears to take advantage of engine torque and horsepower. This gave

2005 911/996 TURBO S CABRIOLET
Mountain roads beg for Porsches. For 2005, Porsche carried over production of its 996 Turbo coupes and cabriolets while it prepared the new 997 models for introduction. Few buyers seemed put off by the wait.

Porsche's wizards the opportunity to address other concerns in both the manual and Tiptronic transmissions that resulted in an all-new six-speed manual gearbox with torque- and horsepower-capacity to spare. Engineers raised gearshift pressure and increased stall speed on the five-speed Tiptronic, enabling faster starts from a standstill, more powerful and spontaneous acceleration, and quicker shifts, especially in lower gears.

"This is a passion we follow," Wolfgang Dürheimer said. "If you get the chance to work on the 911, on the one hand this is a very big opportunity and on the other hand, it's an obligation. The team is very aware of this. The health of the company is affected. Many jobs are at stake. Therefore everybody tries as hard

as possible to get his component, his part, into the target section. We have many engineers at Weissach that make their application to Porsche after they are finished with their university degree. They get hired and they stay at Porsche all during their career, as long as they are engineers. They are deeply into their subjects, aerodynamics, acoustics, basic engine work, and they are constantly asking themselves, 'What can I improve?'"

The engineers and designers filled notebooks and desk drawers with ideas, and when they got the next chance, they were ready. They pulled out their wish lists. Dürheimer chided them: "Don't stop making new suggestions. If you are not successful in bringing it into the present project, bring it next time. Do not abandon it." One idea that engineers brought back to the tables for the 997 was the Porsche Active Suspension Management (PASM), the automatic stability system.

"We tried PASM for the 996," Bernd Kahnau said. Kahnau was project manager for 997, and served the same role for 996 and 993. He had grown up inside Porsche, literally. His father was production manager in the 1950s and Kahnau's earliest technical education came in the back seats of 356s. "But this system now is special for us. Bilstein built it. The Jaguar system back then was too soft, and that was all that was available. It was too soon. The technology wasn't ready for what we wanted the 996 to be able to do."

Achleitner's commitment to 19-inch wheels and tires on the Carrera S motivated Porsche to bring the technology up to its standards.

Ambitions grew bold. The standard suspension always represented a compromise for Achleitner, even under the best of circumstances. At the beginning of the conceptual work on the 997 in late 1998, he formed a team of 20 engineers, designers, and staffers from the predevelopment group, and sales. They had to decide what the new car would look like, how it would be equipped, how much horsepower it would have, and dozens of other questions and variables. They didn't rely only on their own instincts but they also queried 993

Porsche made the X50 performance option standard equipment on the 2005 model. This modified the exhaust system, turbochargers, air intake, engine management computer, and it strengthened the transmission to handle the additional torque. Porsche's ceramic composite brakes (PCCB) are also standard, with six-piston front calipers and four-piston rears.

and 996 owners, as well as some individuals they located who had test-driven a 996 or a 993 but not bought one.

"One thing we noticed was that, for some people, the 996 was a little too soft at that time," he explained. "We had no GT3 yet, no Turbo, no C4S. *We* knew what was coming in the future, but we took this feedback from the market and decided that the 997 should be a little more muscular, a little bit sportier. But not too sporty, not too muscular, because we didn't want to lose all the customers we had gotten from Mercedes-Benz and BMW. These are people who never would have bought a Porsche before. The 993, for example, had been too harsh, or too loud, or too uncomfortable for them.

"Then we had the question of how could we solve this task? You have to think about what makes a car faster, and, on the other hand, what can make the car smoother, more comfortable, without losing sportiness? One thing that came out of this target-conflict was the PASM system for the 997. Except for the 959, which really was a prototype car, this 997 is the first time that we have offered an electronic spring and damper system." (In the cabrio, this was an industry first.)

"At the beginning of the development, meeting the target to make the car comfortable wasn't so hard, because we didn't see a chance to make the car better than the 996. But especially within the last year of our work we learned a lot about what was possible with the software. Even our specialists only understood all the possibilities of this system within the last four or five months, just before the start of production. We could make tiny changes, even to accommodating a single bump in a smooth road."

What PASM and their laptop computers allowed the engineers to do was fine-tune characteristics that made any one Carrera S model (on which this suspension system was standard equipment) into any of a variety of cars. As Wolfgang Dürheimer characterized it, "We have made it possible that two demands which could not be fulfilled in one car in the past could be covered with one new suspension system. It's very sporty on one side. We can make our 'Top Guns' very happy and still bring them on a long distance trip from A to B and get them out of the car relaxed and ready for their next appointment."

Chassis and suspension engineers took cars to Nürburgring *Nordschliefe* to polish the final settings. "In comparison to the standard setup of the 996, the new 911, with its PASM in the 'sports' setting improved the lap time by seventeen seconds," Dürheimer said. "Seventeen seconds! In the past we were happy if we could find three seconds."

For the cabrio this capability redefined what was possible with an open car. Even as Achleitner's engineers

The Turbo carries over the 3.6-liter, water-cooled engine from the earlier performance 996 variants. Porsche quoted a top speed for either Turbo S coupes or cabriolets at 300 kilometers per hour (188 miles per hour).

2005 911/997 CARRERA CABRIOLET

In the winter of 2005, Porsche introduced the next member of the 997 family, the cabriolet. Unlike in previous open-911 developments, Porsche developed the cabriolet first, developing structural rigidity that it then added to the coupes.

replaced the coupe's front springs with those 10 percent softer for the cabrio, they substituted the coupe's rear suspension bushings with some much harder for the open car. Then his staff compressed the range of variability within the PASM to fit the cabriolet's slightly diminished stiffness and the anticipated character of most cabrio drivers. In its stiffest "sport" settings, it came up just about 15 percent softer than the calibration on the coupe, while the softest point is another couple of percent softer than the coupe.

For that coupe, Porsche also offered a full sport suspension for European customers only. This lowered ride height by 20 mm (0.79 inch—too low for U.S. federal standards) and provided a mechanical differential lock on the rear axle of 22 percent under acceleration and 27 percent under deceleration or braking to enhance directional stability. Buyers could order it through Porsche *Individual* as an option on the Carrera or in place of the PASM on the Carrera S. Its ride was much harsher because it was "conceived for the ambitious driver not so much interested in comfort but rather in super performance and agility," Achleitner explained. While it lacked the designation, this was a kind of club sport handling package meant more for track days than best-of-all-worlds compromises.

Bringing these mannerisms to the road was a daunting task. From the beginning, in late 1998, power train manager Stefan Knirsch was part of the 20-member group making concept studies outlining their goals. He recalled the meetings.

"There was not one target for this car, but many. We used individual vehicles for specific targets, performance, fuel economy, exterior package and dimensions, exhaust emissions, interior noise, and its sound." The group

considered Ferrari's F360 and Lamborghini's Gallardo. But each of these had too small a production and too high a price to be useful beyond reinforcing packaging and performance parameters. BMW's new 6 series and its M3 entered into the equations; however the initial 6-series models lacked the performance quotient. The Aston Martin DB9 also had far too small an output to really measure as a target. Both Lamborghini's chief designer Luc Donckerwölke and Aston Martin's design boss Henrik Fisker had stated in published interviews that they had targeted Porsche's 911 for their new cars. For Knirsch then, his goal was clear.

"You always want more power in the next generation of any Porsche," he said. He and his staff came up with intake and exhaust modifications to the familiar 3.6-liter 996 engine that added 5 horsepower to reach 325 brake horsepower at 6,800 rpm and 273 ft-lb of torque at 4,250 rpm for the base Carrera. This engine carried over the VarioCam Plus valve management system comprising two interacting switching cup tappets on the intake side of the engine, driven by two cams of varying size on the intake camshaft.

The 3.6-liter engine that powers the base Carrera is a different engine from the 3.6 that drives the 996 models. This engine is smaller in physical dimensions and allows the car a somewhat smaller rear bulge than the 996's.

The decision to offer 19-inch wheels and tires as an option forced engineers to design a new lighter and wider front and rear suspension. Overall vehicle width increased 38 mm (1.5 inches) from 1,770 mm (69.7 inches) to 1,808 mm (71.2 inches).

Enlarging cylinder bore from 96 mm to 99 but retaining stroke at 82.8 mm brought the new S engine displacement to 3,823 cc, or 3.8 liters. Using 43-mm (1.69-inch) diameter intake manifolds that measure 60 mm (2.36 inches) shorter that those on the 996 on this new Carrera, and by utilizing a two-piece synthetic resonance chamber specially configured to reduce intake noise and enhance airflow between 5,000 and 6,000 rpm, it developed 355 brake horsepower at 6,600 rpm, with torque at 295 ft-lb at 4,600. The new Carrera coupes reached 60 miles per hour in 4.8 seconds (5.2 for the cabriolet), and 4.6 seconds for the S (but 4.9 seconds for the S cabriolet). Porsche quoted top speeds of 177 and 182 miles (283 and 291 kilometers) per hour respectively. This was the first time since 1977 with the 2.7-liter and 3.0-liter engines that Porsche had offered two normally aspirated engine variants simultaneously.

Porsche introduced the 997 Carrera and Carrera S coupes in Europe and the United States as 2004 model. Through the 2005 model year, it continued manufacturing and selling 996 Turbo S and Turbo S cabriolets. Cabriolet versions of the 997 Carrera and Carrera S reached dealers worldwide in April 2005. The first all-wheel-drive models reached dealers in midsummer, with Targas, Turbos, and other models existing as well-known secrets into 2006.

Engineers were not the only ones at Weissach whom Wolfgang Dürheimer encouraged to think ahead and develop ideas. Porsche's design staff points its telescopes 5 and even 10 years into the future. While Pinky Lai slaved to make the 996 form aerodynamically effective without the benefits of a movable wing, Grant Larson created the 986 Boxster alongside Lai in the same studio. As Lai developed the forms for Porsche's 1999 Carrera, Larson began conceiving his own ideas for the next 911. When design chief Harm Lagaay put Larson and Mathias Kulla to work on the 997, their concepts did not just materialize from thin air.

"This is what's important to understand," Larson explained. "If you go to any designer within the department, you can say, 'Do a new 911'. It's not, really *not* a case where ideas have to just pop into our mind . . . that we have to start coming up with new ideas from nowhere. Forget it. We've got it in our head already. So when the word comes, we don't just sit there and spend two years sketching around on it. We put down this idea that we've been thinking about the whole time the department was working on the previous generation."

Except for its back seats, the 997 interior was nearly all new, the work of interior designer Anke Wilhelm and interior chief Franz-Josef Siegert. In the late 1990s, Harm Lagaay hired in designers only to do interiors and still others to attend to the details, the jewelers, as he called them. Wilhelm and Siegert's instrument pod seemed familiar to past and present Porsche owners and Uli Sauter's graphics were quickly comprehensible to those driving one for the first time. The 996 interior was the most comfortable and user friendly of any previous model. Porsche would not shy away from its new enthusiast base. The 997 offered four seat options to satisfy most backs and body shapes. All were comfortable and supportive, with headrests 2 inches higher and angled closer for better support. The new interior looked, felt, and worked as if the 996 were the prototype and this new car was the working model. That was accurate in one sense. Lagaay explained that Porsche now committed two 911 model lives to each new platform. The 996 came first and the 997 was the second. There was much more metal and less plastic in this new interior than ever before. But some plastic remained.

"At the beginning of development," Achleitner recalled, "we had door handles made of aluminum. But in our front crash tests, the weight of that swinging aluminum handle was enough to open the door. One solution we considered involved counterweights but that added costs, and worse to a Porsche, weight. So we chose a composite that we painted to look like aluminum."

For Larson and Kulla, the legacy of the Porsche cabriolet went back generations. Butzi Porsche designed a version in the early 1960s that never left the design studio for reasons already explained here. When the

Porsche fitted 18-inch wheels standard on the base Carrera so the car rides on rear 265/40ZRs on 10-inch-wide wheels, and front 235/40ZRs on 8-inch-wide wheels. Carrera S models ride on 19s, with 8-inch fronts mounting 235/35ZR tires and the 11-inch rears carrying 295/30ZR18s.

production version appeared in 1983, it was part of a larger strategy. Peter Schutz and Dr. Helmuth Bott used it to proclaim that, despite rumors of its demise, the 911 was alive and well. The 1983 cabrio surely was lively, but none of Porsche's current staff of designers thought it looked very well.

Porsche had carried over the same convertible roof from the 911SC and 3.2 Carreras through the 964 series. "The first ones were more functional," Grant Larson explained. "I think that's the best way to describe it." From Tony Hatter's efforts to improve the 993 cabrio roof, came Lai's forms with the 996 and now Larson's with the 997.

"From generation to generation," Larson said, "they've gained so much experience. There are new geometries and things they can work out. We have a lot of magnesium in the new roof. That makes it a lot lighter. We have a new 'Z' folding mechanism that made a whole lot more sense for the 996 and 997 versions. Those early cabriolet roofs took a whole lot of weight and pushed it back further where it shouldn't be on the car. I'm involved heavily in this area of advanced design in cabriolet tops. One of our projects is roof systems, which is a very important consideration for our car, especially when you recognize how many open 911s we sell."

According to Dürheimer and 997 project manager Bernd Kahnau, 40 percent of all 997s for 2005 were cabriolets, and customers tended to steer about 50 percent of those to the United States. The solid, fixed-glass back window with an electric defogger was just one of its bragging points, something introduced at the 996 facelift in 2002 and slightly enlarged with the 997. Unlike the driver of any 996, the driver of a Porsche 997 could raise or lower the roof at speeds up to 31 miles per hour. That process, including dropping and raising side windows, took 20 seconds in either direction.

"There are a couple of parts that work really well with this car, not only the 'moving while it's driving' function in the case of the 997's convertible top," Larson continued. "But it's also important to think about how the top folds into the car without constricting the amount of luggage space. Any car can have a really fantastic system but it may eat up half the trunk. Our philosophy is to stick with a cabriolet roof, not only for reasons of tradition, but also for the considerations of purity, and sportiness, and light weight. That's the reason we're keeping folding roofs rather than going to a folding hardtop. If you added a folding hardtop to the car, you'd put its handling characteristics a little bit in jeopardy with all that added weight on top of the engine. And I don't think our customers are out there screaming for a hard roof. And if they are, we have a hardtop." Unlike the 996, however, the convertible hardtop no longer was standard equipment on the new 997. Weighing 73 pounds, it sold as an option for $2,345. "So many of the U.S. customers left them at the dealers, or never even picked them up," Larson explained. "They all say, 'I bought a cabriolet, not a coupe.'"

Porsche's wholly owned subsidiary Car Top Systems (CTS) developed the mechanism for the 997's top and manufactured the complete system with bows, hinges, motors, inner lining, glass, and outer material. They arrived from CTS fully assembled and, as did everything else on the Zuffenhausen assembly line, just in time for two men to lift it and set it onto the painted car body. Porsche offered it in black, gray, cocoa, and blue. The entire assembly weighs 42 kilograms, or 93 pounds. But weight always was an enemy to Porsche engineers.

Porsche installed steel synchronizer rings on the new transmission, replacing the brass rings in the 996 models. Engineers designed a new shift linkage that shortens throws by 15 percent without increasing lever force.

While the cabriolet gained a total of 135 kilograms over the coupe, diligent management of every single system kept the net weight increase to just 85 kilograms, or 187 pounds.

Because the roofline, even with Grant Larson's efforts and CTS' technology, could not exactly mimic the coupes, August Achleitner's engineers tweaked the performance of the rear spoiler. It rose 20 millimeters higher on the cabriolet than on the coupe to be more aerodynamically effective. However the cabrio's higher rear wing impacted its coefficient of drag numbers. The coupes measured 0.28 drag coefficient, while the cabrios came in at 0.29.

The subtly higher wing was not the only effect that top-down Porsche drivers may have noticed. As with the 996, audio volume changed with road speed. However, an open roof prompted the audio system to reconfigure the entire graphic equalization and front-rear speaker mix. Front-rear balance moved forward something like 20 centimeters, about 9 inches, and the system elevated bass and treble levels.

There was another audio category in which U.S. buyers benefited and open car owners benefited even more. Because of America's relaxed exhaust-noise standards, U.S. buyers got the loudest exhausts of any 997 purchaser. "The exhaust sound was even more aggressive with the cabrio," Bernd Kahnau explained with a broad grin, "because of the open cabin. We wanted our customers to really be able to hear the engine." On the roads, that sound was familiar music to cabrio drivers' ears. It reminded some drivers of the 993 more than a water-cooled 996. Bernd Kahnau knew the sound and explained the reason. "Our exhaust engineers? They are our Mozarts."

For nearly 50 years, Porsche has listened to its engineers and designers as they have worked to deliver Ferry Porsche's dream car to an ever-changing world. The interpreters have ranged from Erwin Komenda and Franz-Josef Reimspeiss, Butzi Porsche and Hans Mezger, Huschke von Hanstein and Helmuth Bott and Ferdinand Piëch, Ernst Fuhrmann and Norbert Singer, Tony Lapine and Paul Hensler, Wolfgang Berger, Tilman Brodbeck, Heinz Branitzki, Peter Falk, Herbert Ampferer, Jürgen Barth, Fritz Bezner, Peter Schutz, Arno Bohn, Harm Lagaay and Hartmut Kristen and Horst Marchart, Wolfgang Dürheimer and August Achleitner, to Wendelin Wiedeking. The mantle of responsibility for thousands of employees, tens of thousands of customers, and hundreds of thousands of enthusiasts has been a burden of such weight that sometimes some of these individuals have staggered and misstepped under it.

The Carrera S runs Porsche's Active Suspension Management (PASM) system. This monitored a variety of conditions up to 20 times a second and could be adjusted from near-racetrack stiffness (even in the cabriolet) to boulevard cushiness with the touch of a button.

"Whatever you do at Porsche," Harm Lagaay said, "there's always a little bit of car history you are making, because Porsche is taken seriously, whatever they do. The 911 concept has a long way to go. There are still many, many improvement possibilities."

The question that launched this book, that opened these discussions, was "Who does Porsche target?" While the engineers and designers keep their eyes open and watch the competition, it is clear that their target is not "who," but "what."

"It takes a lot of passion and heart and feeling and craftsmanship," Wolfgang Dürheimer said. "And this is how I think you can summarize it. The job we try to conduct in Weissach is to do it perfect. Full stop. If it isn't you need to do it again. This is the search for constant perfection."

2005 911/997 CARRERA S CABRIOLET

When Grant Larson and Mathias Kulla designed the 997 coupes and cabriolets, they profited from the hard work that Pinky Lai did with his 996. Both 997 body styles produce lower coefficients of drag than the 996, shaving 0.02 off each, to achieve 0.29 for the cabrio and 0.28 for the coupe.

Porsche may be an old-world company manufacturing automobiles in a surrounding of thousands of years of art, architecture, and culture, but there is nothing about the Porsche's 911's concept, design, engineering, or manufacturing that is not state of the art for the twenty-first century.

ACKNOWLEDGMENTS:

My most sincere thanks go to Michael Baumann, General Manager International Press, Dr. Ing. h.c.F. Porsche Aktiengesellschaft, Stuttgart, Germany. On the eve of the annual shareholders' meeting and the launch of the 997 Cabriolet, Michael found time to arrange and coordinate a series of interviews for me, each of which was essential to telling this story. For several days he devoted time to this book and my needs while maintaining his characteristic grace, humor, and patience.

Equally deep gratitude goes to Bob Carlson, Manager Public Affairs, Porsche Cars North America. He enthusiastically supported this project from our first conversation about it. Bob's invited me to attend the 997 Carrera and Carrera S introduction in Hameln, Germany, which sharpened the focus and the direction of this book.

While the history of Porsche is a story of cars and other vehicles, this book is about the people who created one specific strain of Porsche. A great number of people presently with Porsche or retired from the company gave generously (and repeatedly) of their time. I wish to convey my sincere thanks to: August Achleitner, Director Product Line Management Carrera, Weissach; Jürgen Barth, Customer Motorsport Coordinator, Weissach; Tilman Brodbeck, Director Exclusive Program, Stuttgart-Zuffenhausen; Wolfgang Dürheimer, Executive Vice-President, Research & Development, Weissach; Tony Hatter, Design Manager, Customer and Special Projects, Style Porsche, Weissach; Bernd Kahnau, Manager, Complete Product Line, Weissach; Stefan Knirsch, General Manager Base Engine Development Department, Weissach; Porsche stylist Pinky Lai, Weissach; Grant Larson, Manager Advanced Design Exterior Style Porsche, Weissach; Cristina May, Porsche Leipzig GmbH, Leipzig; Klaus Parr, Manager, Historical Archive, Stuttgart-Zuffenhausen; and Jens Torner, the sharp-eyed photo archivist, Historical Archive, Stuttgart-Zuffenhausen.

I am further indebted to Dr. Norbert Singer, recently retired manager of racing, Weissach, for his time and his memories. In addition, I wish to express my deep gratitude to Harm Lagaay, retired Director, Style Porsche, Inning, Germany, and to Tony Lapine, retired Director of Design, Porsche, Baden-Baden, Germany; as well as to Dick Soderberg, retired designer, Adelaide, Australia; and to Otto Soeding, Birmingham, MI. In addition, I am most deeply grateful to Peter W. Schutz, Naples, FL. Each of these individuals patiently spoke with me about their work and their philosophy.

I am further grateful to Alois Ruf, Ruf Automobile GmbH, Pfaffenhausen, Germany, for his recollections and observations on his role and accomplishments both as an independent automobile manufacturer and as a long time modifier of series-production Porsches. In addition, Bernd Polster, design historian, writer and editor, Bonn, Germany, offered his well-considered observations and gave me the perspective to understand the role the Ulm School of Design played in the visual development of the Porsche 911.

I also must thank Freeman Thomas, Escondido, CA, Kerry Morse, Tustin, CA; and Jerry Reilly, Hardwick, MA; for their thoughts, ideas and insights as this book came together. Each of these three made significant suggestions that further sharpened the focus of this book.

The premise of this book grew from quotes from both Luc Dönckerwolke, chief designer at Lamborghini, S.P.A., and Henrik Fisker, former design director at Aston Martin, that appeared in successive issues of *CAR* magazine stating that their new cars had targeted Porsche's 911. Tim Parker, Motorbooks quiet, observant Senior Vice President of Global Publishing, reported to me the quotes from *CAR*, and posed to me the one question that launched close to a thousand more: Who does Porsche target?

My own frantic schedule completing this book tested the patience of my friend and editor, Darwin Holmstrom, and his boss, Zack Miller, Publisher. I am most grateful to these men for the invitation to look so closely again at the design and engineering of Porsche's cars.

I would be remiss if I did not thank Pete Stout, editor of *Excellence* magazine, for his generous help, numerous introductions, and enthusiastic support of this project.

I want to express my gratitude to fellow photographers Dennis Adler, Dee Lambert, David Newhardt, Patrick Paternie, Dale von Trebra, Bob Tronolone, and Ulrich Upietz, for graciously granting me use of their photographs for this book.

Owners from around the United States and across Europe opened garages and sheds so their cars could appear in this book. I am very grateful to John Acampura, Irvine, CA; Molly Almond, Thousand Oaks, CA; James Alton II, San Dimas, CA; Dick Barbour, San Diego, CA; Mike Baum, Newport Beach,

CA; Tony Callas, Torrance, CA; Joe Carastro IV, Santa Barbara, CA; Chris Clarke, The Blackhawk Collection, Danville, CA; John Clinard, Irvine, CA; Ray Crawford, Costa del Mar, CA; Tom Dalton, Playa del Rey, CA; Steve and Arisa Dovris, Thousand Oaks, CA; Matt Drendel, Hickory, NC; Geoff Escalette, Costa Mesa, CA; Ken Fahn, Sacramento, CA; Ernst Freiberger, EFA-Automobile Museum, Amerang, Germany; Larry Frye, Mountainview, CA; Bart Galloway, Reno, NV; Gary Gasperino, Camarillo, CA; Stuart Gillard, Montecito, CA; Fred Hampton, London, England; Marty Harris, Simi Valley, CA; Scott Hendry, Anaheim, CA; Richard Hille, Santa Ynez, CA; Mike Hodson, Camarillo, CA; Hal Holleman, Newport Beach, CA; Eade Hopkinson, Carlsbad, CA; Dan Jacobs, Wallingford, CT; William Jackson, Denver, CO; John Larsen, Santa Maria, CA; Dirk Layer, Irvine, CA; Jerry Layer, San Diego, CA; Pete Lech, Fullerton, CA; Robert Linton, New York City, NY; Ken Lubell, New York City, NY; Tony Magglos, Thousand Oaks, CA; Don Maluzio, Philadephia, PA; Marco Marinello, Zurich, Switzerland; Patrick Martin, Mahopac, NY; Richard McLean, Santa Barbara, CA; Dick Messer, Director, and Leslie Kendall, Curator, The Petersen Automotive Museum, Los Angeles, CA; John Mann, Thousand Oaks, CA; Gary Moser, Westlake Village, CA; Brent Overacker, New Canaan, CT; Mike Palmieri, Camarillo, CA; Chris Pascoe, Hillsborough, CA; Phil di Pasquale, Las Vegas, NV; Les Quam, Las Vegas, NV; Jerry Reilly, Hardwick, MA; Richard Roth, Long Island City, NY; Jim Schrager, South Bend, IN; Paul Ernst Strähle, Schondorf, Germany; David Stone, Camarillo, CA; John Sturdevant, Mission Viejo, CA; Mike Turek, Oxnard, CA; William Vogl, Santa Monica, CA; Bob de Vries, San Luis Obispo, Roy Walzer, Litchfield, CT; Ranson Webster, Reno, NV; Chester Yabitsu, Agoura Hills, CA;

Finally, to my partner in life, Carolyn, I am deeply grateful for your love, patience, and encouragement as this assignment repeatedly pulled me far from home. I never slacked my pace. I always am anxious to get back to you.

Randy Leffingwell
Santa Barbara, CA

PHOTO CREDITS:

Dennis Adler:
6-7, 30-31,

Dee Lambert:
158

David Newhardt:
5, 21, 23, 24 both, 34-35, 37-38, 69-73, 79-81, 92-94, 112-115, 120-128, 134-138, 152-154, 160-165, 167-169, 173-178, 190, 194-196, 202-211, 213, 228, 250-253, 262-263, 280-281, 284-285, 306-312, 316-319, 322-323, 329, 332-337.

Porsche Archives:
19-20, 39, 44-45, 58, 68, 78, 86, 97, 118, 144-147, 184-185, 197-201, 212, 257, 288-291, 304-305,

Dale von Trebra:
116

Bob Tronolone
129

Ulrich Upietz/Porsche Archives
269-270, 272-273

All others Randy Leffingwell

INDEX

MODELS

25th Anniversary, 130
356, 13, 16, 18, 35, 38, 42, 45, 158, 201, 207
    Cabriolet, 45
    Carrera Speedster, 1957, 10
356A, 9
    Carrera GT, 1959, 13
356C, 28, 29, 31, 38, 41
356SC, 38, 41
    Cabriolet, 1965, 28
40th Anniversary model, 2003, 307, 309
547 Carrera, 84, 94
550-Spyder, 1955, 294
587/1, 28
616, 28, 30
695, 18, 50
745, 30
    T7, 42
753, 28, 30, 37
754 T7, 19
771, 28
804 Formula One, 1962, 16, 17, 36
    901, 20, 23, 31, 35, 38, 69, 112, 119, 212
    901/22, 51
    901/911, 18, 24, 27
    Prototype, 1964 Pilot Production, 6, 7
    1964, 21
902, 42
903 Turbo, 1978, 136
904, 18, 20, 23, 38, 63
    Carrera GTS, 1964, 24
    GTS, 17
906, 59
Carrera 6, 36
908, 231, 234
911/996 Turbo S cabriolet, 2005, 332
911/996, 293
911/997 Carrera cabriolet, 2005, 338
911/997 Carrera S, 2005, 328
    Cabriolet, 2005, 345
911T/R, 1968, 68
912, 42, 52, 63, 64
    E, 133
914, 72, 85, 94, 133
    914/6, 94
917, 72, 87, 94, 100, 111, 118
    917/30, 94
    K, 236
924, 146, 158, 167, 171, 223, 280
    GTP, 174
928, 87, 88, 129, 146, 156, 158, 159, 167, 213, 219, 257, 288
    S4, 237, 262
930, 129, 137, 139, 193
930 Turbo, 127, 139, 147, 223, 288
    1970, 124
    Carrera, 132
930S, 199, 225
    1983, 170
    1986, 191
    Cabriolet, 1990, 214
934, 138, 139, 143
    1976, 131
    Group 4 champion, 1976, 130
    Turbo, 1976, 129
935, 138, 143, 150, 155, 170, 193, 197, 216, 232
    935/71, 155
    935/78 Moby Dick, 146, 148, 151, 171, 185, 189, 191, 195, 275
    K3, 1980, 155
    Kremer K3, 1981, 158, 159
936, 171
    936/78, 144
944, 171, 254
    Turbo, 218
    S2, 213, 237
953, 230–232
    Paris-Dakar Rally Car, 1986, 180

956, 195, 243
959, 185, 189, 195, 199, 207, 212, 215, 216, 222, 223, 269, 271, 275, 277, 279, 334
    S, 198
    U.S. Sport, 1988, 186
960, 187
961, 187
962, 275
964, 206, 212–214, 216, 218, 222, 225, 232, 245, 251–253, 255, 257, 262, 266, 268
    Carrera 4, 218, 257
        Lightweight, 323
    Carrera Cup, 232
    RS Touring, 237
    RSR, 228, 232, 234, 237
965, 214, 219, 222–224, 255
    Turbo, 219, 254
966, 323
968, 254, 288, 300
986 (Boxster), 290, 292, 293, 294
989, 224, 288
993, 251, 252, 257, 260, 262, 266, 271, 274, 275, 279, 280, 283, 287, 288, 300, 322, 333
    C4S, 314
    Carrera cabriolet, 1995, 252
    Carrera Cup, 266
    Pace Car, 1995, 254
    Turbo, 258, 269
    Turbo-Look, 305
996, 283, 288, 290, 292, 298, 299, 301, 304, 305, 308, 309, 311, 328, 331–334, 337, 339, 341, 343–345
    GT2, 322
    GT3, 313
    RUF RGTRS, 318
    Supercup GT3, 313
    Turbo, 304, 323
    S, 341
    2001, 294
997, 283, 327, 328, 330–335, 341, 343, 344, 345
    Cabriolet, 330
    Carrera, 341

Abarth, Carlo, 50
Achleitner, August, 309, 327, 328, 331, 332, 334, 338, 341, 344
Acura, 212
    NSX, 211, 212, 237, 252
Adam, Bill, 261
Aichele, Tobias, 23, 44
Aicher, Otl, 10
Alfa Romeo, 45
    1600 Giulia GT, 57
    Super Sprint, 20
Alpine Renault A110, 36
America Roadster, 237, 238
    GS, 1993, 238
    1992, 228
Ampferer, Herbert, 264, 271, 275, 283, 344
Arkus-Duntov, Zora, 96
Aston Martin, 35, 51, 288
    DB4, 20
    DB5, 35
    DB9, 339
    Vantage, 195
    Virage, 269
    Volante, 195
Ate disc brakes, 31
Audi, 172, 243
    100 model, 216
    Quattro, 182, 193

Bahnsen, Uwe, 252
Bamberg, Konrad, 18
Bantle, Manfred, 186–188, 191, 193, 195, 198, 213, 222
Barth, Jürgen, 87, 106, 155, 182, 212, 218, 228, 230–233, 237, 266, 268, 271, 275, 279, 281, 323, 344
Baüerli, Heinz, 59
Baur, Karl, 57

BBS extractor wheels, 157
Beierbach, Walter, 23, 24, 42
Bell, Derek, 171
Bendel, Hansjörg, 38
Berger, Helmut, 103
Berger, Wolfgang, 94, 95, 100, 103, 107, 139, 143, 344
Bertone 911 Roadster, 1966, 40
Bertone Studios, 62
Bertone, Nubbio, 27, 41, 42, 43, 49, 50
Bertoni, Flaminio, 20
Bez, Ulrich, 223–225, 232, 246, 247, 252, 257, 260, 262, 266, 288
Bezner, Fritz, 213, 218, 222, 225, 257, 344
Bill, Max, 10, 13
Bilstein, 193, 333
Biral cylinders, 100
Blakely, Chantel, 10
BMW, 29, 63, 94, 100, 112, 137, 148, 174, 181, 223, 224, 243, 252, 288, 300, 334
    1800 TISA, 57
    2000CS, 36
    2800CS, 95
    3 series, 323
    3.0CSL, 107, 143
    5 series, 247
    6 series, 323, 339
    633CSi, 159
    645i coupe model, 181
    7 series, 181, 246
    745i model, 181
    8 series, 247
    850Csi, 269
    M1, 159
    M3, 339
    Technik, 223
    Type 507, 13
Boge, 64
Bohn, Arno, 246, 262, 288, 294, 344
Bonomelli, 106
Bosch, 64, 105, 117, 140, 173, 193, 195, 305
    D-Jetronic, 132
    K-Jetronic, 112, 117, 125, 142, 161, 173
    L-Jetronic injection system, 181
    Motronic system, 199
Bott, Helmuth, 19, 27, 31, 42, 45, 51, 64, 84, 85, 89, 95–97, 150, 171–173, 179–184, 186, 189, 191, 193, 195, 196, 198, 203, 204, 207, 216, 218, 222, 223, 243, 252, 257, 343, 344
Boutsen, Thierry, 278
Bovensiepen, Burkard, 95
Boxster, 288, 290, 294, 295, 299, 300, 323
Bracq, Paul, 27
Branitzki, Heinz, 79, 85, 211, 218, 223, 245, 251, 344
Brock, Peter, 27, 96
Brodbeck, Tilman, 79, 90, 91, 95–97, 100, 103, 104, 112, 216, 344
Brose, Eberhard, 295, 309
Brown, David, 288

Canepa, Bruce, 198
Car Top Systems (CTS), 304, 343
Carosserie, Wilhelm Karmann, 27
Carrera, 16, 45, 96, 100, 103, 120, 121, 131, 132, 147, 176, 179, 196, 199, 201, 262, 275, 299, 300, 301, 327, 329, 330, 339–341
    2 (C2), 28, 218, 219, 224, 225, 228, 237, 238, 242, 243, 245, 252, 262
    3.0 RSR, 231
    3.2, 181, 184, 214, 215, 251, 256
        Targa, 1986, 190
        Turbo-Look, 1984, 162, 173
        1986, 206
    4 (C4), 218, 219, 224, 243, 245, 252, 255, 257, 262, 266, 277, 304, 305, 308, 312
        Leichtbau (Lightweight), 232, 233, 237
        RS Lightweight, 1991, 218
        1990, 208, 212

4S, 281, 282, 308, 310, 311
6, 51, 59
904GTS, 17, 36
Cabriolet, 2000, 292
Club Sport, 1989, 195
Cup, 228–230, 257, 266
GTS, 27
RS, 103, 119, 133, 280, 317
   2.7, 111, 119, 231
      1973, 97, 231, 232
      Lightweight, 1973, 99
   2.8, 231
   3.8, 1993, 268
      1973, 196
RSR 2.8, 107
   1973, 103
RSR 3.0, 138
S, 329, 330, 334, 338, 341, 344
   1997, 248, 274
   1998, 282
Targa, 1997, 280
   1974, 112
   2002, 298
Carrosserie Touring, 20
Chandler, Otis, 187, 197
Chapron, Henri, 27
Chevrolet Corvette, 61, 88, 133, 143, 147, 304, 322
   Stingray, 27, 65
Citröen
   ID19, 20
   DS19, 27
Cleare, Richard, 130, 131, 133
Club Sport, 189, 196, 200, 220, 237, 280
Cosworth eninge, 193
Cup Design wheels, 253

de Tomaso, Alejandro, 62
Detroit International Auto Show, 290, 294
Digital Motor Electronics (DME) Motronics 2 engine man-
   agement, 181
Dodge Viper, 322
Donahue, Mark, 100, 119, 120
Donckerwölke, Luc, 327, 339
Dron, Tony, 132
Dürheimer, Wolfgang, 328, 330, 332–334, 341, 344, 345

Earl, Harley, 20
Elford, Vic, 60, 68
Engine, V-8 Indy, 222
Euro Carrera, 131
Evertz, Egon, 131
Exner, Virgil, 20

F1-GTR, 264
Falk, Peter, 55, 57, 60, 94, 100, 170, 228, 252, 253, 257, 271
Ferguson, Harry, 188
Ferrari, 20, 35, 36, 51, 174, 181, 199, 212, 275, 312
   213PB, 107
   275 GTB Berlinetta, 96
   365 GTB-4 Daytona, 94
   Dino 206GT, 62
   F355, 269, 304
   F360, 339
   Modena, 308
   Lusso, 96
   250 GTO, 236
   288GTO, 195
   328GTB, 212
Fiat 850 fastback, 96
Fitzpatrick, John, 156, 159
Flegl, Helmut, 87, 100, 232
Follmer, George, 129
Ford Motor Company, 16, 94, 157, 160
   Capri, 95, 112, 118
   Cobra Daytona Coupe, 96
   de Tomaso Pantera, 94
   GT350 Mustang, 96
   GT40 Mk IV, 96
   GT500 Mustang, 96
   Lotus Cortina, 57
   Mangusta, 62
   RS200

Scorpio, 216
Ford, Henry, 157
Forstner, Egon, 31
Frankfurt Auto Show, 28, 31, 35, 42, 118, 130, 173, 174,
   179, 193, 196
Frère, Paul, 151, 233
Fuchs alloy wheels, 46, 103, 176, 200
Furhmann, Ernst, 84, 85, 86, 87, 94, 95, 100, 101, 103,
   107, 111, 112, 117, 118, 120, 129, 130, 132, 143, 146,
   156—158, 160, 165, 172, 173, 179, 344

Gandini, Marcello, 62
Gelin, Maurice, 61
Gemballa Cabriolet, 1995, 262
Gemballa, Uwe, 262
General Motors, 16, 88
Geneva Auto Show, 50, 62, 63
Getrag, transmission, 190, 199, 201, 293, 297, 299, 304, 315
Glöckler, Otto, 10
Gmund, 9, 42
Goertz, Count Albrecht, 13, 18, 50
Goodyear Bluestreak tires, 143
Greenwood, John, 143
Gruber, Dr. Thomas, 100, 105
Gugelot, Hans, 63
Gurney, Dan, 16

Hall, Jim, 62
Hatter, Tony, 222, 224, 252, 253, 257, 260, 262, 272, 274,
   275, 280, 282, 283, 311, 343
Haywood, Hurley, 171
Helmer, Lars, 85
Henrik Fisker, 339
Hensler, Paul, 51, 59–61, 64, 77, 89, 117, 195, 217, 218, 344
Hermann, Hans, 61
Hershey, Frank, 20
Hetman, Richard, 61
Hild, Wilhelm, 10, 12, 17
Hoffman, Max, 13, 48, 49
Holbert, Al, 197
Honda Motor Company, 211, 212, 288
   Prelude 4WS, 257
Honda, Soichiro, 212

Iacocca, Lee, 157
Ickz, Jacky, 171, 182, 183, 188, 189

Jacobson, Andy, 252
Jaguar, 35, 333
   XJ-S, 195
   XK150, 20
   XK-E, 27, 65
   XKSS, 20
Jenson, Allan, 188
Jenson, Richard, 188
Joest, Reinhold, 278
Jünginger, Albert, 59

Kaes, Ghislane, 61
Kahnau, Bernd, 257, 300, 309, 333, 343, 344
Karmann assembly plant, 31, 41, 43
Kern, Hans, 61
Kinsella, W. P., 270
KKK turbocharger, 128
Klie, Heinrich, 18, 26
Klöckner-Humboldt-Deutz (KHD), 165
Knirsch, Stefan, 299, 338, 339
Komenda, Erwin, 9, 12, 15, 17–19, 21–24, 28, 44, 72, 292,
   331, 344
Koni shock absorbers, 51, 90
Konradsheim, Dr. Georg, 100, 105
Kranefuss, Michael, 94
Kremer, Erwin and Manfred, 155, 156
Kristen, Hartmut, 322, 344
Kulla, Mathias, 252, 331, 341, 345
Kussmaul, Roland, 147, 189, 212, 232, 244, 271, 275, 288,
   303, 312

Lagaay, Harm, 129, 197, 199, 201, 223, 224, 246, 247, 251,
   252, 254, 257, 260, 280, 281, 287, 288, 290, 292, 294,
   300, 309, 341, 344, 345

Lai, Pinky, 199, 252, 288, 290, 292, 294, 298, 299, 301,
   303–305, 309, 313, 323, 331, 341, 345
Lambda-Sonde oxygen sensors, 160
Lamborghini, 51, 195
   2+2, 21
   Diablo, 269
   Ferruccio, 62
   Flavia, 57
   Gallardo, 339
   Jalpa, 212
   Lancia, 174
   S.p.A., 327
Lapine, Tony, 65, 68, 69, 72, 73, 86, 88, 90, 96, 100, 103,
   104, 112, 124, 132, 148, 179, 189, 191, 203, 216, 222,
   292, 344
Larrousse, Gerard, 61
Larson, Grant, 252, 290, 294, 331, 332, 341, 343–345
LeCamel, Patrick, 252
Leiding, Rudolf, 85
Lemoyne, Dominique, 184, 188
Lola, 174
Loos, Georg, 106
Lotus Europa, 62
Lotz, Kurt, 65, 85
Ludvigsen, Karl, 89, 103, 118, 121, 187, 204, 218, 299, 312
Lutz, Bob, 160

MacPherson strut front suspension, 19, 27
Maraj, Dave, 261
Marchart, 344
Marchart, Horst, 257, 282, 288, 298, 300
Maserati, 35, 51
Matra-Simca MS670B, 107
May, Michael, 112, 118
McLaren, 212, 264, 275, 312
Mercedes-Benz, 12, 96, 137, 148, 181, 282, 288, 300, 312,
   334
   190E, 193
   220SE, 35
   230SL, 27, 36
   280GE Gelandewagen, 182
   280SL, 65
   300SEL 6.3, 159
   300SL, 13, 35
   350SL, 100
   450SLC, 159
   500-series SL/SLC, 181
   600SL, 270
   1955 190SL, 13
   CLK, 311
   SL, 304, 323
Metge, René, 184, 188, 189
Mezger, Hans, 23, 29, 60, 63, 59, 100, 105, 111, 118, 155,
   344
MGB, 57
Mickl, Josef, 10, 19, 31
Mimler, Hubert, 17
Minilite wheels, 91
Mitchell, Bill, 88
Möbius, Wolfgang (Walter), 112, 121, 129, 156. 191, 216,
   222
Moretti, Gianpiero, 156
Morse, Kerry, 231, 232
Müller, Herbert, 107
Murkett, Steve, 199, 201, 254, 257, 281
Murray, Gordon, 271

Neerpasch, jochen, 61
Nissan, 275, 288, 312
   300ZX, 213, 237
Nordhoff, Heinz, 61, 63, 65, 68, 72
Notucker, Siegfried, 21, 22
Nye, Doug, 193

Opel, 45
   GT, 65
Options
   M427, 103
   M471, 103
   M491 Turbo-look, 103, 174, 175, 196
   M506 Turbo, 196, 199
   M637 Club Sport, 195

PCCB, 323
Sportkit, 57, 225
Sports Chrono package, 328
X50 performance, 334

Panamericana, 1989, 197
Paris Auto Salon, 64
Paris Auto Show, 103
Paris-Dakar, 230
Paul, John L. Sr. and Jr., 158
Peter, Patrick, 268, 271
Petruschat, Jörg, 11
Peugeot, 37, 42, 182
    Model 201, 36
Piëch, Ferdinand, 30, 50, 53, 55, 57, 59, 61, 69, 72, 78–80, 86,
    89–91, 94, 100, 117, 129, 172, 189, 204, 206, 344
Piëch, Louise, 30, 79, 165
Piëch, Michael, 79
Pininfarina, 20, 21, 62, 86, 96
Pirelli, 233
Plaschka, Fritz, 18
Pohlman, Chuck, 27
Polster, Bernd, 10, 13
Porsche A.G., 165, 166, 197
Porsche Active Suspension Management (PASM), 329, 333,
    334, 338, 344
Porsche Cars North America (PCNA), 197, 279, 300, 303
Porsche Exclusiv, 96, 311
Porsche Individual, 338
Porsche Owner's Club, 230, 255
Porsche Stability Management (PSM), 295, 305, 308, 313
Porsche, Ferdinand Alexander "Butzi", 10, 11, 16–24, 26,
    27, 30, 31, 36, 42–44, 48, 49, 63, 64, 69, 78, 79, 84, 86,
    124, 148, 179, 292, 300, 331, 341, 344
Porsche, Ferdinand, 15, 27, 63
Porsche, Ferry, 10, 12, 13, 16, 18, 19, 23, 24, 26–29, 36,
    41, 42, 49, 50, 52, 78–80, 84, 94, 117, 133, 156, 165, 166,
    174, 179, 197, 199, 254, 262, 269, 281, 331, 344
Porsche, Peter, 79, 80
Programs
    B-Program, 173
    C-Program, 173, 179
    D-Program, 179
    E-Program, 181
    G-Program, 196
    H-Program, 199
    J-Program, 199
    K-Program, 200
    L-Program, 218
    M-Program, 237
    S-Program, 262
    T-program, 279
Prototypes
    754 T7, 28
    695, 69
    911/C20, 1970, 86
    911R, 1967, 50
    936, 138
    996, 288, 289
    Pininfarina 4-seater, 1969, 78
    Targa, 1965, 45
    644 T8, 19
    901, 27
    Pilot production 901, 1964, 30

Rabe, Karl, 10, 12, 16, 28, 72
Raether, Wolfgang, 12, 42, 60
Ratel, Stéfane, 268, 271
Reimspeiss, Franz, 9, 10, 16, 28, 29, 344
Reisinger, Peter, 121
Reitter, Horst, 274, 283, 309, 311
Reutter, 27, 28, 41
Reutter Carosserie (Recaro), 24, 57
Reutter Karosseriewerke, 10
Reutter, Albert, 24
Reutter, Wilhelm, 24
Ricard, Paul, 143
Richards, David, 142, 143
Richter, Les, 119
Rombold, Helmut, 27, 31
Rondeau, 174
Ruf, Alois, 315, 317, 318, 319

Sauter, Uli, 341
Sayer, Malcolm, 27
Schäffer, Valentine, 111, 112, 117, 118
Schmid, Leopold, 9, 10, 12, 19, 26
Schmidt, Lars, 60
Scholle, Inge, 10
Schröder, Gerhard, 43, 44, 179
Schutz, Peter, 165–167, 170–174, 179, 182, 195–199, 201,
    203–206, 218, 222, 271, 343, 344
Schutz, Sheila, 205
Series, A, 18
Series, B, 10, 18
Series, C, 77
Series, E (einspritzung or fuel injection), 62, 64, 73, 78, 79,
    89, 90, 94, 103, 120
    1970, 79
Series, F, 94
Series, G, 120, 125, 262
Series, GT, 55, 328
    GT1, 264, 266, 271, 272, 275, 281
    GT1/96, 269, 279
        Road Version, 1996, 271
        1996, 264
    GT1/97 road version, 1997, 272
    GT1/98, 283, 312
    GT2, 258, 261, 264, 271, 313, 314
        2004, 313
    GT3, 308, 313, 314, 319, 322, 334
        2004, 321
        R, 314
        RS, 2002, 303
Series, H, 130
Series, I, 132
Series, L (Luxury), 53, 54, 57, 61, 62, 64
    1968, 60
Series, R (Race), 50, 52, 53, 54, 55, 59, 61, 64, 68, 89, 100, 101
    1967, 54
Series, RS (Race Sport), 105, 239, 303
    1960, 294
    America coupe, 237
    IROC, 317, 319
Series, RSR, 105, 106, 118, 124, 151, 269, 288
    3.0, 95
    3.8 Supercup, 1993, 232
    IROC, 1974, 119
Series, S (Sport) series, 42, 51, 52–54, 57, 59–64, 69, 70, 73,
    77, 79, 82, 85, 86, 89, 90, 100, 101, 103, 112, 120, 121,
    131, 132, 139, 146, 156, 179, 202, 274, 315, 330, 340, 343
    2.7, 100
    1975, 120
    GT, 1968, 65
    LM, 266
        1994, 271
    Targa
        1967, 46
        1969, 69
        1972, 93
        Tour de France winner, 1971, 87
Series, SC (Super Carrera), 28, 146, 154, 181
    Cabriolet, 1983, 166
    Safari Rally, 1978, 150
    Targa, 1979, 152
    1981, 160
    1983, 262
Series, SC-RS, 142, 219
    1978, 108, 112, 139
    Rothmans, 1978, 140
Series, ST, 55, 57
    1970, 82
Series, T, 54, 62, 64, 68, 73, 78, 79, 82, 89, 90, 100, 117,
    120
Shelby, Carroll, 96
Shinoda, Larry, 27, 88
Show Car Styling Concepts, 1989, 201
Siegert, Franz-Josef, 341
Siffert, Jo, 59
Singer, Norbert, 79, 89, 94, 95, 100, 103, 105–107, 111,
    118–120, 138, 139, 143, 146–151, 155, 170, 185, 189,
    230, 264, 271, 274, 278, 271–283, 309, 311, 344
Soderberg, Dick, 121, 129, 185, 189, 191, 216, 222, 223,
    254, 275

Soeding, Otto, 22, 23
Solex carburetors, 23, 38, 51, 89
Soukup, Emil, 45
Speedline Cup, 247
Speedster, 12, 18, 49, 201, 204, 220, 237
    1989, 203
    1994, 242
Spoerry, Dieter, 59
Sportomatic transmission, 61, 62, 120, 147, 154
Sprenger, Rolf, 215, 217, 238
Steckkönig, Günther, 96, 100
Steinemann, Rico, 59
Stotz, Erich, 26
Strähle, Paul Ernst, 100
Stuck, Hans, 261, 278
Stuttgart Technical Institute, 12, 24, 29, 57, 84, 90, 96,
    112, 157, 165, 317
Styling Concept 959, 1982, 185

Targa, 26, 45, 48–52, 61, 63, 64, 78, 90, 124, 137, 147,
    179, 196, 199, 280, 281, 309, 328, 341
Teague, Richard, 20
Teve, Alfred, 31, 64
Thorszelius, Hans, 151
Tiptronic transmission, 239, 243, 245, 293, 295, 299, 304,
    308, 332, 333
Tomala, Hans, 17, 29
Toyota Motor Company, 59, 261, 275, 288, 312
    Celica, 182
Triumph TR4, 45
Turbo, 119, 131, 138, 156, 170–172, 174, 181, 187, 191,
    193, 199, 201, 214, 216, 219, 222–225, 228, 237, 238,
    262, 275, 280, 282, 297, 301, 308–311, 314, 315, 318,
    322, 334, 337, 341
    Carrera, 111, 137
        RSR, 139, 143
            1974, 117
    S, 238, 245, 271, 279, 333, 334, 337, 341
        1994, 244
        1997, 275
    S2, 238
        1991, 223
Turbo-Look, 175, 196, 204, 228, 237, 238, 242, 281, 308, 312

Ünger, Kendrick, 189

van Lennep, Gijs, 107
VarioCam Plus valve system, 299, 339
VarioRam intake, 274, 280
Vogele, Charles, 59
Volkswagen, 27, 36, 44, 61, 63–65, 68, 69, 72, 77, 94, 96,
    101, 129, 133, 157, 179, 312, 318
Volkswagenwerke, 85, 86
von Hanstein, Baron Huschke, 36, 48, 51, 52, 57, 60, 68, 344
von Neumann, Johnny, 40, 43, 48–50
von Rücker, Klaus, 17, 27–29, 84

WABCO Westinghouse, 193
Wagner, Harald, 42, 45, 48, 49, 60, 61
Wagonbaushcule, 22
Waldegaard, Björn, 85, 100, 151
Weber carb, 38, 51, 56, 57, 73
Weinsberg, Karosserie, 27, 41
Weissach, 77, 86, 96, 121, 138, 157, 170, 171, 189, 199,
    206, 212, 213, 215, 219, 230, 234, 237, 245, 251, 257,
    258, 269, 271, 274, 275, 279, 281, 305, 312, 322, 328,
    333, 345
Welti, Max, 266
Wiedeking, Wendelin, 215, 246, 261, 262, 266, 280, 282,
    294, 299, 312, 323, 332, 344
Wietmann, Julius, 38
Wilhelm, Anke, 341
Wind Tunnel Prototype 959, 1982, 185
Wollek, Bob, 278
Wütherich, Rolf, 55

Yellow Bird, 318

Zuffenhausen production, 38, 44, 53, 60, 65, 67, 78, 85,
    101, 103, 105, 167, 204, 233, 238, 257, 261, 262, 279,
    280, 299, 305, 318, 323